The Confessions of T. E. Lawrence

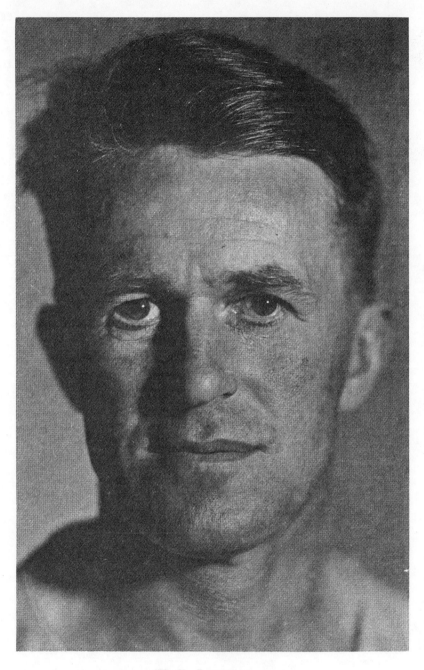

T. E. LAWRENCE

Photograph by Howard Coster. Printed by permission
of British Central Office of Information.

THE CONFESSIONS OF
T. E. LAWRENCE

THE ROMANTIC HERO'S
PRESENTATION OF SELF

BY

THOMAS J. O'DONNELL

 Ohio University Press
Athens, Ohio

Library of Congress Cataloging in Publication Data

O'Donnell, Thomas J 1938-
    The confessions of T. E. Lawrence.

    Bibliography: p.
    1. Lawrence, Thomas Edward, 1888-1935—Criticism and inter-
pretation. 2. Confession in literature. 3. Romanticism. 4. Psychology and literature. I. Title.
PR6023.A937Z83   828'.9'1209   77-92257
ISBN 0-8214-0370-2

To
Kenneth E. Godfrey, M.D.

ACKNOWLEDGMENTS

Portions of this research were supported by grants from the University of Illinois, from the English Department, University of Kansas, and from the General Research Fund, University of Kansas. I am appreciative of the permissions granted by the editors of *American Imago* and *Genre* to reprint parts of my essays which first appeared in these journals. I thank the Letters of T. E. Lawrence Trust, the Seven Pillars Trust, and Jonathan Cape Limited for permission to use unpublished passages from Lawrence's letters and from the Bodleian manuscript of *Seven Pillars of Wisdom*. For permission to use published passages from *The Mint, Seven Pillars of Wisdom*, and *The Letters of T. E. Lawrence*, I am grateful to Mrs. A. W. Lawrence, the Seven Pillars Trust, Jonathan Cape Limited, and Doubleday & Company.

Several people offered valuable suggestions and encouragement at various times in the writing of this book: Ms. Martha Masinton, Mrs. Constance Scheerer, and Professors Edward Brandabur, Charles G. Masinton, Linda O'Donnell, Wayne Pounds, and George Worth. To them I am most grateful.

Three people were especially helpful. At the early stages of my study of T. E. Lawrence, the most useful and perceptive comments came from Ms. Mary Kelly Black. At a later stage, Dr. Laura Weaver spent a great deal of time and energy reading and editing drafts of the manuscript. Her intelligence, patience, and skill were gratifying. Dr. Kenneth Godfrey's advice during the completion of the book was invaluable.

Finally, I wish to thank Ms. Mary Fitzgerald, Mrs. Margaret Guilfoyle O'Donnell, and Mr. Thomas E. O'Donnell.

True there lurked always that Will uneasily waiting to burst out. My brain was sudden and silent as a wild cat, my senses like mud clogging its feet, and my self (conscious always of itself and its shyness) telling the beast it was bad form to spring and vulgar to feed upon the kill. So meshed in nerves and hesitation, it could not be a thing to be afraid of; yet it was a real beast, and this book its mangy skin, dried, stuffed and set up squarely for men to stare at.

—*T. E. Lawrence,* Seven Pillars of Wisdom

PREFACE

Why should we honor those that die upon the field of battle, a man may show as reckless a courage in entering into the abyss of himself.

—*W. B. Yeats*

The unquestioned courage of T. E. Lawrence in battle is paralleled by his courage in entering into the abyss of himself. Lawrence sounded the dimensions of that abyss in his confessions and his letters. But he did not return from the depths with any message to relieve our pain or his. A few months before his death he declared that he had "learned only the word 'No' in 46 years." Lawrence said he did not understand himself and did not want to. His refusal to simplify, to beat himself into a thin, clear, incised design— that refusal is the glory, richness, and humanity of his confessions. He cannot turn his fascinated, hostile eye from himself. But his angry eye need not be mirrored by the eyes of his readers, however much he solicits their condemnation. Lawrence is not the angel of the omnipotent will that he sometimes fantasied himself to be, a will that he began to feel compelled to restrain and ultimately to renounce. Nor is he the beast he sometimes feared he was, Nebuchadnezzar living among the animals. To paraphrase a line from Kierkegaard, his cries make us afraid, but we love his delicious music.

Lawrence's work is frequently treated as an anomaly by literary critics. A primary purpose of this study is to place it in the confessional and Romantic contexts from which it emerges and which inform judgment on it. *Seven Pillars of Wisdom* and *The Mint* comprise a single confessional project. They possess many of the characteristics of classic confessional works, but they bear special affinities to the secular confessions of the Romantics and of twentieth-century writers. The unifying principle of Lawrence's confessions is the Romantic myth of self, particularly as expressed in the writings of Schopenhauer and Carlyle. The hero's development has two stages: expansion of self and contraction of self to the point of annihilation. These stages are not causally related nor sequential but presented side by side throughout the confessions in a revealing and disconcerting manner.

Lawrence's hero is a radical instance of a divided self. The division between the confident, expansive self of the war narrator—the imperialist—and the confused, contracted self of the introspective hero presents the most intractable formal problem of these confessions as well as their main psychological interest. The unpublished Bodleian manuscript of *Seven Pillars of Wisdom,* used extensively in this study for the first time, is more revealing of the confessional hero than the revised work and indicates the extraordinary degree to which this division of self existed in earlier drafts. In unpublished correspondence with Charlotte Shaw and in letters to Edward and David Garnett, Lawrence himself is puzzled by the division and discloses its sources in his character. The notions of sadism and masochism parallel the hero's stages of expansion and contraction, and this book explores Lawrence's complex integration of psychological and Romantic myths of self.

CONTENTS

REFERENCE ABBREVIATIONS

References to four of Lawrence's works are made in parentheses within the text:

L   *The Letters of T. E. Lawrence*, ed. David Garnett (London: Spring Books, 1964). The pagination of this edition is the same as that of the Jonathan Cape edition of 1938 and the Doubleday, Doran edition of 1939.

M   *The Mint* (New York: Norton, 1963).

Seven Pillars of Wisdom: a triumph (London: Jonathan Cape, 1935). Page numbers to this edition are given without any other designation.

MS   "The Seven Pillars of Wisdom," Bodleian MS. Reserve d.33.

The Confessions of T. E. Lawrence

I

T. E. Lawrence and the Confessional Tradition:
Either Angel or Beast

T. E. LAWRENCE WROTE NO SIGNIFICANT FICTION OR POETRY. His major literary works are autobiographical. *Seven Pillars of Wisdom* is a personal narrative of Lawrence's role in the Arab Revolt of 1916-1918; *The Mint* is a journal describing his postwar years as a common airman in the Royal Air Force. *Seven Pillars* and *The Mint* comprise a single confessional project and are in the tradition of the great confessions of Augustine, Bunyan, Rousseau, and Adams. Despite his activity in other spheres, Lawrence considered this writing his most important work of the postwar decade. During the years of their composition he used the confessions both to express and to shape his life according to a Romantic pattern. The only other work of his that Lawrence himself considered literature was his translation of Homer's *Odyssey*. The rest of his writings are archaeological studies, scientific and technical reports, political essays, reviews, and pseudonymous translations of contemporary French novels. Several volumes of letters, extraordinary in range and quality, were published posthumously. In this study these minor writings are discussed only when they clarify *Seven Pillars* and *The Mint*.

One of Lawrence's last essays, his Translator's Note to *The Odyssey of Homer*, reveals indirectly his attitude toward his own works.[1] If *Seven Pillars* has the "stink of personality," "stinks of me" (*L* 813, 462), so does Lawrence's interpretation of *The Odyssey*. With one eye on his own writings, he savages Homer's. Remarkably, Homer's style, critical temperament, alleged coterie, and deficiencies in characterization parallel Lawrence's notions of his own confessions at virtually every point. *The Odyssey* is "neat, close-knit, artful, and various; as nearly word-perfect as

3

midnight oil and pumice can effect. Crafty, exquisite, homogeneous—whatever great art may be, these are not its attributes. . . . The author misses his every chance of greatness. . . ." Lawrence sees Homer's perfection as a misunderstanding of the ends of art, for man's purpose "properly existed only in unending effort toward unattainable imagined light" (549). Faultlessness is "a meiosis for some faultiness" (L 542). The perfection of Homer is a triumph of technique over spirit: "the tight lips of archaic art have grown the fixed grin of archaism. Very bookish, this house-bred man. His work smells of the literary coterie, of a writing tradition." Only by such "self-criticism can talent rank beside inspiration."

Homer's characterizations are "thin and accidental. . . . He thumb-nailed well; and afterwards lost heart." Only the central family is well-drawn—"the sly cattish wife, that cold-blooded egotist Odysseus, and the priggish son. . . . It is sorrowful to believe that these were really Homer's heroes and exemplars." But Lawrence finds other interests in the epic and tries "to deduce the author from his self-betrayal in the work." He implies, curiously enough, that his own circumstances closely resemble Homer's. In an oblique reference to his own low status as an airman, Lawrence imagines that Homer was "(like writers two thousand years after him) the associate of menials, making himself their friend and defender by understanding." Homer too is an adventurer, "neither land-lubber nor stay-at-home nor ninny." Lawrence intimates that his own experience is superior to Homer's, for he, the masterful leader of Bedouins in Arabia, would not be "all adrift when it comes to fighting," and he alone had "seen deaths in battle" (cf. L 710). Yet in the war narrative of *Seven Pillars* he resembles more the cold-blooded egotist that he imagines Homer created.

Lawrence's letters expose the extent to which the Translator's Note is self-regarding. If *The Odyssey* is crafty, artful, word-perfect, then *Seven Pillars* has an "old-maidish neatness and fastidiousness about the style, and that pleases me, even where it passes over the edge into priggery" (L 380).

Yet this "literary-priggishness . . . sets an open-aired man's teeth on edge" (*L* 431). The Arab Revolt offered Lawrence a subject for "literature, the techniqueless art," but he was "excited only over mechanism" (549). He finds his worrying of technique and diction positively destructive: "No revision makes an incomplete thing into a creation. Life comes either at once, or not at all. The snag about all my writing is that it is immensely careful and quite two-dimensional." Lawrence accepts Romantic notions of creation; a genius does not labor so: "the subconsciousness does the work in the darkness, without the mind's being aware, or sharing the labour. Most of us have to plough and harrow the upper mind, deliberately and of malice prepense."[2]

Lawrence's works are shaped by intense self-criticism: "That's the analytic vein in me. Ineradicable." More critic than artist, the "walking embodiment of the critical temperament,"[3] he is an artist still, for "a critic in conscious creation is . . . an artist."[4] *Seven Pillars* is "compiled out of memory (squeezing the poor organ with both hands, to force from it even the little lively detail that there is)" (*L* 456). On the one hand, he proudly declares that not a word of *The Mint* "is careless or uncalculated" (*L* 624); on the other, he finds that he failed in his "ambition to become an artist . . . by taking thought. Creative work isn't achieved by dint of pains."[5] Lawrence's endless elaboration, his overwrought style is "the vice of amateurs tentative in their arts" (562). Homer's notebooks are "stocked with purple passages and he embedded these in his tale." So too are Lawrence's confessions and "every purple passage is intentional. In my experience purple things are a conscious straining upwards of the mind."[6] If Homer incessantly relies on "tags of epic," everywhere in *Seven Pillars* there are "borrowed phrases and ideas, not picked out by footnotes and untidy quotation marks" (MS 8).

Remarkably, Lawrence argues that both he and Homer possess Decadent characteristics of style. Perhaps recalling accusations that his own style is pseudo-archaic, Lawrence calls *The Odyssey's* diction "Wardour-Street Greek."

Lawrence is critical of Homer's conformance to the very
Decadent ideals he himself emulates; both writers are
"crafty, exquisite." In fact the Translator's Note is a
thorough reading of Homer in Decadent terms. Although
the Note implies censure of the Decadents, elsewhere he
vigorously defends them: "the nineties were very rich, very
strong, very successful."[7]

In *The Odyssey* "every big situation is burked"; if the epic
is gay, fine, and vivid, it is "never huge or terrible."
Analogously, Lawrence condemns himself for making the
reader do his "top scene" or emotional climaxes for him in
Seven Pillars. He "shies off all the 'popular'
moments . . . stressing detached points" (*L* 380). Lawrence most admires the few men who "had honestly
tried to be greater than mankind: and only their strainings
and wrestlings really fill my stomach" (*L* 370). He has
"collected a shelf of 'Titanic' books (those distinguished by
greatness of spirit, 'sublimity' as Longinus would call
it) . . . *The Karamazovs, Zarathustra,* and *Moby Dick.*
Well, my ambition was to make an English fourth" (*L* 360).
Apparently the greatest works must possess a quality beyond
the human (*L* 462). Neither *Seven Pillars* nor *The Odyssey*
portrays Lawrence's ideal inhuman or superhuman Romantic hero, Zarathustra or Ahab; neither writer can portray the
heroic. If Homer "lived too long after the heroic age to feel
assured and large," Lawrence found the epic mode alien to
him "as to my generation. Memory gave me no clue to the
heroic . . . " (549).

Seven Pillars is an epic, Lawrence feels, but it is an
"introspection epic" (*L* 621). Homer's pages are "steeped in
a queer naïvety; and at our remove of thought and language
we cannot guess if he is smiling or not. Yet there is a dignity
which compels respect and baffles us, he being neither simple
in education nor primitive socially." This too defines
Lawrence's Decadent ideal: "sophisticated simplicity.
That's decadence. If a man is not simple by nature he cannot
be simple by art, and if he tries he only achieves a falseness"
(*L* 377). Modern man must accept his complexities and gain
strength by exploring them: "I could have written a simple

story, but only fraudulently, since by nature and education and environment I'm complex. So I tried to make my reactions to experience as compound as they were in reality. I don't agree with your implied hint that simplicity is ethically better (when it would be false): or in any circumstances more artistic."[8]

Lawrence possesses the deficiencies in characterization he imputes to Homer: he thumb-nails well and afterwards loses heart. Though he can present himself, he cannot create the characters of others because, like the Lady of Shalott, his "nature persists in seeing all things in the mirror of itself, and not with a direct eye" (M 195). His analysis of his war diary is applicable to his confessions: "it showed clearly that my interest lay in myself . . . " (MS 364). Lawrence's appropriation of Homer in the Translator's Note is representative. In *Seven Pillars* and *The Mint* Lawrence appropriates the characters of the Bedouins and the common airmen as thoroughly as he does Homer's. The initiates, literary friends who had read the private edition of *Seven Pillars* and who knew the identity of T. E. Shaw, the pseudonym under which Lawrence translated *The Odyssey*, would have been amused by his arrogance. It is this audience whose esteem he sought, though he coveted a very different kind of recognition from the masses.

The Translator's Note reveals that Lawrence had "enormous pretensions" in literature as well as an acute grasp of his limitations.[9] He confesses that "it's only in trying to write that my whole heart has ever been engaged. . . ."[10] He believes he will "be appraised rather as a man of letters than as a man of action";[11] even in Arabia he craved only "the power of self-expression in some imaginative form" (549). Critics consider Lawrence an anomaly in literary history—intriguing, a master of prose, but a writer who resists classification.[12] They most frequently note his affinities to travel literature. But he had greater aspirations: "If mine had been simple stuff it wouldn't have mattered. It could have gone into the Hakluyt category as a good yarn; but it is elaborate and self-conscious: ambitious if you like: and that makes failure a discredit. It doesn't matter missing if you don't aim . . ." (*L* 359). Among Lawrence's contemporaries, *Seven Pillars* was art, not history, and Lawrence generally wrote of it as art, even "an artificial straining after art."[13]

Seven Pillars and *The Mint* can best be understood in the context of the confessional tradition in which they originate. Lawrence knew well literary precedents; he had read and admired, for example, the rare prewar edition of Henry Adams' confession.[14] Like other works in the genre, Lawrence's confessions are book-length, nonfictional narratives in prose exploring an aspect of the writer's life which determines his moral standing in a system of belief. The belief is public and shared in the religious confession, private in the secular. Highly selective, the writer reads his life under one sign or organizing principle. The prominence of the principle is deceptive, for it provides occasion for the writer's review of his entire life focusing on those aspects he deems most significant and revealing. "Did my mind select at the time . . . ," Lawrence asks anxiously of *The Mint*, "or is there no truth that art is selection . . . or does my book lack selection [?]" (*L* 619).

The confessional writer establishes a pattern or myth by means of which he defines himself. In discussing the genre in the Afterword to his confession *Manhood* (1946), Michel Leiris suggests that the author intends to make himself "the mouthpiece of the great themes of human tragedy."[15] The self must be explained indirectly by its relation to an idea or a pattern that is greater than the self, or at least outside the self. If the writer attempts to distinguish the self from the pattern in which it is embodied, he either establishes a new pattern or becomes incoherent and soon falls silent; the latter process Lawrence clearly illustrates in the final books of *Seven Pillars*. Arthur Schopenhauer, with whose works Lawrence's confessions have close affinities, writes in *The World as Will and Idea*: "as soon as we turn into ourselves to make the attempt, and seek for once to know ourselves fully by means of introspective reflection, we are lost in a bottomless void; we find ourselves like the hollow glass globe, from out of which a voice speaks whose cause is not to be found in it, and whereas we desired to comprehend ourselves, we find, with a shudder, nothing but a vanishing spectre."[16]

The organizing principle may be religious, as in Augustine and Bunyan, or secular, as in Wilde and Lawrence. The confessions of Wilde and Lawrence are imitative of clearly established Romantic literary patterns. Just as the narrative of an exemplary conversion unifies Augustine's confession, so the process of growth and contraction of self endured by a late Romantic hero unifies Lawrence's. In *The Mint* Lawrence delineates the Romantic myth his confessions embody: "Man, who was born as one, breaks into little prisms when he thinks: but if he passes through thought into despair, or comprehension, he again achieves some momentary onenesses with himself" (*M* 179). "Onenesses" indicates Lawrence's constant ambivalence about the validity of the pattern he imposes.

The confession has a didactic purpose inseparable from its myth; the hero becomes the exemplar of the teaching. Augustine traces the steps of his conversion and shows his difficult pilgrimage from pagan to Christian; Rousseau discovers and professes the new religion of Romanticism, using his own life to prove the validity of his theories about a man "true to nature"; Adams propounds a deterministic view of history which, he believes, explains his life and character. According to Northrop Frye, "Nearly always some theoretical and intellectual interest in religion, politics, or art plays a leading role in the confession. It is his success in integrating his mind on such subjects that makes the author of a confession feel that his life is worth writing about."[17] But in the best confessions the ordering myth and the lesson are not securely held or fully understood; the integration is tentative. There is constant tension between the narrator's assertion of his uniqueness and his attempts to show himself as representative. The myth develops in writing the confession and threatens to succumb to other principles of order during composition. The confession creates the myth and then defends it against other orientations. It presents ongoing thoughts and feelings, not a finished product. "By putting all the troubles and dilemmas on paper," Lawrence writes, "I hoped to work out my path again, and satisfy myself how wrong, or how right, I had been. So the book is the self-argument of a man who couldn't then see straight . . . " (L 692).

The confessional writer brings his life up to the moment at which he is engaged in writing the work, then perspective is lost. Even Augustine discovers he must "confess both what I know of myself and what I do not know." He must record "not what I once was, but what I am now, . . . now, at this moment, as I set down my confessions." Augustine achieves no spiritual security; after all of his introspection, perhaps because of it, he admits, "I have become a problem to myself, and this is the ailment from which I suffer."[18] More than fifteen hundred years after Augustine, Genet writes in *The Thief's Journal*, "If I attempt to recompose with words what my attitude was at the time, the reader will be no more taken in than I. . . . [This journal] is meant to indicate what I am today, as I write it. It is not a quest of a time gone by, but a work of art whose pretext-subject is my former life. It will be a present fixed with the help of the past, and not vice versa. Let the reader therefore understand that the facts were what I say they were, but the interpretation that I give them is what I am—now."[19] In the confession the present myth of self, inverting historical determinism, defines the past and threatens at every point to transform or distort it; the past can be understood only by virtue of the present. The writing of a confession is an act intended to perceive the order in one's life, but it becomes a review which, at least in the traditional confession, makes that order or fixes the chaos. The confession also affects the future; it is, according to Leiris, "an *act*, a drama by which I insist on incurring, positively, a risk—as if this risk were the necessary condition for my self-realization as a whole man." *Seven Pillars*, Lawrence declared, is both "an apology for my first thirty years, and the explanation of the renunciation which followed on them."[20] Lawrence was planning and achieving this "renunciation" during the writing of *Seven Pillars*, a renunciation that was to determine the course of the rest of his life.

Though the form of the genre remains influential, the twentieth-century confession departs radically from its religious origins, for there can be no moral norm common to author and reader. Henry Adams, following the lead of John Stuart Mill in his *Autobiography*, broadens the theme of the hero's conversion to that of his education. In a comment on his own confession, *The Education*, Adams admirably summarizes the difference: "his great ambition was to complete St. Augustine's 'Confessions,' but . . . St. Augustine, like a great artist, had worked from multiplicity to unity, while he, like a small one, had to reverse the method and work back from unity to multiplicity. The scheme became unmanageable as he approached his end."[21]

The public, Christian myth is useless as an organizing principle for twentieth-century writers. As in other literature of this century, the myths used to present a concept of self become increasingly esoteric and idiosyncratic; even the ability to create a private myth has atrophied. Leiris argues that the modern writer can and should avoid establishing any unifying pattern: "From the strictly aesthetic point of view, it was a question of condensing, in the almost raw state, a group of facts and images which I refused to exploit by letting my imagination work upon them; in other words: the negation of a novel. To reject all fable, to admit as materials only actual facts (and not only probable facts, as in the classical novel), nothing but these facts and all these facts, was the rule I had imposed upon myself." Yet a few pages earlier Leiris admits his actual practice in writing his own confession; he employs "psychological myths which affected me by their revelatory power and constituted, for the literary aspect of the operation, not only motifs but intermediaries. . . ." Leiris uses the Freudian myth of sadomasochism to unify *Manhood*.

Faced with his isolation from larger social and moral spheres, the writer is forced to contemplate the adequacy of his instrument. "Even as I write," Leiris complains, "the plan I had devised escapes me, and one might say that the more I look into myself the more confused everything I see becomes, the themes I originally hoped to distinguish proving inconsequential and arbitrary. . . ."[22] Such statements, common in the modern confession, serve as persistent evidence of the natural and moral chaos the writer perceives and intends to express; frequently, as in Lawrence's confessions, conflicting presentations of self are left unresolved in the face of such confusion. The modern confessional writer, like his counterparts writing poetry and fiction, becomes obsessed with himself and the act of composition. Leiris writes that it is "as if the *creative* aspect of a literary work were subordinate to the problem of *expression*, the object produced merely accessory to the man who conceals—or parades—himself behind it." Within the confessions themselves there are copious reflections on the motive, significance, and manner of confessing. *The Mint*, for example, constantly portrays Lawrence recording events in the midst of its narrative. The heroes of *The Education of Henry Adams, Manhood*, Fitzgerald's *The Crack-Up*, and Mailer's *The Armies of the Night* are similarly engaged. The act of writing the confession becomes a way to cope with the moral chaos the writer perceives, a vital instrument to which he clings and which enables him to survive.

Didactic, public motives for writing decrease as private intentions to use confessions to make sense out of one's life or to change its course increase. The modern confession's purpose is, as Leiris says, "to elucidate . . . certain still obscure things." Leiris' intention is "to engage myself completely. Within as without: expecting it to change me, to enlarge my consciousness, and to introduce, too, a new element into my relations with other people, beginning with my relations with those close to me, who could no longer be quite the same once I had exposed what may have been already suspected, but only in a vague and uncertain way. This was no desire for a brutal cynicism, but actually a longing to confess everything in order to be able to start afresh, maintaining with those whose affection or respect I valued relations henceforth without dissimulation." Analogously, Lawrence's writing of *Seven Pillars* slays the will of its author: "it was a real beast, and this book its mangy skin, dried, stuffed and set up squarely for men to stare at" (564). Lawrence argues that the creation of *Seven Pillars*, not the war, destroyed his will and forced his postwar enlistment as an airman; the book took "all my nights and days till I was nearly blind and mad. The failure of it was mainly what broke my nerve, and sent me into the RAF . . ." (*L* 456).

Twentieth-century confessions are, in D. H. Lawrence's phrase, "art for my sake." Art is T. E. Lawrence's primary source of value: "Writing has been my inmost self all my life, and I can never put my full strength into anything else" (*L* 758). Through his confession a modern writer attempts to create value, to discover a private myth with which he can identify or which he can use to express the self, one analogous in function to the earlier Christian myth of conversion. The confession, even if it cannot sustain its shaping myth in the face of opposing presentations of self, incorporates these oppositions and thus gives its creator some solace, purpose, and sense of unity.

In the modern confession the relationship between reader and author is more ambivalent than it was for Augustine and Bunyan. Whatever his overt stance, the writer needs his audience and has a certain responsibility to it. The justification for the existence of the confession is dual; as Leiris emphasizes, one must "*illuminate certain matters for oneself at the same time as one makes them communicable to others.*" The modern confession is primarily written for a coterie or addressed to a single individual and is often published privately, as *The Education of Henry Adams* and *Seven Pillars*, or posthumously, as Wilde's *De Profundis*. Frequently the confessional writer defines himself in opposition to a public code of morality. He apparently assumes that his intimate audience identifies with him rather than with the imaginary general reader, for he sets out to outrage and antagonize this wider audience. Arthur Adamov's "The Endless Humiliation" is characteristic: "For what follows I do not expect sympathy or even understanding. I know that most of you will soon abandon me, paralyzed by an insuperable disgust. You will be the same ones who, confronted with the deepest conflicts of sexuality and neurosis, either maintain a stubborn silence or burst into odious sniggers to protect your meanness of spirit and your fear of facing a horrible and unspeakable problem."[23] The humiliation of Adamov is a consequence not only of the acts he narrates but also of the putative audience to which he exposes himself. Lawrence's attitude toward his readers vacillates between abasement and exalted egotism, and in this he closely resembles Rousseau and Adamov.

The general reader is assumed to have moral values antithetical to the author; he establishes his own values as an ethical norm and escapes the pessimism and bondage in which the author finds himself. Augustine and Bunyan wrote in triumph, indeed because of triumph, but secular confessions after Rousseau dramatize failure and humiliation. The self-integration characteristic of the religious confession now yields to portrayal of distintegration. "Pray God," Lawrence begins, "that men reading the story will not, for the love of the glamour of strangeness, go out to prostitute themselves and their talents in serving another race" (31).

Despite their declarations, the secular writers still seek absolution from the reader by means of their confessions. The confession, as Leiris writes, is an attempt "to seduce my public into being indulgent, to limit . . . the scandal by giving it an aesthetic form, . . . to find in my neighbor less a judge than an accomplice." According to Stephen Spender, all confessions are "from the individual to the community or creed. Even the most shamelessly revealed inner life yet pleads its cause before the moral system of an outer, objective life. . . . The essence of the confession is that the one who feels outcast pleads with humanity to relate his isolation to its wholeness. He pleads to be forgiven, condoned, condemned even, so long as he is brought back into the wholeness of people and of things."[24]

As seen clearly in Augustine's *Confessions*, the genre's archetype, both religious and secular writers reveal an inordinate and growing contempt for flesh and an increasing overvaluation of spirit and mind. This tendency reflects the religious origins of the genre, but may also be an inevitable consequence of intense self-observation, attempting to distinguish the core of one's identity from the acts and flesh which veil it. "Indeed," Lawrence concludes, "the truth was I did not like the 'myself' I could see and hear" (566). Confessions are Puritan in temper, yet their writers assume an erotic viewpoint, for sexuality is the most obvious and central denial of the primacy of spirit. Confessional writers, particularly the modern ones, are deeply wounded in their sex. One must triumph over the sexual, sublimate it, or prostrate oneself to it. Sexuality is central to the confessions of Augustine, Abélard, Rousseau, Lawrence, Leiris, Adamov, Genet, and Mailer, central not only to their lives but to the shape they give their lives.

Psychology is a discipline in the Christian heritage of self-scrutiny, the tradition of Augustine, Abélard, and Bunyan.[25] The modern confessional writer discovers a self in pain and bondage. Introspection is the cause of the suffering, for it is the introspective power, not God, that must be appeased. To look inward is a punishing experience, but the reward is in the pain, in discovering an exemplary sufferer or sinner. Lawrence writes eloquently, "Saint and sinner touch—as great saints and great sinners" (*M* 179), and he sometimes sees the agony which the introspective self endures as a crucifixion.

As Susan Sontag notes, in the nineteenth and twentieth centuries the artist has replaced the saint as exemplary sufferer. "One used to think," Lawrence writes bitterly of his confessional impulse, "that such frames of mind would have perished with the age of religion: and yet here they rise up, purely secular. It's a livid flash into the Nitrian desert: seems almost to strip the sainthood from Anthony. How about Teresa?" (*L* 416). H. M. Tomlinson argues in a letter to Lawrence that no critic of *Seven Pillars* "got near his formidable job, which might have been about a crucifixion, with himself as the sinner for whom this was done. . . . Sometimes I wonder what would happen if full light fell on the scene and the words—so that all might get the revelation—'Father, forgive them.' " Lawrence annotates Tomlinson's letter: "I did have that crucifixion motif in the back of my head. Christians often forget how many thousands of people have been crucified."[26] The hero of *Seven Pillars* endures a period of purification in the desert, preaches publicly the religion of nationalism, makes a triumphal entry into Jerusalem, suffers despair and betrayal, is flagellated. But Lawrence's use of the motif of crucifixion is derivative, suggesting that he acquired the pattern more through literature than religion. If the pain is real, the crucifixion is imitative, as even Lawrence understands by Book IX of *Seven Pillars*: "When the expiator was conscious of the under-motives and the after-glory of his act, both were wasted on him" (551). Lawrence records in *Minorities*, a private anthology of lyrics he admires, an F. L. Lucas poem that ends, "Only our pain is never masquerade."[27]

As the confession becomes secularized, soul becomes a vague concept of "self," a shrinking core or citadel to which identity withdraws. Bunyan's *Grace Abounding* provides several revealing comparisons to Lawrence's work; both *Seven Pillars* and *The Mint* are in the English Puritan confessional tradition—the former in spirit, the latter in spirit and form. In the works of both writers act and self, what you do and what you are, are irremediably separated. Grace and redemption are given, not earned; damnation and salvation are foreordained. But there are significant differences. As Bunyan is to God, Lawrence is to an aspect of himself which judges, which is implacable, and which remains independent—untouched and uncorrupted by good or evil acts. For Lawrence no appeal beyond the self and its phantasms is conceivable. Adamov summarizes the psychological loss accompanying such secularization: "Thus the great gods who once governed all together became the tiny and absurd demons that tyrannize each of us separately. . . . The suppression of rites, the decay of festivals, of every ceremony practiced in correspondence with the rites of the world itself, indicates the end of an era of sovereign equilibrium between exterior and interior. . . ."[28] The absolute now must be sought inside. In twentieth-century confessions there is constant struggle among the absurd demons inside each writer rather than with the great God outside.

In both religious and secular confessions, extremes within the self are frequently defined and opposed. For example, both Bunyan and Lawrence vacillate perpetually between extremes. Lawrence asks, "What was this hoarding of extremes, this laying up of the highest and lowest . . . ?" (MS 393). Perhaps this is caused by the hypersensitivity of the writers. With his exquisite sensibility Bunyan identifies the feeling that generates the vacillation; his "former frights and anguish were very sore and deep, therefore it did oft befall me still as it befalleth those that have been scared with fire: I thought every voice was Fire, fire—every little touch would hurt my tender conscience." To Bunyan security "is the very kingdom and habitation of the wicked one." The vacillatory narrative rhythm of both confessions is expressed in Bunyan's statement that "sometimes I should lie under great guilt for sin, even crushed to the ground therewith, and then the Lord would show me the death of Christ . . . that in that conscience where but just now did reign and rage the law, even there would rest and abide the peace and love of God through Christ."[29]

A struggle between extremes exists for Montaigne and Pascal, but it is not the norm, not a condition to be admired or tolerated. "Man," Pascal writes in the seventeenth century, "is neither angel nor brute. . . ." The internal war of "reason against the passions has made a division of those who would have peace into two sects. The first would renounce their passions, and become gods; the other would renounce reason, and become brute beasts." Pascal argues that one must seek the *via media*: "Man must not think that he is on a level either with the brutes or with the angels, nor must he be ignorant of both sides of his nature. . . ."[30] But Lawrence and his contemporaries can live only at one extreme or the other: "Once I fancied I was very near the angels. . . . Angels, I think, we imagine. Beasts, I think, we are" (*L* 554). Lawrence argues that his own confessions are divided in this way: "The S.P. [*Seven Pillars*] was man on his tip-toes, trying very hard to fly. These notes [*The Mint*] are men on their very flat feet, stumbling over a sticky and noisome earth."[31] Lawrence, however, records no passage between the extremes, establishes no cause-effect relationship; he simply judges the same acts differently. In the sixteenth century, Montaigne identified a similar process: "I have ever observed that supercelestial ideas and subterrestrial conduct are singularly suited to each other. . . . People try to get outside of themselves, and escape from the man. That is foolishness: instead of transforming themselves into angels, they transform themselves into beasts. Instead of raising they degrade themselves."[32]

The author of *Seven Pillars* and *The Mint* first presents his hero as angel, then beast, as war narrator, then introspective self. Which is the true angel, which the proper beast is a problem he cannot resolve. These presentations of self are never linked; no transition between them is psychologically possible for either self. Lawrence vacillates between the two and is unable to extinguish one or the other pole or to desire a middle position. The war narrative of *Seven Pillars* portrays the hero's attempt to expand the boundaries of the self, to assume "another's pain or experience, his personality" (550). The introspection of *Seven Pillars* and *The Mint* portrays contraction of self, dissolution of the self under pressure of analysis. The main formal problem of Lawrence's confession is this division. Lawrence's attempts to bridge the division by means of structure are relatively ineffective, and the various manuscript versions of *Seven Pillars* attest to the vagaries of this attempt. Lawrence, while never abandoning the war narrator and his pride in his power to act, increasingly comes to emphasize the introspective hero and his paralysis. The opposing concepts of self are allied to the classic psychological notions of sadism and masochism, though these simplify the complexities of Lawrence's vision to some degree. In traditional literary terms, the war narrator begins in the optimistic, expansive stage of the young Romantic protagonist. After a time his will is thwarted and he must withdraw, contract the boundaries of self to the point of annihilation; this second stage is most clearly presented in the introspection of *Seven Pillars* and in the first two sections of *The Mint*. In his final stage the hero rejects personality and says he feels absorbed by society and by matter, ideally achieving "a oneness of himself with his fellows: and of them with the stocks and stones of his universe" (*M* 179). This stage is asserted in an unconvincing, contradictory manner in Part Three of *The Mint* and is never adequately dramatized. In significant respects, aspects of this three-stage pattern are common to Wordsworth, to Byron's early protagonists, to Carlyle's Diogenes in *Sartor Resartus*, to Mill himself in his *Autobiography*. In Chapter II I discuss Lawrence's intentions for *Seven Pillars* and how these are revealed by its manuscript states and embodied in its form. In later chapters I analyze Lawrence's dramatization of the two unintegrated selves of his Romantic hero, the expansive self of the war narrator and the contracted self of the introspective hero, as the author works them out within the limitations of the confessional genre.

NOTES TO CHAPTER I

1. New York: Oxford University Press, 1956. First published under the name of T. E. Shaw in 1932.

2. *Shaw-Ede. T. E. Lawrence's Letters to H. S. Ede, 1927-1935*, ed. H. S. Ede (London: Golden Cockerel Press, 1942), pp. 24, 27.

3. Letter to Edward Garnett, 10 June 1927, T. E. Lawrence Collection, Humanities Research Center, University of Texas at Austin (subsequently referred to as Texas Collection).

4. Letter in Vyvyan Richards, *Portrait of T. E. Lawrence* (London: Jonathan Cape, 1936), p. 186.

5. Letter to Charlotte Shaw, 17 June 1926, British Museum Additional Manuscripts 45903-04. Subsequent references to Lawrence's correspondence with Mrs. Shaw are to this collection.

6. Letter in Richards, *Portrait*, p. 187.

7. Letter to Charlotte Shaw, 31 May 1925.

8. Letter to Vyvyan Richards, undated [1923], Texas Collection. See also Richards, *Portrait*, pp. 185-88, where excerpts from this letter are quoted.

9. *T. E. Lawrence to His Biographers, Robert Graves and Liddell Hart* (London: Cassell, 1963), II, 177. See also quotation in B. H. Liddell Hart, *'T. E. Lawrence': In Arabia and After* (London: Jonathan Cape, 1964), p. 405.

10. Letter to Charlotte Shaw, 20 November 1928.

11. Letter to Edward Garnett, 23 December 1927, Texas Collection.

12. In *The Wounded Spirit: A Study of Seven Pillars of Wisdom* (London: Martin Brian and O'Keeffe, 1973), p. 139, Jeffrey Meyers, while acknowledging some of the influences on *Seven Pillars*, concludes that Lawrence "creates a unique literary form, a blend of imaginative and historical writing." For an excellent review of significant literary criticism of Lawrence's works see Stephen E. Tabachnick, "The T. E. Lawrence Revival in English Studies," *Research Studies*, 44, No. 3 (September 1976), 190-98.

13. *T. E. Lawrence to His Biographers*, II, 68.

14. Letter to Charlotte Shaw, 31 December 1928. Lawrence writes: "Do you know the 'education of Henry Adams'? Will you some day see if it has been cheaply republished? It used to be rare: yet everybody should read it."

15. *Manhood: A Journey from Childhood into the Fierce Order of Virility*, trans. Richard Howard (New York: Grossman, 1963), p. 161. Unless otherwise noted, subsequent Leiris references in this chapter are to the Afterword, pp. 151-62. There is no standard book-length study of the confessional tradition; among the most useful discussions, besides Leiris', are the following: Francis R. Hart, "Notes for an Anatomy of Modern Autobiography," *New Literary History*, I, No. 3 (1970), 485-511; Jon Lanham, "The Genre of *A Portrait of the Artist as a Young Man* and 'the rhythm of its structure,'" *Genre*, X, No. 1 (1977), 77-102; John N. Morris, *Versions of the Self* (New York: Basic Books, 1966); James Olney, *Metaphors of Self: The Meaning of Autobiography* (Princeton: Princeton University Press, 1972); Roy Pascal, *Design and Truth in Autobiography* (Cambridge, Mass.: Harvard University Press, 1960); Henri Peyre, *Literature and Sincerity* (New Haven: Yale University Press, 1963); Louis A. Renza, "The Veto of the Imagination: A Theory of Autobiography," *New Literary History*, IX, 1 (1977), 1-26; Robert F. Sayre, *The Examined Self: Benjamin Franklin, Henry Adams, Henry James* (Princeton: Princeton University Press, 1964); W. David Shaw, "*In Memoriam* and the Rhetoric of Confession," *English Literary History*, 38 (1971), 80-103; Susan Sontag, *Against Interpretation* (New York: Dell, 1969); and. Lionel Trilling, *Sincerity and Authenticity* (Cambridge, Mass.: Harvard University Press, 1972).

16. Trans. R. B. Haldane and J. Kemp, 3 vols. (London: Routledge and Kegan Paul, 1883), I, 358n.

17. *Anatomy of Criticism: Four Essays* (New York: Atheneum, 1968), p. 308.

18. *Confessions*, trans. R. S. Pine-Coffin (Baltimore: Penguin Books, 1961), Bk. X, Chapters 5, 3, and 33.

19. Trans. Bernard Frechtman (New York: Grove Press, 1973), p. 71.

20. Letter to Charlotte Shaw, 31 August 1924.

21. Editor's Preface, *The Education of Henry Adams: An Autobiography* (Boston: Houghton Mifflin, 1961), p. xxi. Though signed by Henry Cabot Lodge, the Editor's Preface was written by Adams.

22. *Manhood*, p. 83.

23. Trans. Richard Howard, *Evergreen Review*, 2 (Spring, 1959), 64. See also Genet, *The Thief's Journal*, p. 111.

24. "Confessions and Autobiography," in *The Making of a Poem* (New York: Norton, 1963), p. 69.

25. For development of these ideas see Susan Sontag, "The Artist as Exemplary Sufferer," in *Against Interpretation*, pp. 49-57.

26. This passage is included in a letter to Charlotte Shaw, 31 December 1928. Tomlinson's letter is in *Letters to T. E. Lawrence*, ed. Arnold W. Lawrence (London: Jonathan Cape, 1962), pp. 189-92.

27. *Minorities: Good Poems by Small Poets and Small Poems by Good Poets*, ed. J. M. Wilson (Garden City, N. Y.: Doubleday, 1972), p. 220. Wilson's Introduction to this collection is a concise, perceptive review of Lawrence's biography.

28.   Adamov, p. 65.

29.   *The Pilgrim's Progress and Grace Abounding*, ed. James Thorpe (Boston: Houghton Mifflin, 1969), pp. 59, 41, 34.

30.   *Pascal's Pensées*, trans. W. F. Trotter (London: J. M. Dent, 1932), pp. 99, 109, 111.

31.   Letter to Charlotte Shaw, 16 February 1928.

32.   *The Essays of Montaigne*, trans. E. J. Trechmann (New York: Oxford University Press, 1927), II, 599-600. Northrop Frye, in *Anatomy of Criticism*, p. 307, argues that the "confession, too, like the novel and the romance, has its own short form, the familiar essay, and Montaigne's *livre de bonne foy* is a confession made up of essays in which only the continuous narrative of the longer form is missing." Montaigne's essays are to the confession proper what the short story is to the novel.

II

Confession and History:
"The Interests of Truth and Form Differ"

LAWRENCE GAVE THE BEST-SELLING ABRIDGMENT OF *Seven Pillars of Wisdom* an antithetical title, *Revolt in the Desert,* which precisely suits the public voice of a war memoir and delineates the subject of his history. These contrasting titles reveal the ambiguity of Lawrence's intentions. He considered *Seven Pillars of Wisdom* "a perverse work. I shy off all the 'popular' moments . . . off the obvious . . . " (*L* 380). The allusive title of *Seven Pillars* illustrates this preference. An exchange of titles would grossly misrepresent both works, for the abridgment differs radically from the original. The intellectual, personal, and anti-heroic elements of *Seven Pillars* are systematically eliminated or disguised in *Revolt in the Desert,* the only relatively complete version of the war narrative to appear in a public edition in Lawrence's lifetime.

As the titles of the original and abridgment suggest a division in narrative purpose, so too *Seven Pillars* has a similar division between its title and subtitle, "a triumph." The opposition between title and subtitle is indicative of that split between introspection and action which permeates the stylistic, thematic, and formal aspects of the work. Lawrence's most extensive comment on the title is addressed to an enlisted man during postwar service: "*The Seven Pillars* is a quotation from *Proverbs*—'Wisdom hath set up her seven Pillars'—meaning a complete edifice of knowledge. It was the title of a book I wrote before 1914 and destroyed when I joined up: and I put it on to my war diary because I couldn't think up anything short and fit. The figure 'seven' implies completeness in the Semitic languages" (*L* 514). Lawrence gives three bases for his use of the title: *Seven Pillars of Wisdom* was the title of a travel

22

manuscript he destroyed; it is symbolic; and, closely allied to symbol, it alludes to a Biblical passage.

Characteristically, Lawrence's analyses of the title vary in emphasis and completeness depending on the correspondent, for each letter directs itself "towards my picture of the person I am writing to: and if it does not seem to me (as I write it) that it makes contact—why then I write no more that night" (*L* 813). Addressing R. V. Buxton, once Commander of the Imperial Camel Corps in Arabia, Lawrence displays a certain aristocratic arrogance, as in much of his work. The title is arbitrary, individual, and not to be taken seriously. *Seven Pillars* "is used as a title out of sentiment: for I wrote a youthful indiscretion-book, so called, in 1913 and burned it (as immature) in '14 when I enlisted. It recounted adventures in seven type-cities of the East (Cairo, Bagdad, Damascus, etc.) and arranged their characters into a descending cadence: a moral symphony. It was a queer book, upon whose difficulties I look back with a not ungrateful wryness: and in memory of it I so named the new book . . . " (*L* 431). Arnold W. Lawrence summarizes the limited interpretation given above in his preface to the first public edition of *Seven Pillars*: T. E. "transferred the title as a memento" (21).

Lawrence's analyses of the title become increasingly elaborate after the book's completion. In 1927 writing to his editor Edward Garnett he explores more fully his reasons for giving *Seven Pillars* the same title as a piece of juvenilia. Hardly is it a memento: "The title of my book was a reminiscence, for my ear, of a destroyed book of mine. But it fits the new *S. P.* better than it fitted the old. Perhaps [Herbert] Read is not fond of Jewish symbolism?" (*L* 548).[1] In 1933, in response to a question from his biographer Liddell Hart, Lawrence suggests the title is "More fully elucidated in Jewish Rabbinical embroideries (medieval Jewish) beginning with 'M.' " Hart selects several explanations of the phrase from the Midrash and, as befits a biographer of military and political aspects of Lawrence's career, considers the following quotation most relevant: "If man . . . is righteous and keeps the Law he will inherit seven lands; and if not, he will be dispersed into seven lands.''[2] Lawrence's dedicatory poem to S. A., which sets "our work, the inviolate house, as a memory of you". (5), supports this political interpretation. He also entitles Book X "The House is Perfected." The epilogue shows he had hoped to free and then unite into a "new Asia" (661) these seven type-cities of the Middle East which he visited in his early travels. For centuries these lands had been under Turkish domination.

Lawrence suggests still other interpretations of the title. In *Seven Pillars* he remarks that it is his "seventh consecutive summer in this East" (518). In the years after his enlistment he is obsessed with the length of his service in the ranks, a balance for his "seven years' labour of one head" in Arabia: "It's an odd penance to have set oneself, to live amongst animals for seven years" (*L* 412, 410). *The Mint* repeatedly calls to mind the number: "Seven years now before I need think of winning a meal" (*M* 21).

Lawrence compares a simple tale of Arabian adventure with his work and asserts he might have published a similar narrative if he had completed his prewar travel book: "Later I went to the very bottom of Arab life—and came back with the news that the seven pillars were fallen down."[3] The title of the unfinished book was intended to be literal, to indicate the full measure of wisdom to be found in the seven lands. To a suggestion that he might have made *Seven Pillars* a perfect lyrical triumph, he responds: "Yes, but that was only the superficial aspect of the campaign, and it would be superficial to write it as a triumph. The word [triumph] on my title page is ironic."[4]

Seven Pillars is not the book or house of complete wisdom. The military victory becomes both a personal and a political defeat. The clearest irony in the title is political. In the dedicatory poem the narrator attempts to earn "Freedom, the seven pillared worthy house" for S. A., "But for fit monument I shattered it, unfinished." He refuses to unify the seven Arab lands. The book is not even the narrative of victory (also symbolized by the number seven). Rather, "The practice of our revolt fortified the nihilist attitude in me" (468). During the war "it became clear that nothing was worth doing, and that nothing worthy had been done" (307). The narrator ends in despair, for "anyone who pushed through to success a rebellion of the weak against their masters must come out of it so stained in estimation that afterward nothing in the world would make him feel clean" (659).

Irony is also implicit in Lawrence's selection of the title from Proverbs IX, which contrasts the house of wisdom with the house of folly. Lawrence thought he was in the house of wisdom, and *Seven Pillars*, at least in its introspection, shows how he comes to know the place for the first time. The visitor to the house of folly "knoweth not that the dead are there; and that her guests are in the depths of hell." Nor does the confident and victorious narrator of the early books of *Seven Pillars*, the narrator who eschews introspection, know that in the penultimate scene of his Arabian Revolt he will end in "the charnel house . . . burying those bodies of ultimate degradation" rotting in the Turkish hospital in Damascus (659). But to recognize his residence in the house of folly is to transform it into the house of wisdom. William Blake's epigram in *The Marriage of Heaven and Hell* (his finest poem according to Lawrence)[5] is applicable: "The road of excess leads to the palace of wisdom." The Biblical house of folly is knowledge to Lawrence, "a complete edifice of knowledge" (*L* 514), because "what we call knowledge is the opposite of 'wisdom.' "[6] True wisdom is nihilism: "I have learned only the word 'No' in 46 years."[7] Wisdom is the extinction of reason and will, pulling down the house upon the self. If folly is the assertion of the will, wisdom and triumph are in its denial.

The qualities of the title represent the introspective side of *Seven Pillars*: its allusions to other literature, its self-consciousness, its pretentiousness, its irony, its "ring within ring of unknown, shamefaced motives, cancelling or double-charging their precedents" (552). Like its title, the work "is intensely sophisticated: built up of hints from other books, full of these echoes to enrich or side-track or repeat my motives" (*L* 371). The subtitle "a triumph," printed uncapitalized and in small, light type directly below the massive title, immediately establishes a tension which reinforces the ironies of the title. In 1922, the year Lawrence completed the surviving manuscript, he declared that the work is "in essence, tragedy—a victory in which no man could take delight" (*L* 360). As the title points toward the complex self, the subtitle states the outcome of the Arab Revolt in simple-minded terms. It delineates a story which "will appeal to Boy Scouts" (*L* 311).

Thus the major rhythm of *Seven Pillars* is found in microcosm on its title page. The title symbolizes the private self, the subtitle the public self. The complex, introspective, preciously literary Lawrence is the antithesis of the direct, epic, military Lawrence. He feels that what he is is independent of what he does. *Seven Pillars* fails to link the introspective to the epic, the unconscious self to the social self, the subjective to the objective, emotion and intellect to act. These crude polarities are merely suggestive not exhaustive, but there are subtler groupings to which the primary split between self and act leads. For instance, the complex private self identifies with the primitive Bedouin and the cyclical form of history he represents, while the man of action identifies with the civilized English and a progressive view of history.

Edward Garnett hoped Lawrence could unify self and act: "It's *all* there, except the relations of your inner world to it, the expression of which is to *harmonize* the whole. . . . Don't worry about 'the giving of myself quite away.'" But Garnett finally realized that "the whole character of the book reflects and is governed by the laws of your own character. . . . Your instinct of keeping yourself and your emotions so much down and under is justified by the result, and even the glaring beam you suddenly throw on yourself in 'Myself' [Chapter CIII], fits into its place. . . ." Nonetheless Garnett demonstrates that he does not fully grasp the significance of the division between private and public self: "The version you have preferred is . . . the official you which might have been supplemented by the revelations of the unofficial you. . . ."[8]

Similarly E. M. Forster realizes that readers are bewildered by contrary effects in *Seven Pillars* and clearly identifies the conflicting tendencies. Lawrence "has discovered that he can lead an Arab army, fight, bluff and spy, be hard and disciplinary, and this is exhilarating; but the course of his inner life runs contrary. . . . Personal ill-luck and ill-health, particularly a horrible masochistic experience, emphasize this, so that when he analyses himself it is as a spiritual outcaste, on the lines of Herman Melville's Ishmael. To the attentive reader, something has gone wrong here, the analysis has reached one conclusion, the text keeps implying another."[9] The Lawrence of the war narrative is Ahab to this introspective Ishmael.

Lawrence came to perceive the split more clearly than his critics. In an analysis of his own style, he declares that many "find the variations of my writing . . . confusing. But in narrative one goes full speed ahead, and in judgement one goes very slow, and in introspection one looks back at one's tale every pace so of course my manner changes. . . . Forster hates passages where words stick together in mimicry of thinking, but that's how I think— inch by inch, circumspectly, and agglutinatively."[10] Lawrence's attack on the poetry of Laurence Housman is a good illustration of the dichotomy in style he himself exhibits in *Seven Pillars:*

> Two voices are there; one is of the deep
> And one is of an old half-dizzy sheep
> And "Housman" both are thine![11]

Lawrence accepts and elaborates others' views of the split: "Garnett said once that I was two people in my book: one wanting to go on, the other wanting to go back. That is not right. Normally the very strong one, saying 'No,' the Puritan, is in firm charge, and the other poor little vicious fellow can't get a word in, for fear of him." He would like to make the public and private self agree, but is "too shy to take the filthy steps which would publicly shame me. . . . I want to dirty myself outwardly, so that my person may properly reflect the dirtiness which it conceals. . . ."[12] He resents "the doubleness of my shape."[13] Lawrence even projects his psychological conflict onto the lives and works of other writers: Dostoevsky "lived over-much within himself. Not many people are happy enough to strike the balance between inside and outside, and achieve a harmony" (*L* 492).

The contrast between sophisticated title and simple subtitle is a valid measure of the division between self and act which determines the style and influences the form of *Seven Pillars*. An earlier subtitle was struck from the manuscript: "An personal essay in Rebellion."[14] The word "personal" was inserted above the line, as if it were an afterthought. At first this subtitle seems more appropriate than "a triumph." A personal essay is what the title itself emphasizes; but the original subtitle fails to establish the division between self and act and does not stress the irony of the pretentious title. The emphatic "Rebellion" seems to refer more to Lawrence's attempt to rebel against English standards of thought and conduct than to describe the political and military machinations of the Arab Revolt.

Is the work a "personal essay in Rebellion"; that is, is it primarily confessional? Or does it narrate the history of a military "triumph"? Lawrence, as well as his readers, was puzzled by these questions. His belated insertion of "personal" in the manuscript is evidence of indecision. Now he sees one side of the conflict, calling the work personal, now another, calling it a chronicle or a history. Though he exaggerated when he insisted the abridgment was made "in seven hours . . . with the assistance of two airman friends" (*L* 518), he easily separated confession from history in writing *Revolt in the Desert*.

Lawrence on occasion believes that

> personal revelations should be the key of the thing: and the personal chapter [Chapter CIII] actually is the key, I fancy: only it is written in cypher. Partly it's a constitutional inability to think plainly, an inability which I pass off as metaphysics, and partly it's funk—or at least a feeling that on no account is it possible for me to think of giving myself quite away. There would be only two ways out of this—one to do like Pepys, and write it in cypher, as I have done—one to write what is not true, or not complete truth—and the second I don't like. . . . I think it's all spiritually true. (*L* 366)

Thus he considers the heart of the book confessional. He argues that it is indirectly a portrayal and estimation of his entire life: "For this the whole experience, and emanations and surroundings (background and foreground) of a man are necessary. Whence the many facets of my book, its wild mop of side-scenes and side issues: the prodigality and profuseness: and the indigestibility of the dish. They were, when done, deliberate: and the book is a summary of what I have thought and done and made of myself in these first thirty years" (*L* 370-71). *Seven Pillars* is no military memoir or history, but "sums up and exhausts me to the date of 1919" (*L* 431). Indeed, he writes in a passage struck from the first pages of the manuscript that it "is not the history of the Arab movement but just the story of what happened to me in it. It is the narrative of what I tried to do in Arabia, and some of what I saw there" (MS 8). Lawrence considers the work "an individual thing. Few books reflect their authors so much."[15]

At times he goes even further and argues that *Seven Pillars* is a psychological casebook. Its history is not objective: "I was wrapped up in my burden in Arabia, and say things only through its distorting prism. . . . It wasn't meant: just the inevitable distraction of a commander whose spirit was at civil war within himself" (*L* 432). It is "a pessimistic unworthy book, full of the neurosis of the war" (*L* 429). Both *Seven Pillars* and *The Mint* have only "the psychological interest of souls in travail."[16]

The manuscript of *Seven Pillars* is mute evidence of Lawrence's attempt to judge himself. It is written in a massive leather account book where he totals up his moral assets and debits. Lawrence "wrote it in some stress and misery of mind." He seeks his "own moral standing. . . . By putting all the troubles and dilemmas on paper, I hoped to work out my path again, and satisfy myself how wrong, or how right, I had been" (*L* 692). A passage struck from the first chapter of the manuscript suggests he is puzzled by the disparity between action and reflection and intends to work out the problem in writing *Seven Pillars*: "I am fully conscious that, as in my heat I sometimes did ill, and saw imperfectly, so also I must have thought wrong"

(MS 12). Lawrence later comes to realize that feeling, not thought, is the difficulty.

The emphasis of the book appears to change during its composition from act to self, from history to confession. According to Lawrence the change was forced upon him by events:

> In the S.P., I started out to write a history of the Arab Revolt: and the first of the book is an elaborate building up of the atmosphere and personality of the Revolt. After the capture of Akaba things in the field changed so much that I was no longer a witness of the Revolt, but a protagonist in the Revolt. So the latter third of the S.P. is a narrative of my personal activity. If I were going to re-write the book tomorrow I would hardly do it differently. The interests of truth and form differ, there as generally.[17]

Thus Lawrence is aware of the book's increasing obsession with self. Yet the self emphasized at the end of the work is not the self presented in the war narrative, whose acts, as Lawrence presents them, appear to remain independent of the one who feels and reflects.

The change which the hero undergoes is more apparent than real. Forster seems to recognize development (or deterioration) in the introspective self: the course of Lawrence's inner life "is turbid, slow, weighted by remorse for victory, and by disgust against the body," while his power over other men steadily increases.[18] The psychiatrist John Mack, who sometimes views *Seven Pillars* as the case study in the abnormal Lawrence occasionally believed it to be, finds that a "tone of failure and despair comes increasingly to mark the pages of *Seven Pillars* as the book advances and seems to parallel the widening gulf between the debased reality of Lawrence's experiences and the exalted nature of his dream. Simultaneously, statements of his conscious purpose—to bring about a magnificent epic revolution—give way to a searching inward for lowlier, more personal motives."[19] Yet Lawrence really presents no process; rather he emphasizes one presentation of self at the expense of the other to give the illusion of a process.

To summarize, in many of his statements Lawrence finds personal revelation the key to *Seven Pillars*; the book is a psychological study of his first thirty years. There is nothing remarkable in these assertions by Lawrence except his insistence that the entire book is subjective, even neurotic. Yet the frontispiece of the 1926 Subscriber's Text, the only edition prepared by Lawrence, is a portrait of Feisal, not Lawrence as in the posthumous 1935 text. Analyses of *Seven Pillars* as history appear less frequently in Lawrence's letters than comments on the book as art, confession, catharsis, or a case study in the abnormal. Lawrence could more readily separate introspection from history than the reverse. Introspection sometimes penetrates history, but the war narrative is segregated from introspective passages, and in the narrative Lawrence freely disregards the reflections made in introspection. He presents contradictory positions, perhaps with unfeigned conviction.

Whether or not he can write a book in which thought and feeling are independent of act, his letters commenting on the book separate introspection and history. *"Seven Pillars,"* he insists, "was a historical necessity: I don't call it an option."[20] In 1922 he writes G. B. Shaw that he "was brought up as a professional historian, which means the worship of original documents. To my astonishment, after peace came I found I was myself the sole person who knew what had happened in Arabia during the war: and the only literate person in the Arab Army. So it became a professional duty to record what happened." He insists the book "is history, and I'm shamed forever if I am the sole chronicler of an event, and fail to chronicle it" (*L* 356-57). In 1924 he writes Forster that the book "was forced from me not as a poem, but as a complete narrative of what actually happened in the Arab Revolt. . . . If I invent one thing I'll spoil its raison d'être: and if there are invented conversations, or conversations reconstructed after five years, where will it be?" (*L* 455-56). In 1927 in an angry response to a critic he asks, "Isn't he slightly ridiculous in seeking to measure my day-to-day chronicle by the epic standard? I never called it an epic, or thought of it as an epic, nor did anyone else, to my knowledge. The thing follows an exact diary sequence, and is literally true, throughout. . . . [Herbert] Read talks as though I had been making a book, and not a flesh-and-blood revolt" (*L* 550).

Nevertheless Lawrence had no confidence that objective history could be written. He deletes an observation that having helped produce history in the East, he had developed "a contempt for our science, seeing that its materials were as faulty as our private characters which supplied them" (MS Chapter CXVIII). He argues that "the manner is greater than the matter, so far as modern history is concerned. . . . The historian is retired into a shell to study the whole truth; which means that he learns to attach insensate importance to documents. The documents are liars. No man ever yet tried to write down the entire truth of any action in which he has been engaged. All narrative is *parti pris*. And to prefer an ancient written statement to the guiding of your instinct through the maze of related facts, is to encounter either banality or unreadableness" (*L* 559). Lawrence's view of history, as of other aspects of life, is total relativity: the only absolute is the individual Romantic will. History is made by the historian.[21] While Lawrence sees the war narrative as *parti pris*, he has no similarly predetermined opinions of private self.

Frequently Lawrence vacillates between labeling the book history and insisting it is confession; he will contradict himself in the same chapter. In the suppressed introduction to *Seven Pillars*, he finds it "historically needful to reproduce the tale. . . . The record of events was not dulled in me and perhaps few actual mistakes crept in. . . ." Two pages later he insists that "the history is not of the Arab movement, but of me in it. It is a narrative of daily life, mean happenings, little people. . . . It is filled with trivial things, partly that no one mistake for history the bones from which some day a man may make history. . . ." He ends the chapter by arrogantly challenging the validity of his own account. For political reasons, "I began in my reports to conceal the true stories of things. . . . In this book also, for the last time, I mean to be my own judge of what to say." J. B. Villars naïvely condemns Lawrence's executors for publishing such contradictions and needlessly alarming historians.[22] On the other hand Lawrence alarms students of his confession when he remarks that *Seven Pillars* is historically accurate, except for minor errors and many "things I was ashamed to tell of, because they were sentimental, or too good, or weak, or horrible, or just simply insane. We were mad, off and on: and I've suppressed these incidents or motives; even where they were of great importance. . . ."[23] However, conflicts between truth and fiction, confession and history, introspection and act exist not only in isolated sentences: they are inherent in the whole. Incongruities are found not only in what Lawrence says he is doing, but in what he does.

Lawrence contradicts himself even more sharply in his letters. Emphasizing the work as history, he says he "tried to draw a movement, and a country, and a race at war." Two paragraphs later he argues: "I put much of myself into it. . . . The *S.P.* is unbearable to me, because of the motley I made myself there for everyone's seeing. That's why it won't be published, in my living." In the final paragraph he writes that the work "was given a restricted circulation, because it was historical—the only record of its experience . . ." (*L* 608-9).

Rarely does Lawrence see the book as a harmony of act and self, history and confession: "You say 'record of fact' or 'work of art' [of *The Mint*] . . . When I had writing ambitions, they were to combine these two things. *The Seven Pillars* was an effort to make history an imaginative thing. It was my second try at dramatizing reality" (*L* 603). In another letter he integrates political and personal aspects: "It is meant to be the true history of a political movement whose essence was a fraud—in the sense that its leaders did not believe the arguments with which they moved its rank and file: and also the true history of a campaign, to show how unlovely the back of a commander's mind must be" (*L* 427).

Lawrence's most sensible and detailed comment relegates history to a secondary or subsidiary place. *Seven Pillars*, he writes Robert Graves, remains unpublished "because it is a full-length and unrestrained portrait of myself, and my tastes and ideas and actions. I could not have deliberately confessed to so much in public. . . . Yet to tell the whole story was the only justification for writing anything at all."

It is "all spiritually true" (*L* 366). Norman Mailer develops a similar view of the superior truth of confession to history in *The Armies of the Night: History as a Novel, The Novel as History*. By "history as a novel" Mailer means that the history of self, the personal narrative, alone is true, even though it is written under the guise and form of a novel. By "the novel as history" Mailer means that an objective account of events is in fact fictionalized, a novel disguised as history.

Lawrence comes closest to asserting the harmony of self and act when he calls *Seven Pillars* an "introspection epic" (*L* 621). Yet he finds the two genres mutually exclusive. War narrative and introspection are generally found in separate chapters in the text, though the manuscript isolates the two more thoroughly than the revision. The reader is confused about the work's purpose because Lawrence is confused. *Seven Pillars* is both history and confession, confession gradually relegating the history to a secondary position, but never becoming integrated with it, never absorbing it.

A multitude of relationships exist in *Seven Pillars* between history and confession, act and self. Lawrence knew this, of course, but finds in both literature and life that it is "a hard task for me to straddle feeling and action" (549). He consistently discovers that the public self "wasn't even a caricature, much less a likeness, of the private one" (*L* 605). Villars' desire for consistency would have been destructive if applied. The virtue of the book lies in its presentation of conflicting motives, in Lawrence's inability or refusal to blend himself into a smooth consistency. The most complete manuscript version of *Seven Pillars* is superior to the published text to the degree that it does not try to impose a logical pattern on the self and experience.[24]

Lawrence considers the introspection extraneous and easily detachable in various published and unpublished states of the work. The first published record of Lawrence's wartime experiences is in *The Arab Bulletin*, an intelligence journal founded in 1916 by the Arab Bureau and edited by Lawrence for a time. Several entries in the journal are incorporated verbatim in *Seven Pillars*. His first ride up

country to meet Feisal in Book I and his reflections on the
Syrian character in Book V are substantially unchanged
from essays on these topics in *The Arab Bulletin*. Most of his
accounts of the war in diaries and private letters were
thoroughly mined for passages in *Seven Pillars*. The earliest
postwar accounts were published in periodicals: *The Times*,
The World's Work, *Royal Engineers' Journal*, *The Army
Quarterly*, and *The Round Table*. These dealt primarily
with the events of the war or with matters of military
strategy. Sometimes they served as propaganda for the Arab
cause. In these accounts Lawrence kept himself decidedly in
the background. Some of these articles, particularly those
published after 1919, seem to be based on one or the other of
three manuscript versions Lawrence describes in his Preface
to *Seven Pillars* and his notes in the surviving manuscript in
the Bodleian.[25]

MS 1 was written from January to July 1919; Lawrence
claims he lost most of this version in November. He
estimates its length was approximately 250,000 words and
insists his "war-time notes, on which it was largely
constructed, were destroyed as each section was finished."
MS 2 was written from December 1919 to May 1920; it was
"corrected and added to slowly for nearly 2 years." This
version, by now approximately 400,000 words, was burned
by Lawrence in May 1922. "The Arab Revolt," a radical
abridgment which still remains in manuscript at the
University of Texas, is probably based on this text. The
abridgment was published in part and with significant
variations in *The World's Work*. It deals wholly with the
events of the war and was intended to be a popular account.
MS 3 was written from September 1920 to May 1922. It was
deposited by Lawrence in the Bodleian; he considered it the
"only sound text." Lawrence estimates that MS 3 has
approximately 330,000 words, but its actual length is over
400,000.

Eight crude copies of the Bodleian manuscript were
printed in 1922 on the press of the *Oxford Times*. The copy
of the Oxford Text in the British Museum has many
typographical errors and contains a multitude of variants

and autograph corrections in the hand of Lawrence. Frequently Lawrence introduces a word or sentence that differs from any other version. The Subscriber's Text was published in December 1926, and January 1927; 211 copies were printed. A condensation, bowdlerization, and grangerization of the Bodleian manuscript, the Subscriber's Text has approximately 280,000 words by Lawrence's estimate. Included is an appendix of photographs by Lawrence and portraits, commissioned by him, of Arab and English war heroes. *Revolt in the Desert,* published March 1927, is a substantial abridgment of the 1926 text; Lawrence estimated it contained 130,000 words. The public edition was published posthumously in 1935. Except for a few minor changes, the text is the same as that of the 1926 edition, but a substantial number of the photographs, cartoons, and paintings have been omitted. Those illustrations that remain, unlike the 1926 edition, are integrated with the text.

Lawrence added the most important books of introspection (Introduction, VIII, IX) to his manuscript after the war narrative was completed (21). *Revolt in the Desert* demonstrates that the sections on war tactics cannot be removed as easily as the introspective sections, and in the abridgment his reflections on military tactics appear integrated with the plot to which the whole of *Seven Pillars* is reduced. The fate of the introspective passages is curious. They seem so separate from the structure, or appear to have so much a structure of their own, that Lawrence can insert them in the body of the war notes and expand them substantially in the second and third manuscript versions. He begins to reduce the introspection in the privately published text of *Seven Pillars* and finally and radically does so in *Revolt in the Desert*. He adds introspection gradually, removes it gradually; the war narrative, however, remains a constant.

Lawrence is quite conscious of the extraneous quality of the introspection. In December 1920 he writes to Robert Graves, sending him "literal extracts from a book I wrote: but all the personal (subjective) part is left out for dignity's sake" (*L* 324). Later, revising the finished text, he left in these personal sections in Book IX (e.g., Chapters XCIX-C) against the advice of Edward Garnett:

> You will observe with pleasure that *none* of your suggested avoidance of the stodgy patches of this section have been adopted. . . . However, I've done a little, in this draft, to improve it. One special lump of stodge has been cut off from the bulk, and isolated. So a once-bit reader can shy off it ever after. The other chapter, that about myself [Chapter CIII], has lost a quarter of its bulk. It too, being concentrated, can be skipped. Whereas had I embodied its matter in incident, as you suggest, the poor worms would have had to read it all. (*L* 479-80)[26]

Clearly Lawrence believes the style and form of the introspection run counter to that of the narration. However flippant his explanation, he admits that he cannot embody the introspective self in events.

Lawrence's letters show that the introspection was an afterthought, that during the war self-analysis was periodic, not pervasive, and that an indistinct but real opposition exists between act and private self: "The war was good by drawing over our depths that hot surface wish to do or win something. So the cargo of the ship was unseen, and not thought of" (*L* 334). Thus he implies that the relationship between his acts and his sense of self was perceived afterward and grafted onto the war narrative.

The surviving manuscript of *Seven Pillars* (MS 3) supports Lawrence's conviction that he changed intention as he worked and began with no fixed preconception of the morality of his role in the Revolt. Lawrence says in the Preface to the 1926 text that the manuscript of *Seven Pillars* was "condensed (the single canon of change being literary). . . . I had learnt my first lessons in writing, and was often able to combine two or three of my 1921 phrases into one" (22). He lists a few exceptions to this rule, but these are misleading and represent only a fragment of the substantial excisions made. Approximately 50,000 of 400,000 words were deleted by Lawrence. For instance, an entire chapter (MS Chapter XLII) is omitted and not entered as an exception on his allegedly complete list. Privately he admits he bowdlerized the book (*L* 548).

The manuscript version of the dedicatory poem differs only slightly from the text, but the changes are representative of those throughout *Seven Pillars*. The earlier version more strongly emphasizes the will and immediacy of its speaker. "Death was my servant" becomes "Death seemed my servant" (MS 4). The manuscript "I" becomes "we," and "my" becomes "our"; the earlier version reads, "When I came . . . Men prayed me to set my work. . . ." The text, and this is true of the entire final version, consistently dulls and distances the sense of power and control the speaker reveals in the manuscript.

There are several types of manuscript changes in addition to the literary or stylistic emphasized in Lawrence's Preface. Tense is frequently changed from the journal or diary present to the autobiographical past, and dates are moved from the text to the margins, but these are hardly the most prominent. The significant changes are, first, that political attacks on both men and policy are made less biting in the text, whether on English or French, and there is less patronizing of the Arabs in the published version. The attacks and condescension remain, but are dulled, consistently becoming more impersonal or general. These excisions domesticate the "real beast" of the will (564). Second, and most relevant, a great number of personal reflections are either suppressed or made abstract.

Lawrence notes in the published text that he became more concerned with the self after the fall of Akaba in Book IV. Increased focus on introspection is much more dramatic in the manuscript and the pattern Lawrence imposes much clearer. The number of passages of any sort cut from the manuscript increases markedly in the latter half of the work; three quarters of the revisions are in its final third. The great majority of these revisions concern reflections on his motive and character and his contemplation of an honorable course after the war. Frequently the substance of these reflections remains in the text, but transformed into Lawrence's Pepysian cypher. The increase in the proportion of passages excised parallels the degree to which Lawrence changes from initiation and control of an historical action to domination

by it, from detachment to entanglement, from the impersonal to the obsessively personal, from war to self.

The dichotomy in *Seven Pillars* is evident in its process of
composition, its style, and in Lawrence's intentions. The self
who acts and the self who reflects are perceived as
irreconcilable in the deserts of will in Arabia, if not in the
deserts of flesh in the postwar R.A.F.: " 'Body and soul',"
Lawrence writes, "I'd like to believe—I built my Arabian
practice on the belief—that they are antitheses."[27] Lawrence
throughout *Seven Pillars* presents himself in two ways: in
the war narrative he is dominant, opportunistic, intelligent,
feared, successful; in introspection he is victimized, impo-
tent, confused, frightened. The reader may choose to
emphasize one or the other of the presentations of self,
ignoring the fact that one self cannot absorb or transform the
other. Or he may confront the contradiction and declare the
book is poor because it has no unity, certainly a frequent
judgment by critics. Perhaps the best approach for the reader
is to see this dichotomy as characteristic of Romantic
literature of the nineteenth and twentieth centuries.
Coleridge in "Christabel," Wilde in *The Picture of Dorian
Gray*, Conrad in *The Secret Sharer*, D. H. Lawrence in
Aaron's Rod, Yeats throughout his poetry and in *A Vision*
present divided selves. George Bernard Shaw writes that
"you masqueraded as Lawrence and didn't keep quiet; and
now Lawrence you will be to the end of your
days. . . . Lawrence may be as great a nuisance to you
sometimes as . . . Frankenstein found the man he had
manufactured. . . ." The comparison is apt, for Mary
Shelley's novel is a complex instance of the theme of the
divided self in Romantic literature.[28]

T. E. Lawrence proves as subtle in exploiting the
technique of self-division as many of these writers. Certainly
the self-division in his confessions is thorough and radical.
R. D. Laing argues that the division of self reflects the split
between behavior and experience in modern life. In extreme
cases, in schizoids, the body and many mental processes are
severed from the core of self. Actions become the province of
the severed body and cannot touch the citadel of feelings and

of identity, the self. But the self, cut off from any possibility of authentic action, atrophies.[29] *The Mint* portrays a similar annihilation of self, "the burning out of freewill and self-respect and delicacy" (*L* 419). But unlike Carlyle and Mill, writers whose patterns of spiritual death he imitates, Lawrence's annihilation does not lead to regeneration.

If the "interests of truth and form differ," then the validity of Lawrence's experience as expressed in the dichotomy is offset by the structure of *Seven Pillars*. The form at first seems designed either to veil the dichotomy or to bridge the chasm within its hero. *Seven Pillars* has often been compared with Charles M. Doughty's *Arabia Deserta*, though Lawrence vigorously repudiated the comparison. After reading a draft of *Seven Pillars* in 1924, Doughty wrote, "I am able to view your vast war-work near at hand, with its almost daily multifarious terrible & difficult haps, experiences, physical and mental strains, & sufferings & dark chances that must needs be taken, in meeting & circumventing enemies, in the anxious Leadership of an Armada of discordant elements, as often naturally hostile among themselves of Arab Tribes; until, after two years, you won through to the triumph of Damascus, after enduring all that human life can endure to the end."[30] No matter how curious his style, Doughty does summarize the war narrative of *Seven Pillars*. Yet Doughty's description gives a sense of inevitable but chaotic action, seizing in narrative form and historical act the given chance, a quality more characteristic of Doughty than Lawrence. Unlike *Arabia Deserta*, Lawrence's work does have an intricate structure. Doughty, according to Lawrence, had an unworthy idea of form,[31] "no sense of design" (*L* 534). Nonetheless *Arabia Deserta* was his best work because "his sense of design could express itself only in the aimlessness of his wanderings" (*L* 534). The true artist should care only for formal aspects, Lawrence asserts extravagantly.[32]

Lawrence divided *Seven Pillars* into ten books of unequal length prefaced by a substantial book-length introduction. A book is the important structural unit, and Lawrence's analysis of the form of *Seven Pillars* is expressed in terms of it. He wrote the work rapidly in book-length stages and divided it into chapters only after he had completed the first version.[33] At times Lawrence despairs of his attempts to impose a structure on the narrative: "artistically it has no shape" (*L* 384). He argues that its proportions are "the worst side of *The Seven Pillars*: and was determined that . . . whatever else I wrote should be, at any rate, calculated" (*L* 612). Echoing his own attack on Doughty, he writes that his own book has "no structural design."[34]

If *Seven Pillars* has no design, it is not for lack of effort. The work "is partly theatre" (*L* 775). During composition and revision he frequently analogizes the structure of *Seven Pillars'* last six books with drama; from these analogies the structure of the first four books may also be inferred. Lawrence's intentions are clear, but how far they express a valid or tenable commentary on its inherent structure is debatable. Lawrence makes at least three approaches to structure; the dramatic is merely the most prominent. None of the three contradicts the others, but each has certain liabilities and requires qualification.

The first four books describe two military campaigns in which Lawrence figured prominently. Book II concludes with the capture of Wejh, and the war enters a new phase. Book IV ends with the capture of Akaba, the most brilliant military victory in the Arab Revolt. In an early article on the Revolt, Lawrence says that after Akaba the "abandon of the early days, when each man had his camel and his little bag of flour and his rifle, was over. The force had to be organized and become responsible."[35] He describes Book V as "carrying on from the capture of Akaba through our establishment there to the first experiments upon the Railways (a marking-time book after the heat and adventure of the march to Akaba). . . ."[36] The climax is Book VI; *Seven Pillars'* "top note comes in the earlier chapter of our ride to the Bridges and failures after them" (*L* 520). The title of Book VI is "The Failure of the Bridges," but the most significant personal action in the book is the beating and homosexual rape of Lawrence at Deraa. In a letter describing the genesis of *Seven Pillars*, Lawrence notes that "Book VI was written first of all the seven pillars: and has only been twice re-written: except the Deraa chapter, which is about its ninth revise. Not that the many revises have changed its essence." Book VI was meant, Lawrence notes sardonically, to be "less gay."[37] The rape at Deraa is intended as the third-act climax (or turning point) in a five-act tragedy; it occurs precisely two-thirds of the way through *Seven Pillars*.

Lawrence seldom comments on Book VII, though he calls it "better than the average of the stuff"[38] and speaks vaguely of its "comparative excitements" (23), probably because, like X, it emphasizes the war narrative rather than introspection. Book VII describes the ineffective campaigns of the winter of 1917-18. Of Books VIII and IX, the most directly introspective and least active in the work, he writes: "Don't spend too much time on VIII and IX; they are only incidental."[39] He feels these comprise a dull description of a dull period.[40] Book VIII is "intended as a 'flat,' to interpose between the comparative excitements of Book VII and the final advance on Damascus" in Book X. He shortens an earlier version of Book VIII because readers "complained of the inordinate boredom of the 'flat' " (23). In Book IX he gives "birth to a long summary of myself; and there is a political argument, with much discussion upon the ethics of sacrifice."[41] The activity of the book falls "into a trough for twenty pages, to give my imaginary reader a rest before piling up the agony of the last advance upon Damascus" (*L* 457).

Lawrence fears the final books have not carried out his plan for a climactic ending: "I've never got them in perspective: and I've always had a lurking fear that they were flatter than the VIth and VIIth parts (the failure of the bridge and the winter war) and formed an anticlimax—a weak ending" (*L* 368). Most books "end with the big bang with only a word or two, short as a benediction, to tell us what happened to the bits. In nearly all the cases there is a deliberate effort at a final climax, except in the realism-hunting very 1900 sort, which just dragged grayly, without hills or valleys. I'm speaking of novels of course." Perhaps he is recalling his favorite Romantic novel, *Moby Dick*: "I have an ache in me for the big bang at the very last."[42]

On the basis of these comments, Lawrence's view of the

dramatic structure of the narrative can be summarized in the terms Gustav Freytag used to analyze a tragedy. Each of the first six books of *Seven Pillars* can be grouped in pairs. Books I and II constitute Act I, exposition: entry into Arabia, introduction of the central characters, and the first campaign. Books III-IV, Act II, present the rising action: Lawrence's Akaba victory and a few hints of the personal (as opposed to military or political) difficulties which are to come. Books V and VI, Act III, portray the climax: military failure at the Yarmuk Bridges, followed by Lawrence's will being broken at Deraa. They form a recognizable unit of narrative which begins with the aftermath of the capture of Akaba, Lawrence's proudest triumph, and ends with his beating and loss of "integrity" at Deraa, his greatest humiliation. Unlike the previous books, V and VI portray failures: military and political in the ride to the Yarmuk Bridges, personal at Deraa. Books VII-IX comprise the falling action, Act IV, as Lawrence recognizes in IX stating that "the next was probably the last act" (542). They are replete with nihilism and introspection after Deraa. Despite the movement from action in VII to introspection in IX, these books possess unity and are bracketed before by Deraa and after by the advance on Damascus. Lawrence intended to make Act V or Book X "more warm with excitement than . . . the frigid procession of all the other chapters."[43] Book X portrays the catastrophe: Lawrence's alienation from both Arab and English, which ends in hysteria in a charnel house at Damascus. Yet it also shows the Arab forces triumphant and exultant. Lawrence expresses the ambiguity of triumph and tragedy perfectly in a letter to Edward Garnett: "Yes, I saw that you were shaken: and ascribed part-cause of it to my writing. So, it was a half-compliment, but only half for great tragedy plays a catharsis and leaves its readers calm at the end. I looked on *The Seven Pillars* as in essence tragedy—a victory in which no man could take delight" (*L* 360).

If we accept his comment that Deraa is his "top scene" and the climax of the drama, then obviously Lawrence intends *Seven Pillars* to have an introspective or personal climax, for Book VI is among the least significant militarily. In fact the structure reflects primarily the introspective side of *Seven Pillars*—personal agony and failure rather than military triumph. The whole rhythm of the narrative of action is radically opposed to that of the narrative of self. Lawrence could not make the structures of action and introspection complement one another nor could he integrate them by establishing a cause-effect relationship between the two structures.

Revolt in the Desert is primarily a narrative of the war's events and in it Lawrence identifies a different climax: "*Revolt*'s top note now comes during the retreat about Deraa and Tafas" (*L* 520). In *Seven Pillars* the retreat and destruction of the Turkish army is narrated in the middle of Book X; in *Revolt in the Desert* it is also one of the final scenes. Lawrence realizes the extent of the revision he did for the abridgment: "If you read *Seven Pillars* you'll see that it's entirely different to *Revolt. Revolt* parodies *S.P.*" (*L* 520). By "parody" he means that *Revolt* is "a bowdlerising of the story and the motives of it, and would give the public a false impression . . . a favorably false impression" (*L* 374).[44] The abridgment deliberately is a "half-true story."[45] It is "full of quaint smiles and mock simplicities" (483). *Revolt in the Desert* presents a war without tears and becomes again the Boy Scout book *Seven Pillars* was in its early drafts. Lawrence carefully considers the proportions of *Seven Pillars* and *Revolt in the Desert*. He finds that the advance on Damascus "reads very weak . . . as though I was exhausted. . . . I put it all, disproportionately, into *Revolt in the Desert*, to give it a chance by itself with all the best bits of the early sections cut out" (*L* 512-13). Unlike the abridgment, *Seven Pillars* "is in excess . . . as regards intensity and breadth. . . . There's a clamour of force in it which deafens. A better artist would have given the effect of a fortissimo with less instrumentality. It's unskilled craftsmen who are profuse" (*L* 368). He wishes to avoid a personal "emotional climax at the end of *Revolt*" and eliminates the scene in the charnel house in Damascus (Chapter CXX): "*The Seven Pillars* is altogether higher in key than *Revolt*, and could carry the hospital chapter without its seeming in any way conspicuous. Whereas it would have stuck out of *Revolt* like a raisin in a sponge cake. My sense of proportion made me sacrifice purple bit after purple bit, in selecting the pages to comprise *Revolt* . . ." (*L* 520). In Damascus Lawrence ends in hysteria after seeing Turkish dead and wounded in a hospital. This emotional climax has nothing to do with the fortunes of the war, affecting only him.[46]

Lawrence appreciates the consequences to his history of these efforts to give the narrative form: "I want a diary, or record of events to be as near slice-of-life as can be. Imagination jars in such instances. In novels, however, slice-of-life jars because their province is the second remove, the sublimation of the theme. One is eyewitness, the other creative mind. In the first the photograph cannot be too sharp, for it is the senses which record: in the second, you need design. Any care for design renders the record infect."[47] *Seven Pillars,* unlike *The Mint,* is recollected "in tranquility—or rather in changed conditions" and is a "rationalisation of experience" (*L* 611).

Though Lawrence obviously considered structure a paramount means of imposing order and unity on the narrative, his analysis of *Seven Pillars* in the terminology of drama seems inadequate. The introspective hero, the "Myself" he struggles to define in Chapter CIII, does not in fact change before or after Deraa. There is no turning point in either his personal or military fortunes. Arab and English seem to progress inexorably toward the triumph at Damascus.

In a second approach to structure Lawrence declares that *Seven Pillars* is comprised of two balanced halves. The first half is completed with the capture of Akaba in Chapter LIV at the end of Book IV. The longest consecutive passages in *Seven Pillars* of the war narrative are Chapters IV-LIV, and these constitute nearly half the entire work. The chapters are preceded by introspection and succeeded by a shift from primary focus on the events of war to increasing focus on the self. In his letters Lawrence clearly perceives that the book

begins as a history, but after Akaba it becomes "a narrative of
my personal activity."[48] The second half is " 'a human
document': meaning a thing which a decent person would
not have written and a determined person would have torn
up after writing."[49] Told that *Seven Pillars* had the making
of great tragedy because it did not portray his personal
triumph, Lawrence responds, "I tried to bring this out, just
this side of egotism, as a second note running through the
book after Chapter V., and increasing slowly towards the
close, but it would be a fault in scale to represent the Arab
Revolt mainly as a personal tragedy to me."[50] In a letter to a
compatriot in the Revolt, he indicates the moment of change
with less precision and more emotion: "After you left us the
Arab Adventure got rather too black and heavy and the gaiety
died out: while the end of it left a nasty taste in my mouth.
Hence partly my disgust for my war personality" (*L* 399).
Lawrence also notes this change in the text:

> I had no concern with the Arab Revolt in the beginning. In the end I
> was responsible for its being an embarrassment to its inventors. Where
> exactly in the interim my guilt passed from accessory to principal,
> upon what headings I should be condemned, were not for me to say.
> Suffice it that since the march to Akaba I bitterly resented my
> entanglement in the movement, with a bitterness sufficient to corrode
> my inactive hours, but insufficient to make me cut myself clear of it.
> Hence the wobbling of my will, and endless,vapid complainings. (552)

The clearest illustration of Lawrence's changing intentions is revealed by study of the quantity, type, and place of
introspective passages in *Seven Pillars*. Before Akaba, only
the first three chapters of *Seven Pillars* are primarily
introspective. The next fifty chapters contain relatively little
reflection or analysis of self, and what does occur is quite
brief and fragmentary. He meditates on death and wishes for
it (e.g., laying out dead Turks at Aba el Lissan, 289). He
frequently compares Bedouin to English, supporting,
though not developing, the observations of Chapters II-III
(e.g., 147, 187, 219-20, 256, 259, 261-62, 282). Substantial
excisions of introspection from the manuscript are often
reintroduced in substance after Akaba. Thus an early
comment on his inadequacies as a leader (MS 102, struck

from text 145) is moved to Chapter CIII. Lawrence's early discussion of the proper attitude of an Englishman among Arabs and of his own cold-blooded use of an ideal (MS 120, struck from text 169) is taken up at many points in the last half of the book, particularly in Chapters XCIX-C. He suppresses a description of a long ride through Syria on an intelligence-gathering mission (MS 186, struck from text 275). In the passage he concludes, as he is later to do in Book IX, that he has become "almost the chief crook of our gang." He also declares prematurely that he hates being a man of action: "So many men craved action, detested thinking. It was an irony that I should fill one of their places unwillingly." Prophetically, he hopes for a bodily wound which "would have been a grateful vent for my internal perplexities." These examples by no means exhaust the changes he made of a similar nature. Lawrence probably removed such passages and inserted them in the final books to create a pattern of increasing introspection and a growing sense of personal failure in the midst of military triumph. If the passages remained in the first four books, the reader would realize that the self was not being changed by the events he was undergoing, that there was no growth in the hero.

Between the victory at Akaba and his torture at Deraa, reflections directly or indirectly related to the introspective self increase, though important changes in the manuscript are few. The most significant subjects are nihilism (314, 412-13), the effect of military discipline in making men social outcasts (337-40), and self-division (346, 451-52).

After Deraa, the increase in introspection is astounding. Implicit is an admission on Lawrence's part that he has failed to present the private self in action and now must approach it directly. In Books VIII and IX entire chapters are devoted to direct introspection for the first time since Chapter I. Book X has less introspection than the two immediately preceding it, but more than any other book except these. After Deraa significant suppressions of introspective passages in the manuscript are much more frequent than before it. Yet the increase in introspection in the final books is only quantitative; the qualities of the introspection do not change. Lawrence fixedly presents the attitudes and themes of Chapter I; there is elaboration of them but no development.

Seven Pillars seems crudely balanced on the fulcrum of Akaba, though Lawrence probably intended the balance to be thorough and complete. Lawrence contrasts Chapter II-III of the Introduction with Chapters LVIII-LIX of Book V. The first three chapters of V give Lawrence's immediate reactions to the Akaba victory and describe his return to Egypt and preparations for the northern campaign. The southern war ends with the securing of the Hejaz. Lawrence intends to begin the new "campaign as we had begun that in Wadi Ais, by a study of the map, and a recollection of the nature of this our battleground of Syria" (328). The next two chapters on the Syrian character (LVIII-LIX) parallel Lawrence's exposition of the geography and psychology of the Arabs, particularly the Bedouin of the desert, in the opening chapters of *Seven Pillars* (II-III). The Syrian chapters are a formal sign he has begun the second half of the work.

His analysis of the peoples of Syria recalls his approach to those of Arabia. He again discusses geographic divisions, language differences, and religion. As he plans the next stage of the Revolt, he at first tries to appear dispassionate, though he scarcely conceals his contempt for the Syrian or his love for the Bedouin: "Aims and ideas must be translated into tangibility by material expression. The desert men were too detached to express the one; too poor in goods, too remote from complexity, to carry the other. If we would prolong our life, we must win into the ornamented lands; to the villages where roofs or fields held men's eyes downward and near . . ." (328).

In passing from the Arabian campaign to the Syrian, Lawrence moves from emulation of his ideal back toward the debased reality which he sought to escape in Arabia, from anti-self back to self: "The difference between Hejaz and Syria was the difference between the desert and the sown" (328). The transformation of Lawrence's attitude toward the war is generated not only by his becoming involved with the townspeople of Syria, but also by the growing alliance of Arab and English. His sense of alienation is augmented by his re-entry into the company of Englishmen and their disciplined conduct of war; he now realizes that he is estranged from both English and Arab. Later he writes that the Arab Movement "had lived as a wild-man show, with its means as small as its duties and prospects. Henceforward Allenby [the English Commander] counted it as a sensible part of his scheme; and the responsibility . . . removed it terrifyingly further from the sphere of joyous adventure" (507). Thus the Syrian digression sets the stage for the personal disasters to come: he has returned to Western standards of conduct and responsibility, from the ideal world of the Bedouin to the pragmatic world of political expediency. This is the content of the formal division of the book into halves.

Another approach to the structure of *Seven Pillars* has already been mentioned. Lawrence intends to alternate books of high and low emotional intensity: "Books should be all up and down, like this ᴧᴧᴧᴧwith easy places between their heights."[51] Thus the form reflects his conviction expressed on the first page of *Seven Pillars* that "We lived always in the stretch or sag of nerves, either on the crest or in the trough of waves of feeling" (29). The movement between extremes is the rhythm of the book and permeates its structure, style, and theme. But Lawrence appears without transition at one extreme, then the other, like a burrowing beast who arbitrarily shows himself at one opening of his den, then at the other. In his presentation of self there is no process or passage evident between highest and lowest, active and passive, angel and beast.

NOTES TO CHAPTER II

1.   Herbert Read, rev. of *Seven Pillars of Wisdom, The Bibliophile's Almanack*, 1928, p. 36, writes: "Why an affectation of mystery? Why give this title to your book to which it has no relevant or perceptible application?"

2.   *T. E. Lawrence to His Biographers*, II, 130; also see Meyers, pp. 46-47.

3. Letter to Charlotte Shaw, 19 June 1928.

4. Letter in Richards, *Portrait*, p. 187.

5. Letter to Charlotte Shaw, 14 April 1927; revealingly, this reference to Blake's poem is recorded in a letter in which the primary subject is the union of his parents.

6. *T. E. Lawrence to His Biographers*, I, 65.

7. Letter to Charlotte Shaw, 31 December 1934.

8. *Letters to T. E. Lawrence*, pp. 88, 94.

9. *Abinger Harvest* (New York: Meridian Books, 1955), p. 138.

10. Letter to David Garnett, 30 February 1927, Texas Collection.

11. Letter to Charlotte Shaw, 18 July 1928. "Failure," a poem by Laurence Housman, is anthologized in *Minorities*, p. 76 (see also pp. 248-49), and is recorded at the end of the Bodleian manuscript of *Seven Pillars*. Lawrence's lines are a comment on "Failure" and are derived from a parody by J. K. Stephen of Wordsworth's "Thoughts of a Breton on the Subjugation of Switzerland."

12. Letter to Charlotte Shaw, 28 September 1925.

13. Letter to Charlotte Shaw, 3 June 1926.

14. Perhaps Lawrence was only following a convention of travel writers. For example, he is familiar with Richard Burton's *Personal Narrative of a Pilgrimage to Al-Madinah and Meccah*.

15. Letter to Charlotte Shaw, 18 January 1928.

16. Letter to Charlotte Shaw, 4 January 1928.

17. *Shaw-Ede*, p. 11. In a letter to Charlotte Shaw, 29 July 1927, Lawrence argues that in the Akaba ride he first became "conscious of my aim in Arabia. It represents the change over of the book from accident to intention. 'Revolt' hides that purposely."

18. *Abinger Harvest*, p. 138.

19. "T. E. Lawrence: A Study of Heroism and Conflict," *American Journal of Psychiatry*, CXXV (1969), 1086.

20. *T. E. Lawrence to His Biographers*, I, 155.

21. For a discussion of this idea, see E. H. Carr, *What Is History?* (New York: Knopf, 1961), Chapter I.

22. *T. E. Lawrence: or, The Search for the Absolute*, trans. Peter Dawnay (London: Sidgwick and Jackson, 1958), pp. 297-98. The suppressed chapter is in *Oriental Assembly*, ed. Arnold W. Lawrence (New York: E. P. Dutton, 1940), pp. 139-46.

23. *T. E. Lawrence to His Biographers*, I, 117-18.

24. Wayne Shumaker develops this notion in *English Autobiography* (Berkeley: University of California Press, 1954), pp. 44-45.

25. See also Lawrence's record of the writing, printing, and distribution of *Seven Pillars* reproduced in *Texas Quarterly*, V (Autumn, 1962), 48.

26. This seems to be Lawrence's general attitude toward the suggestions of critics such as Edward Garnett and Robert Graves. He is not the deferential writer R. P. Blackmur and Stanley Weintraub would have him be in their critical studies of him. Though he sometimes assumes an obsequious role before famous writers, in the end he does not carry out their suggestions.

27. Letter to Charlotte Shaw, 30 April 1924.

28. *Letters to T. E. Lawrence*, pp. 168-69. For a study of this theme in the novel, see Harold Bloom's Afterword to Mary Shelley, *Frankenstein* (New York: New American Library, 1965). Recent general studies of the subject are Masao Miyoshi, *The Divided Self: A Perspective on the Literature of the Victorians* (New York: New

York University Press, 1969), and C. F. Keppler, *The Literature of the Second Self* (Tucson: University of Arizona Press, 1972).

29. Laing explores these patterns in *The Divided Self* (Baltimore: Penguin Books, 1965) and *The Politics of Experience* (New York: Ballantine Books, 1967).

30. *Letters to T. E. Lawrence*, p. 54.

31. Letter to Charlotte Shaw, 2 February 1928.

32. Letter to Eric Kennington, 29 April 1926, Texas Collection.

33. Letter to Charlotte Shaw, 16 February 1928.

34. Letter to Charlotte Shaw, 29 July 1927.

35. *Evolution of a Revolt: Early Postwar Writings of T. E. Lawrence*, eds. Stanley and Rodelle Weintraub (University Park: Pennsylvania State University Press, 1968), pp. 45-46.

36. Letter to Charlotte Shaw, 16 May 1925.

37. Letter to Charlotte Shaw, 30 July 1925.

38. *Ibid.*

39. Letter to Charlotte Shaw, 7 October 1925.

40. Letter to David Garnett, 21 June 1925, Texas Collection.

41. *Ibid.*

42. Letter to Charlotte Shaw, 10 May 1926.

43. Letter to Charlotte Shaw, 4 July 1925.

44. Lawrence was discussing an earlier abridgment of *Seven Pillars* made by Edward Garnett in 1922. Garnett's draft was more frank than *Revolt in the Desert* and Lawrence refused to publish it, in part because he considered it too revealing.

45. Letter to David Garnett, 30 November 1927, Texas Collection.

46. Meyers, in *The Wounded Spirit*, pp. 66-67, 147, provides a detailed comparison of *Seven Pillars* and *Revolt in the Desert*.

47. Quoted by John Brophy in *T. E. Lawrence by His Friends*, ed. Arnold W. Lawrence (London: Jonathan Cape, 1937), p. 441.

48. *Shaw-Ede*, p. 11.

49. Letter to Eric Kennington, undated [c. October 1926], Texas Collection.

50. Letter in Richards, *Portrait*, p. 188.

51. Letter to David Garnett, 16 February 1928, Texas Collection.

III

War Narrator: "Joyless Impunity"

*All of them, through incapacity or timidity or liking, allowed
me too free a hand. . . . they gave me licence, which I abused
in insipid indulgence. Every orchard fit to rob must have a
guardian, dogs, a high wall, barbed wire. Out upon joyless
impunity! (565)*

WHEN LAWRENCE ANALYZES HIMSELF AT THE END OF *Seven
Pillars* he argues that only "too good an actor could so
impress his favourable opinion. . . . I began to wonder if all
established reputations were founded, like mine, on fraud"
(562). The form of *Seven Pillars*, the increasing desire to turn
from the war narrative to introspection, reveals the strength
of Lawrence's feeling that he cannot get himself into the
action, that the self with which he identifies is not defined by
these acts. He finds that "it was and is very hard to *write
about oneself* in action."[1] He declares that his participation
in the war was "more acting than action" (*L* 693) and tears
off the mask of this role in chapters of introspection (563).
Nonetheless the role rather than the introspection may
represent the true self he has sought all along, the self he
cannot acknowledge.[2] Hegel insists that "the individual
being *is* what the *act is*. . . . when his performance and his
inner possibility, capacity, or intention are opposed, the
former *alone* is to be regarded as his true reality, even if he
deceives himself on the point and, after he has turned from
his action into himself, means to be something else in his
'inner mind' than what he is in the act."[3] The introspection
in *Seven Pillars* is a veil thrown over the act not merely to
prevent the reader from grasping its true nature, but for
Lawrence's sake. Once Lawrence comes upon an Arab
victim of a Turkish atrocity. Bayonets had been "hammered
through his shoulder and other leg into the ground, pinning

him out like a collected insect" (633). Impaled on his acts, Lawrence too is fixed and wriggling, seeking escape.

Before examining the pattern of Lawrence's introspection in subsequent chapters, I want to turn (as the form of *Seven Pillars* does) to his presentation of self in action. The narrative self differs from that analyzed in the introspection. Though self-conscious, it can act and define itself by action, can understand the cause-effect relationships between what it does and is, can grasp its motives. It is not a victim, but in charge. Lawrence's account in Chapter XXXI of his execution of Hamed the Moor is representative. After the capture of Wejh, the first great Arab victory, Lawrence rides south to Wadi Ais to see Prince Abdulla. He is ill and unfit for a long march: "Dysentery of this Arabian coast sort used to fall like a hammer blow, and crush its victim for a few hours, after which the extreme effects passed off; but it left men curiously tired, and subject for some weeks to sudden breaks of nerve." The party camps and he falls asleep. Suddenly Lawrence is awakened by cries that Hamed has murdered Salem in a fit of anger; he arrests the murderer. The focus of attention is not the murdered Arab or Hamed, but Lawrence: "I sent out to search for Hamed, and crawled back to the baggage, feeling that it need not have happened this day of all days when I was in pain." Fearing that suppressed tribal blood feuds would break out, Lawrence alone is qualified as executioner, for he is "a stranger and kinless."

Throughout the execution the narrator is cold, has a detached attitude toward the victim, yet is full of self-pity, as if he has a sadist's view of Hamed, a masochist's view of himself. Pain for you and pain for me is the mood. The narrative alternates between hard and soft, strength and weakness, naturalistic and romantic. The scene of the murder is Gothic: "I made him enter a narrow gully of the spur, a dank twilight place overgrown with weeds." But the description of the death is precise, vivid, as clear as Hemingway's deaths in battle, but with less feeling for the victim. Hamed is given "a few moments' delay which he spent crying on the ground. Then I made him rise and shot him through the chest. He fell down on the weeds shrieking, with the blood coming out in spurts over his clothes, and jerked about till he rolled nearly to where I was. I fired again, but was shaking so that I only broke his wrist. He went on calling out, less loudly . . . and I leant forward and shot him for the last time in the thick of his neck under the jaw. His body shivered a little, and I called the Ageyl; who buried him in the gulley where he was."

Hamed is described as coldly as if he were an animal, and Lawrence's eyes are obsessed, not averted. He follows this passage with an account of his own wakeful night; in the morning, "They had to lift me into the saddle." The incongruity between Lawrence's concern for his own dysentery and his lack of sympathy for Hamed is blackly comic. Lawrence is not feeling well, but then neither is Hamed. Hamed crawls about waiting for the next bullet and Lawrence says that all this makes him a little sick. He is saying how sensitive he is, showing his insensitivity. Apparently what he feels is at a distance from, alien to, the imputed reader's feelings. Lawrence never characterizes Salem or Hamed, never sets the stage for the action, except by describing his own sickness. Since the Arabs involved have no individuality, the reader's attention is entirely on Lawrence's pain and his act. Lawrence shows emotion and becomes involved only when he considers his own predicament. His control of the narrative belies protestations of weakness and nerves at the breaking point. The focus is intensely on the self, but a self very different from that in introspective passages in *Seven Pillars* and *The Mint*.

An extreme instance of this focus on self occurs in Lawrence's narrative of a long camel trek across a forbidding desert. In the desert Gasim falls behind and is lost, but Lawrence leaves the safety of the group to rescue him. However, he has little concern for Gasim and makes no real attempt at characterization. Gasim is an object who comes to represent Lawrence's Bedouin identity and honor, "a single worthless man" (254) who provides opportunity for a test of his courage and endurance. Interest is solely in his test of will with the desert. Whether Gasim is saved is a matter of indifference—we have not heard of him before the rescue and he never again appears in the book. The war narrator's repeated feats of endurance define his sense of self. Self becomes quantitative: Lawrence can ride this many miles a day, abide this many lashes, go without water this many hours: "Because physical prowess is measurable with a rod, Englishmen exaggeratedly respect it" (*M* 177).[4] "My body's reluctance to ride hard," he notes elsewhere, "was another (and perverse) reason for forcing the march . . ." (450). Lawrence seems to come alive, to feel authentic only when testing the outer limits of his endurance.

The narrator of the Gasim rescue is in control, knows the psychology of leadership, and clearly defines himself against the lost man. He is identified with Auda, the classic Bedouin leader. Auda explains to a townsman the moral of the act: "the collective responsibility and group-brotherhood of the desert, contrasted with the isolation and competitive living of the crowded districts" (256). The narrator now is not a muddled man crucified by events. Rather he seems to accept and be accepted by Bedouin society, his ideal community, which is both more individual and less isolated than the city. He is proud of the rescue, as his bantering with Auda on his return reveals. He understands the immediate benefits such acts have in furthering the Revolt, and he is not averse to coldbloodedly using them to increase his authority (MS 120). But earlier when he had contemplated attempting the rescue he found his "temper was very unheroic, for I was furious . . . with my own play-acting as a Beduin" (254). His emotional and intellectual judgment is that the act is imitation, valueless by some vague metaphysical standard. Yet his account stresses convincingly its importance, his description outweighing his overt appraisal of its significance.

While Lawrence was riding with the Arabs, his "mind went making pictures of them on the road, or rather tried always to discover what effect upon myself their pictures made" (MS 183). In a discussion of *The Mint* he describes this technique more vividly; these notes are

heavily passionate: the product of red-hot moments, when all those bruises on my spirit were aching. They could hardly fail to convey passion: and with it a courage and humour and honesty, for I'm convinced the fellows had all that. What I wonder if they convey is my isolation in their crowd: the chiel taking notes, using my feelings just as pegs to tune my strings. I pretended to be one of them, that I might write down what they said they felt. Oh, that was the difficult part. If I'd forgotten my reproducing business, and gone properly with them, I'd have been dumb, too.[5]

Vanity and obsession with self are Lawrence's most consistent criticisms of his work. "I *meant* the abridgement to feel modest," Lawrence writes of *Revolt in the Desert*. "Anything loud was excised, and little odd bits left in, as it were accidentally, to show the readers that, though not stressed, I was really in the middle of things. And if the modesty is deliberate, or even conscious, then it's really a clever man's improvement upon pride."[6] D. H. Lawrence clearly understood this technique; when an artist effaces himself, "one is far more aware of his interference than when he just goes ahead. . . . Because self-effacement is, of course, self-conscious. . . ."[7] T. E. Lawrence remarks of a book he is reading, "It is old-fashioned in the sense that the traveller does not keep one eye on himself . . ." (*L* 815). Lawrence's own "eyes are always busied in looking at myself."[8] Even in ostensibly impersonal description he stresses "detached points, which a one-eyed man (or a man with his heart in the job) would not have seen" (*L* 380).[9] In the war narrative the very absence of explicit or implicit emotion paradoxically reveals the strength of his feelings. In *The Mint* he would "like to choke out everything: hence that guard over my lips."[10] Whether Lawrence felt normal emotions at moments of tension in battle is conjecture. If he feels them, he does not or cannot communicate them. Frequently situations of stress "put reason on the throne. This was peculiar to myself in company, when I felt fear, disgust, boredom, but anger very seldom; and I was never passionate. Only once or twice when I was alone and lost in the desert, and had no audience, did I break down" (MS 344). The war narrative reflects this view; he never becomes passionate writing about himself in company, only when alone, when he looks inward, for there is the real danger and excitement.

The war narrator's characteristic control is seen clearly in his dramatization of guerrilla attacks on Turkish trains. The central event of Book V is a raid which culminates in a train mining. Lawrence has a "personal need to justify the new prominence and authority I had assumed in the Arab Movement in accordance with my decision during the march to Akaba. . . . to prove my fitness as a leader I must be active after the manner of a Beduin champion; something dramatic was called for. . . . My notion was to mine a train" (MS 228). Masterful in its clarity, the mining is one of Lawrence's most accomplished pieces of narrative. There is no hint of aestheticism in the style. It is a "private battle" (374), not one of trench warfare or massive troop movements. He establishes the remoteness of the scene by presenting an elaborate series of long, slow, peaceful marches to reach the railroad. The action occurs in a world isolated from contact with civilization, where anything is possible. The mining follows an abortive raid upon a station and thus is a tactical anticlimax, an emotional climax.

Lawrence's domination is reflected in both manner and matter: he controls everything that happens. Unlike earlier battles where he defers to Arab leaders, he now positions the mortars and machine guns, stations the men, and gives the signal to detonate the mine. Lawrence's self-possession contrasts sharply with the uninhibited behavior of the Arabs: "I could hear the racket coming, as I sat on my hillock by the bridge to give the signal to Salem, who danced round the exploder on his knees, crying with excitement, and calling urgently on God to make him fruitful. . . . I had not thought of two engines, and on the moment decided to fire the charge under the second, so that however little the mine's effect, the uninjured engine should not be able to uncouple and drag the carriages away" (367). He maintains this focus on himself and limits his narrative to what he does and sees.

After the explosion, he inspects the damage to the

locomotives. He stands calm and detached in the whirl of the wreck while the Arabs loot it. He is both our consciousness of the scene and theirs, for they have no "spare mind to see themselves in action."[11] But there is no implication that he condemns their looting; on the contrary, he seems to approve of their freedom to the degree he disapproves of his own consciousness, which would not let him be free. Perhaps the freedom of polymorphous perversity is also part of his admiration for the Bedouin character, for it is a world in which everything is permitted except, curiously, rape. They are unfallen beings, and he makes no attempt to compare their behavior unfavorably with "civilized" modes of conducting war. The Arabs, "gone raving mad, were rushing about at top speed bareheaded and half-naked, screaming, shooting into the air, clawing one another nail and fist, while they burst open trucks and staggered back and forward with immense bales, which they ripped by the railside, and tossed through, smashing what they did not want" (369). They are so possessed with greed that they "lost their wits, were as ready to assault friend as foe. Three times I had to defend myself when they pretended not to know me and snatched at my things" (371). The victorious Bedouins are now no more a military unit than the defeated Turks. They desire only to return home with their spoils: "Victory always undid an Arab force" (374).

Lawrence graphically expresses his contempt for the Turks. He is virtually without sympathy for the enemy or, indeed, for anyone besides the thesis and antithesis of Bedouin and English with whom he attempts to identify. He demands a different code of behavior from these westernized Turks; when they become as hysterical and undisciplined as the Arabs, he feels revulsion: "To one side stood thirty or forty hysterical women, unveiled, tearing their clothes and hair; shrieking themselves distracted. . . . Seeing me tolerably unemployed, the women rushed, and caught at me with howls for mercy. I assured them all was going well: but they would not get away till some husbands delivered me. These knocked their wives off and seized my feet in a very agony of terror of instant death. A Turk so broken down was a nasty spectacle: I kicked them off as well as I could with bare feet, and finally broke free" (369). His assurance that "all was going well" is brutally ironic. The fears of the Turks and the Austrian officers are well founded, for soon "some dispute broke out between them and my own bodyguard. . . . My infuriated men cut them down, all but two or three, before I could return to interfere" (370).[12] Of the ninety prisoners who did survive the wreck, only sixty-eight reached Akaba, some dying, some escaping (MS 246). His attitude toward the captives foreshadows the massacre he orders in Book X of two hundred Turkish prisoners (633).

The train is carrying "refugees and sick men, volunteers for boat-service on the Euphrates, and families of Turkish officers" (369). Lawrence exposes his indifference to the majority by helping a single passenger, an aged, aristocratic Arab woman, whom he unites with her lost slave: "Months after there came to me secretly from Damascus a letter and a pleasant little Baluchi carpet . . . in memory of an odd meeting" (371). The grotesque chivalry, the reunion of mistress and slave, underlines the general brutality. By contrast, he opens a door upon a carload of Turks, perhaps originally victims of typhus, and finds that the explosion "had rolled dead and dying into a bleeding heap against the splintered end. . . . So, I wedged shut the door, and left them there, alone" (368).

The war narrator's callousness is dramatized by an Englishman and an Australian whom he brings with him, the first non-Semitics to accompany him into the desert. Each "reacted to the type expected" (345), for they have no definite characters; their purpose is to reveal Lawrence's. The Australian, a machine gunner, responds as coldly to the mining as Lawrence. He "grimly traversed with drum after drum, till the open sand was littered with bodies" (368). Finally he "went out east of the railway to count the thirty men he had slain; and, incidentally, to find Turkish gold and trophies in their haversacks" (371). The other stranger, the Englishman, is clean and contrasts with a man like Lawrence, who, "subtle and insinuating, caught the characteristics of the people about him, their speech, their conventions of thought, almost their manner." The Englishman is the representative imperialist, the "John Bull of the books, [who] became the more rampantly English the longer he was away from England. . . . Abroad, through his armoured certainty, he was a rounded sample of our traits." The Englishman "was driven by the Arab strangeness to become more himself; more insular. His shy correctness reminded my men in every movement that he was unlike them, and English" (346). He cannot see the effect of the mortar shells as he launches them over the derailed train. Afterwards he "strolled through the wrecked bridge, saw there the bodies of twenty Turks torn to pieces by his second shell, and retired hurriedly" (371). Lawrence condescends to the Englishman's quaint sensitivity in this private battle where the broken flesh is all too apparent. By attributing the only feelings of horror to the Englishman, the sole agent possessing the refined sensibilities of the Empire, Lawrence indicates that he himself does not react strongly.[13]

The Englishman decently takes no pleasure in what he has done, but accepts medals for it (376). Lawrence refuses medals and takes delight. A week after the mining he describes this "last stunt" of his, displaying a tone which is only slightly masked in the text: "I hope this sounds the fun it is. The only pity is the sweat to work them up and the wild scramble while it lasts. It's the most amateurish, Buffalo-Billy sort of performance, and the only people who do it well are the Bedouin. Only you will think it heaven, because there aren't any returns, or orders, or superiors, or inferiors; no doctors, no accounts, no meals, and no drinks."[14] In part Lawrence's pleasure in such adventures derives from the fact that neither the organization nor materials of Western civilization are present in the desert. The railroad itself is the only fixed artifact of modern society. First opened in 1909, the railroad "at once put an end to the great army which used to perform the pilgrimage [from Damascus to Medina] by road." This is not to Lawrence's romantic taste, for "the annual pageant of the camel-caravan is dead. The pilgrim road . . . is now gone dull for lack of all those feet to polish it, and the kellas and cisterns . . . are falling into ruin, except so far as they serve the need of some guard-house on the railway."[15] His joining with the Bedouins permits him not only to abstract himself from Western civilization, but actually to attack its constructions while theoretically defending them.

The narrator's detachment from the consequences of his acts is vividly demonstrated in a later mining: "I touched off under the first driving wheel of the first locomotive, and the explosion was terrific. The ground spouted blackly into my face, and I was sent spinning, . . . the blood dripping from long, ragged scratches on my left arm. Between my knees lay the exploder, crushed under a twisted sheet of sooty iron. In front of me was the scalded and smoking upper half of a man. When I peered through the dust and steam of the explosion the whole boiler of the first engine seemed to be missing" (431). The shock of seeing the divided human body is felt by the reader rather than Lawrence; and a major component of this shock is Lawrence's apparent callousness and composure. Lawrence juxtaposes the half-man and the half-locomotive as if the two are of comparable value. He is more interested in the half-locomotive.

Lawrence does of course have feelings during action, but these are dismay over his own wounds, regret for a friend killed, delight in success. His typical emotions are only slightly exaggerated in his account of still another mining: a Turk "let the tail of the train slip back down the gradient. I made a languid effort to get behind the wheel with a stone, but scarcely cared enough to do it well. It seemed fair and witty that so much of the booty should escape. A Turkish colonel from the window fired at me with a Mauser pistol, cutting the flesh of my hip. I laughed at his too-great energy, which thought, like a regular officer, to promote the war by the killing of an individual" (379). His expressed feelings are of self-control and mastery. His guilt after the war seems generated by vague unconscious forces inaccessible even to the most searching introspection, not by such minings. Long after the war he cries in bed at night in his barracks, but the "only grief I know is my insufficiency."[16] Lawrence's later mental anguish seems to come primarily from indefinable causes which predate the war.

The minings reveal an even stronger delight in mastery than that displayed earlier in his execution of Hamed. If the war narrator does change after Akaba, it is only to become more masterful and self-assured. He expresses no feelings of remorse or regret while narrating these scenes of slaughter or, indeed, afterwards. Late in *Seven Pillars* the narrator's role in the battle of Tafileh recalls earlier minings and battles, though there are significant differences in the event. Tafileh is not a guerrilla raid. On the contrary, the battle signals the end of the Bedouin style of warfare and a return to Western methods; it anticipates Lawrence's subsequent submission of the Arab force to English control. Tafileh is the only traditional battle Lawrence conducts. As in most of his narratives of combat, he presents Tafileh in two chapters, the first stating the problem, the second its resolution.

The narrative has the directness of his field dispatches on which it is based.[17] A thousand Turks launch a surprise attack on Tafileh. Though Lawrence considers the town strategically valueless for either army, he decides to stand and fight because he is irritated by the stupidity of the Turks. Characteristically, he attributes the source of his anger to an affront to intellect, to an idea. He should have avoided casualties: "This was villainous, for with arithmetic and geography for allies we might have spared the suffering factor of humanity; and to make a conscious joke of victory was wanton. We could have won by refusing battle, foxed them by maneuvering our centre as on twenty such occasions before and since: yet bad temper and conceit united for this time to make me not content to know my power, but determined to give public advertisement of it to the enemy and to everyone" (476). Ostensibly as a consequence of his broken will under torture at Deraa, Lawrence asserts his will even more strongly externally: outer control and inner decay is the paradigm he intends to exhibit. The pattern is not new, even if Lawrence's awareness of it is. He cannot extinguish or even wholly disguise his delight in mastery; he can say, but not demonstrate, that the source of his energy or motive is base, coming from beast not angel. He illustrates at Tafileh the sadomasochistic moral he suppresses in a later section of the manuscript: cruel punishment "provoked only wilder lawlessness" (MS 393). The battle ends in a "massacre and I should have been crying-sorry for the enemy; but after the angers and exertions of the battle my mind was too tired to care to go down into that awful place and spend the night saving them" (482).

Tafileh is a "verbal triumph" (482). Usually he could restrain himself from putting into effect his sharp words: "a certain physical indolence and dreg of wisdom held me from action of a like untimely suddenness. With the odd difference in kind between word and deed it had grieved me always, not saying a thing, but never not doing one: yet on this occasion, open-eyed, deeds and words had gone together, to my lasting shame" (MS 305). Supposedly his loss of will at Deraa is directly responsible for this act: "To be charged against my conceit were the causeless and ineffectual deaths of those 20 Arabs and 700 Turks in Wadi Hesa. My will had gone, and I feared longer to be alone, lest the winds of circumstance, or absolute power, or lust, blow my empty soul away." His "sin" at Tafileh took the "last gloss" from his leadership of the Arab Revolt (MS 315; cf. text 502).

At Tafileh Lawrence's whim determines whether the battle is fought. His overt conclusions about the action run counter to the feelings implicit in his narrative. He endeavors to bridge the dichotomy between public and private self, to demonstrate that the battle is to his "lasting shame." He argues that this victory is not only perceived as a personal failure of will, but is actually a consequence of Deraa, a previous failure. Yet he cannot hide his delight: "The day had been too long for me, and I was now only shaking with desire to see the end; but Zeid [an Arab prince and the putative commander] beside me clapped his hands with joy at the beautiful order of our plan unrolling in the frosty redness of the setting sun" (481-82). Evidently, from the satisfaction implicit in the narrative, it is Lawrence as well as the vulgar Zeid who enjoys the battle.[18] At Tafileh in mastery, as at Deraa in humiliation, Lawrence possesses an identity, knows clearly who he is, and can present that self.

Novels of World War I portray the chaos of battle, Lawrence its order. In Hemingway's *A Farewell to Arms*, Manning's *The Middle Parts of Fortune*, Remarque's *All Quiet on the Western Front*, the hero is a victim of forces beyond his control or ken, forces to which he reacts and for which he is not responsible. As Tafileh vividly reveals, Lawrence is no victim of the war. Even Tafileh, which purports to be evidence of a broken will, is intentional, willed, cold-blooded. In *Seven Pillars* the hero is a victim of an aspect of himself, the introspective self the victim of the active self.

In the final book of *Seven Pillars* the war narrator is still expansive and confident, and Lawrence endeavors to heal the split between the presentations of self in action and in introspection by de-emphasizing, in the published text, this confidence. He excises from the manuscript indications of his expansive mood, adds passages which are antithetical to it. In the narrative of Book X, Lawrence is still the redeemer, despite the laceration of self for this role in Book IX's introspection. In a remarkable passage he writes:

> A shiver of self-assertion and self-confidence ran across the camp. I had made myself the magnet of their hidden longings, and knew that they were ready to do any service we asked of them. The whole country lay willing to our grasp, and I determined to . . . go through with it completely: though my lethargy also made me happy there, lying on the ground, reluctant to rise or do the routine work, while quite prepared to do the unreal myself, and to drag the changed hopes and loves of half a nation madly after my whim. (MS 396; cf. text 618)

In Book X Lawrence describes the triumph of the Revolt in imagery redolent of the sexual; he "could feel the taut power of Arab excitement behind me. The climax of the preaching of years had come, and a united country was straining towards its historic capital. In confidence that this weapon, tempered by myself, was enough for the utmost of my purpose, I seemed to forget the English companions who stood outside my idea in the shadow of ordinary war. I failed to make them partners of my certainty" (583). In the manuscript he is even more emphatic adding, "I was walking by an inner light of experience and foresight: but my sureness seemed to them luck, and my clearness heady" (MS 376).

Lawrence still implies that he can absorb others, can will for them; he liked "to have another, unprompted, announce my secret beliefs: [it] confirmed me in them, and exasperated my mind to rush them forward to an unwarrantable extreme of credulity. In a little while one fool would make his company all of them follies . . ." (MS 397). He identifies with those who "served a mastering idea, and then to it they would offer a general sacrifice, willingly fitting others as tesserae into the common design which comprehended all their consciousness." He still feels god-like: "the powerful infection of general praise swept away the defences of our dissatisfaction, so that we thought we had ordered all that fortuitously passed, and no more than passed!" (MS 377). He denies the obstacles which would hurt flesh, and in his preaching makes his men "eager for some remote, unintelligible, unearthly ideal (in this Arab instance freedom was what we called it) . . ." (MS 404).

Introspection seems not to have affected the war narrator, who to the last is "very spiny and high" (636). He finds it "uplifting to be engaged in a thing of scale" (MS 379). He still believes in the purifying effect of the desert wilderness and finds the cities "stifling with the exhalations of too many trees, too many plants, too many human beings: a microcosm of the crowded world in front of us" (644). Lawrence displays aggression, in contrast to the wishes of his fellow officers, when he presses vigorously a plan to station Arab irregulars astride the path of the Turkish armies retreating from the Palestine front. An English officer, Sabin, argues that the army has already done its duty, while Lawrence, "jealous for the Arab honour," is willing to "go forward at all costs" (624).[19] The war narrator is convinced of the effectiveness of the government he imposes on Syria, which endured, he boasts, "for two years, without foreign advice, in an occupied country wasted by war, and against the will of important elements among the Allies" (651). He

declares that the "harsh days of my solitary battling had
passed. The lone hand had won against the world's
odds . . ." (659).

Side by side with claims of self-expansion, the introspective writer asserts atrophy of will and contradicts the
psychological state of the war narrator at every point.
Everyone is "stout and in health. Except myself" (586). He
denies his eagerness for battle, rests in a pastoral setting, and
thinks of England, wishing "very much to be safely there,
out of it all" (MS 378). His "nerve had broken; and I would
be lucky if the ruin of it could be hidden" (586). He adds to
the text, "when body and spirit were as wearily sick as mine,
they almost instinctively sought a plausible avoidance of the
way of danger" (616).[20] A strong active man would be worn
down by the war, but also "a book-reader like myself" (MS
414).

Lawrence's deprecation of the efforts of the war narrator is
thorough in Book X's introspection. Victory is "a lanky,
white-skinned, rather languid woman" (621), and he
despises women. He declares his gift to the Arabs is "this
false liberty drawn down to them by spells and wickedness"
(MS 411). He dramatizes his isolation from the English by
wandering among them in Arab disguise (641). Yet only for
him is the Arab call for a victory prayer in Damascus
"sorrowful and the phrase meaningless" (652). Now his
image of Bedouin life ignores their elaborate social
organization and emphasizes contraction of self, even death:
"The essence of the desert was the lonely moving individual,
the son of the road, apart from the world as in a grave" (638).
Lawrence constantly analyzes the extinction of self in the
ranks, his future course. He is decidedly negative, declaring
that the troops wear "death's livery" and are "below
humanity" (641), "unlike the abrupt wholesomeness of
Beduin" (638).

Lawrence attempts to show the convergence of the
narrators of war and introspection at the end of *Seven
Pillars*. In the penultimate chapter he describes the Turkish
hospital in Damascus, where the dead "crept with rats, who
had gnawed wet red galleries into them." The living were
not much better off: "I thought these too were dead, each

man rigid on his stinking pallet, from which liquid muck had dripped down to stiffen on the cemented floor" (655). In the manuscript he intimates that this death is to symbolize his future: not death as a strong spirit with quiet hands and wings, but "slow physical corruption, a piecemeal rotting of the envelope of flesh about the hopeless spirit, longing to escape" (MS 413). Later, as Lawrence contemplates his achievement in restoring the hospital to a semblance of order, an officer discovers him in charge and finds the place disgraceful. Lawrence cackles out "with the wild laughter of strain" (659). The officer calls him a "Bloody brute" and smacks him. Lawrence decides the officer's judgment is correct, if not in this instance, at least as a general conclusion, for he is now "so stained in estimation that afterward nothing in the world would make him feel clean" (659). He intends the moral to be clear: his role in the Revolt produces his degradation; act determines self and the dichotomy is annihilated. But Lawrence's hysteria is contrived, contrasting crudely with the extraordinary self-possession which the narrator had previously exhibited in public.

Seven Pillars attempts to disguise, perhaps from Lawrence himself, his love of war and of domination of other men. In the book he protests repeatedly that he had been content with his job in Cairo and is unhappy to leave it, that he is ready at every stage to yield his power. There is a radical difference between the attitude toward war he professes in his letters and that expressed in *Seven Pillars*. In October 1914, he is dismayed that "Turkey seems at last to have made up its mind to lie down and be at peace with all the world. I'm sorry, because I wanted to root them out of Syria, and now their blight will be more enduring than ever" (L 187). In March 1915, he has a seemingly grandiose plan: "I want to pull them [the small Arab powers] all together, and to roll up Syria by way of the Hedjaz in the name of the Sherif. . . . we can rush right up to Damascus, and biff the French out of all hope of Syria. It's a big game, and at last one worth playing. . . . Won't the French be mad if we win through?" (L 195-96).

The realities of the war do not immediately dim his

enthusiasm; at first Lawrence sounds like Lord Jim a few days before he leaps from the *Patna*. In January 1917, in the midst of the period narrated in the first four books of *Seven Pillars*, he finds that "things in Arabia are very pleasant, though the job I have is rather a responsible one. . . . However it is very nice to be out of the office, with some field work in hand, and the position I have is such a queer one—I do not suppose that any Englishman before ever had such a place." In February after the Wejh campaign, he is having "by far the most wonderful time I have had. I don't know what to write about! . . . have become a monomaniac about the job in hand. . . . It's amusing to think that this will suddenly come to an end one day, and I take up other work." In August he finds that it is more restful in Arabia than Cairo, "because one feels so nervous of what may happen if one goes away." The war, "if it ever works out to a conclusion[,] will be imperishable fun to look back upon." But by March 1918 things have changed, for "after four years of this sort of thing I am become altogether dried up. . . . It will be great comfort when one can lie down and sleep without having to think about things; and speak without having one's every word reported in half a hundred camps. This is a job too big for me."[21]

Yet even in late September 1917, after a year in the field, he has a curiously ambivalent response to the war: "I'm not going to last out this game much longer: nerves going and temper wearing thin. . . . I hope when the nightmare ends that I will wake up and become alive again. This killing and killing of Turks is horrible. When you charge in at the finish and find them all over the place in bits, and still alive many of them, and know that you have done hundreds in the same way before and must do hundreds more if you can." But in the middle of the letter he writes: "However while it lasts it's a show between Gilbert and Carroll, and one can retire on it, with that feeling of repletion that comes after a hearty meal. . . . Ripping, to write about—" (*L* 238). In July 1918, he analyzes his psychological state, a "reaction from four years opportunism," which requires a "long quiet like a purge." This letter illustrates perfectly his vacillation and the dichotomy which permeates *Seven Pillars*: "I hate being in front, and I hate being back and I don't like responsibility, and I don't obey orders" (*L* 245-46).

Lawrence's change from enthusiasm about the war to ambivalence is expressed only by indirection in the war narrative, for it is not only *Revolt in the Desert* which bowdlerizes his motives. After the war Lawrence said he would be "wild with delight" if he could satisfy his appetite for action while believing its productions had an absolute value.[22] Unlike the frankness of his letters, Lawrence cannot bring himself to say openly in *Seven Pillars* that he loves war and loves to dominate others and to act. He cannot show or explore directly in introspection the consequences of his domination, but his wild delight in action can only be disguised, not eliminated.

The form of the book is clear. On the one hand, in narratives of battle he loves war and action shamelessly. On the other hand, in introspection he expiates his love. But Lawrence cannot understand this dichotomous pattern in life, though he sees that he has embodied it in *Seven Pillars*. He cannot attribute his guilt to specific acts; he finds it inherent in himself, not in his social relationships. That is, he does recognize the dangers of his powerful will, but does not find what he has done a source of guilt. It is as if the introspection is designed to veil from the self, rather than reveal, the sadism, ambition, and aggression which he exhibits in the war narrative. As Lawrence understands it, guilt inheres in his introspective self; it is the result not of something he has done, but of what he is. The execution of Hamed does not produce introspection because he cannot connect this act with what he feels he is. He can order the execution of hundreds of prisoners or blow up a trainload of women and sick Turks without a word of regret. Yet being buggered produces a horror that even Lawrence finds inordinate and inexplicable. Horror generated by his private acts, not public ones, destroys him. Perhaps the strength of this horror is aggravated by his conduct of the war, for the buggery at Deraa seems an insufficient motive.

In discussing a character in Harley Granville-Barker's

The Secret Life, Lawrence, obviously also referring to himself, divides the figure into a public and a private self: "There is a luxury in keeping outside [of the public role], but it is a poor man who will lie asleep in that: and you don't express the fear he must have had of being *pulled* back [,] . . . the conviction that he'd have to sell the part of himself which he valued, for the privilege of giving rein to the part of himself which others valued, but which he despised or actually disliked" (*L* 453). The self Lawrence valued is the private self, the introspective self. The self others valued is the leader, the active man. But the phrasing is ambiguous; he fears "the privilege of giving rein" to the public self. That is, he must constantly hold the public self in check with the private, for he is attracted to being "pulled back" to the public role.

Lawrence's opinion of the value of these aspects of self was reversed during the war. In a remarkable passage describing the quality of life in the ranks, he writes: "Yes, it is very near the beast. Once I fancied I was very near the angels, and the coming so abruptly to earth was a jar—and a very wholesome jar. Angels, I think, we imagine. Beasts, I think, we are. And I like the beasts for their kindliness and honesty: without really managing to make myself quite like them." Yet he goes on to controvert this favorable view of the beast: "But meanwhile the beast remains, sometimes supine, but sometimes rampant. You will find it taking charge of you, at some weak second of your will: and after that you will either be very charitable and forgiving to others, or you will hide it and be superior" (*L* 554-55). The freedom, the unrestrained expansion of self in the war years, was pernicious: "When men take the governors off their spirits, the spirit seems to fly away, and the animal to creep out of its den, and come snarling into daylight. . . ."[23]

The realization that beast and angel are one is the subject of Lawrence's introspection in *Seven Pillars*. But he cannot express the unity of these opposites clearly because he remains ambivalent about their relationship throughout his life. *Seven Pillars* reverses his war values; in it he attempts to understand his motives, the unseen cargo of the war. I thought I was an angel, but I was really a beast, he argues. Thus the self others value, the angel or the will which can only be expressed in action, comes in the introspection of *Seven Pillars* to be differentiated from the beast or the introspective self. The angel is illusory. But throughout the war and during the first books of *Seven Pillars* there is no introspective self. In the first four books the self he valued during the war is not different from the self others value. Only later do they diverge. As the history of manuscript and text demonstrates, Lawrence put in *Seven Pillars* the self he now values, the introspective self, to veil his early belief in the angelic origins of the man of action and his masterful will. In Freudian terminology, he finds to his dismay that his angel, or superego, is really identical in its aims with his beast, or id. Revealingly there is no ego, no mediating principle: he must be the self others value or the self he values, angel or beast. He is either the dominating, sadistic being of the war narrative or the masochistic being of *The Mint* and of the introspective chapters of *Seven Pillars*, who turns aggression inward and who has an overt desire for extinction of the personality.

During the war Lawrence set up a false antithesis between angel and beast.[24] First, the self he values and the self others value are unified and are considered angelic during the prewar and war period. It is this expansive mood he portrays in his war narrative. Second, the public and private evaluations of self separate late in the war or in the immediate postwar period. The public self others value, his angelic will and his power to act in society, is recognized for the beast it is (564). Discovering this makes the writing of *Seven Pillars* destroy his power to act as much as did his experiences during the war itself. The self he now values is the introspective self which reins in the will. It realizes the will's true nature and thus can control it; he now knows

the truth behind Freud. Sex is an integer in all of us, and the nearer nature we are, the more constantly, the more completely a product of that integer. The fellows [in the ranks] are the reality, and you and I, the selves who used to meet in London and talk of fleshless things, are only the outward wrappings of a core like these fellows. They let light and air play always upon their selves, and consequently have grown very lustily, and have at the same time achieved health and strength in their growing. Whereas our wrappings and bandages have stunted and deformed ourselves, and hardened them to an apparent insensitiveness . . . but it's a callousness, a crippling, only to be yea-said by aesthetes who prefer clothes to bodies, surfaces to intentions. (L 414)

The self he values eventually becomes wholly the power of restraint, desires its own extinction, and vanquishes both angel and beast. It seeks perfect stability: "the equilibrium between conditions and expectations is so fine that I shun all disturbances."[25] He admires fish who "are always perfectly suspended, without ache or activity of nerves, in their sheltering element. We can get it, of course, when we earth-in our bodies . . ." (L 421).

The omission of the directly introspective in the war narrative is revealing of the narrator. It constitutes a formal assertion that the self who judges these acts is absent. "Every man," Lawrence declares, "has the power to look in or out, as he wishes: and circumstances naturally force one to be active, and the other passive."[26] But not every man has the power to unify what he sees. Indeed, it is this contradiction in the two ways of perceiving that makes Seven Pillars modern and determines its style and form. Lawrence fails to make the fortunes of the private self an effect of the events of the war. Since he cannot see the relation of self to history, he emphasizes how different their patterns are. He can give the war narrative structure, design, but not the introspective chapters. He gives the narrative a vigorous, direct, clear style, but introspection the phrasing of fin de siècle aesthetes. In short, he finds the dichotomy between social man and private self unbridgeable.

The dominance Lawrence exhibits in the actual control of men and material in the war is echoed in his assertions of intellectual superiority. Intellectual analysis belongs to the war narrator and his presentation of self and shares these qualities of style, control, dominance. The mind is separate from the introspective self, the feeling. In an account of the schizophrenic personality in The Divided Self, Laing states that the "individual's being is cleft in two, producing a disembodied self and a body that is a thing that the self looks at, regarding it at times as though it were just another thing in the world. The total body and also many 'mental' processes are severed from the self. . . ."[27] Lawrence is hardly schizophrenic, but Laing's description is apt: the "mind" is not what he uses in introspection nor does he identify with it. The mind is bound to the angel, stained by the angel's aspiration and fall.

The functioning of the body seems to be inversely related to the mind. Body atrophy produces mental hypertrophy: "About ten days I lay in that tent, suffering a bodily weakness which made my animal self crawl away and hide till the shame was passed. As usual in such circumstances my mind cleared, my senses became more acute, and I began at last to think consecutively of the Arab Revolt, as an accustomed duty to rest upon against the pain" (188).[28] Historically as well as personally, this is the case: "The printing press, and each newly-discovered method of communication favoured the intellectual above the physical, civilization paying the mind always from the body's funds" (195).

The clearest instance of the application of intellect independent of introspective self, and ostensibly independent of the war narrative, occurs in Chapter XXXIII. Lawrence presents the military and political theory behind the Revolt, supposedly as he thought it out early in the war. Riddled with the Romanticism of Nietzsche, the self he presents here is immensely confident of his powers and excited by the ideas he is expounding: "my personal duty was command, and the commander, like the master architect, was responsible for all." The final "victory seemed certain." In perhaps the most arrogant assertion in the book, he declares there "were many humiliating material limits, but no moral impossibilities." Lawrence later writes, "What I was trying to do, I suppose, was to carry a superstructure of ideas upon or above anything I made" (*L* 853). The idea rather than the effusion of blood is of salient importance, for "Ours should be a war of detachment."

Even his presentation of nature in the war narrative shows preference for what the mind shapes or dominates. Rare is it that "the lack of design and of carefulness in creation no longer irritated" (515). J. K. Huysmans' hero in *Against Nature* is an extreme example of this sensibility; he prefers hothouse flowers to natural ones, machines to women, ingesting food through enemas to eating, for "artifice was considered by Des Esseintes to be the distinctive mark of human genius."[29] Rumm is the most admired of Arabian places. Lawrence's description illustrates Wilde's dictum that nature imitates art, for the "giant hill-shapes are full of design and as far above Nature as great architecture, but beautiful too, as though God had built them ready for some great pageant to which the sons of men were insufficient" (MS 258). The hills "fell short of architecture only in design" (394). He sees Rumm as symbolic the first time he rides up it and adds nothing later; Rumm reduces man and is a passageway toward the absolute, the way made straight: "Landscapes, in childhood's dream, were so vast and silent. We looked backward through our memory for the prototype up which all men had walked between such walls toward such an open square as that in front where this road seemed to end" (351-52). In truth Lawrence evinces little genuine affection for nature. He must distance it by science or literature, make it intellectual, digest and dominate it before he can respond to it. Nature, seen with the eyes of a geologist and cartographer at the beginning of *Seven Pillars*, now becomes an imitation of architecture. An idea must mediate between Lawrence and Rumm.

The presentation of others is based on the model of the self. Lawrence's actions never expose the private self; in his confessions neither do the actions of others. His techniques of characterization draw a veil over the depths of other people. Since Lawrence feels that what he does cannot reveal what he is, he finds this principle operating in others. At best he can only use their characters to mirror aspects of himself. Others possess a rigid and unchanging character, like Lawrence himself in the war narrative. They are beings as fixed and certain as mountains which he can burrow through or fly over or go around if necessary. He can react unexpectedly to their rigidity, but their responses are predictable. There is no process involved, virtually nothing revealed of a character, English or Arab, subsequent to Lawrence's first encounter with him, even of those few characters who appear for more than a single book—Feisal, Auda, Nasir, Ali, Allenby, Farraj, and Daud. There is a quality of domination in his treatment of others which contrasts strongly with his view of himself in introspective chapters. As he seems to control events and the behavior of others, so does he grasp once and for all their characters. There is no contingency present, no mysterious quality that cannot be encompassed.

The only relatively successful characterizations in Lawrence's work occur in figures who have no public role and who bear close relationship to the private self of the confessional hero. Lawrence openly acknowledges his appropriation of his bodyguards: " . . . I knew each of them very well, and his motive and pleasures and character, and liked them, as a body and individually, proud of myself for being their master, proud of them for serving my whims composedly. Self-love and pride and greediness entered into this affection for subordinates—since by liking them so much we made them in a way our flesh and blood, and cast reflections of their high-light upon ourselves" (MS 389). Ali is the most important character, Arab or English, to whom Lawrence is attracted in the final half of the book. He is Lawrence's Arab double. Ali loved adventure, "was physically splendid: not tall nor heavy, but so strong that he would kneel down, resting his forearms palm-up on the ground, and rise to his feet with a man on each hand" (388). He could leap into the saddle of a running camel and he was "impertinent, headstrong, conceited; as reckless in word as in deed; impressive (if he pleased) on public occasions." These observations have repeatedly been applied to Lawrence by himself or by others.[30] Ali has an ideal male-to-male relationship with Turki, an old love: "the animal in each called to the other, and they wandered about inseparably, taking pleasure in a touch and silence" (406). Lawrence himself establishes a similar bond with Ali: "He and I took affectionate leave of one another. Ali gave me half his wardrobe. . . . I gave him an equivalent half of mine, and we kissed like David and Jonathan, each wearing the other's clothes" (449). Their love is juxtaposed to the Deraa homosexual rape, which immediately precedes this scene of parting. Lawrence never shows this tender, yielding, feminine self among the English.

A portrait of Ali in Book VI summarizes the qualities of Lawrence's private self which are to be developed in the remaining books of *Seven Pillars*:

> The lunatic competitor of the wilder tribesmen in their wildest feats was now turning all his force to greater ends. The mixed natures in him made of his face and body powerful pleadings, carnal, perhaps, except in so far as they were transfused by character. . . . He dressed spotlessly, all in black or all in white; and he studied gesture.
> . . . the huge eyes . . . emphasized the frozen dignity which was his ideal carriage, and to which he was always striving to still himself. But as ever the bubbling laugh would shriek out of him unawares; and the youth, boyish or girlish, of him, the fire and deviltry would break through his night like a sunrise.
> Yet, despite this richness, there was a constant depression with him, the unknown longing of simple, restless people for abstract thought beyond their minds' supply. His bodily strength grew day by day, and hatefully fleshed over this humble something which he wanted more. His wild mirth was only one sign of the vain wearing-out of his desire. These besetting strangers underlined his detachment, his unwilling detachment, from his fellows. Despite his great instinct for confession and company, he could find no intimates. Yet he could not be alone. (437-38)

Ali has an idealized physique. But both Ali and Lawrence have mixed natures, alternate at times between boyish and girlish behavior, wear white (though Ali also wears black to dramatize his vacillation between extremes), possess frozen dignity in carriage, have a compulsive giggle at moments of extreme tension, and share a childish sense of humor. Both suffer from depression because the mind could not be silenced; both have an instinct for confession, but no intimates. Both want knowledge rather than power, to know rather than to act and feel. Lawrence places on the Arab the Western crown of thorns—introspection. This is a radical instance of Lawrence's constant technique of seeing only his own image. Significantly, he does not show Ali in action.

With few exceptions, in confessions the author alone is a

credible character. The author, particularly the Romantic author, darkens others by his size, his immensity making unreal the others, suffocating them, depriving them of light. Others are used for the purpose of defining the self, are drawn in and absorbed by the self. Characterization in non-fiction admittedly presents difficulties not inherent in fiction. Norman Holland believes that "except in biography and history, nonfiction has no characters as such, only a drama of thought."[31] But in other confessions Monica, Héloïse, Mme. de Warens, and Lord Alfred Douglas are developed as no figure in Lawrence's works is. Lawrence's difficulty may be explained as lack of talent for characterization, lack of skill in giving others life, but his skill is not the most important or relevant issue. Rather, is his presentation of others consistent with his convictions and his world view? Could he, believing what he does, conceiving of himself as he does, have developed characters who lived outside the life they borrowed from his image or his fantasies?

Lawrence himself is more real among the unnatural poses of the other figures, his contingencies alive among their certainties, his protean character vivid by contrast to their unchanging roles. He never achieves the offstage view of the Arab which Doughty presents in *Arabia Deserta*, a work to which *Seven Pillars* has been frequently compared. Doughty's characterization of Zeyd, for example, has a depth and authenticity lacking in any character in *Seven Pillars* because Doughty recognizes Zeyd's independence. Zeyd is not Doughty's creature, for Doughty is observing him, not assimilating him. But in *Seven Pillars* virtually every scene or reflection seeks actually or symbolically either to advance the narrative or to reveal the narrator. The latter quality is also apparent in Lawrence's *Diary of a Journey Across the Euphrates* and in *The Mint*. According to Lawrence, Doughty has no such dominating purpose; for travelers like Doughty "the seeing Arabia was an end in itself. They just wrote a wander-book and the great peninsula made their prose significant." Now the classical age of Arabian travel writing is past: "The rest must frame excuses for travelling. One will fix latitudes, the silly things, another collect plants and insects (not to eat, but to bring home), a third make war, which is coals to Newcastle. We fritter our allegiances and loyalties."[32]

Doughty can show Zeyd's domestic quarrels vividly because he is interested in everything in Arabia—topography, cairns, the construction of tents, domestic quarrels. In a memorable scene, the Arabs gossip and laugh about the disaffection of Zeyd's wife, Hirfa. The couple "sat daily sporting lovingly together before us, for we were all one family and friendly eyes, but oftentimes in the midst Hirfa pouted; then Zeyd would coldly forsake her. . . ."[33] Later Doughty comes upon the despairing Zeyd, slumbering "with his head in the scalding sun." Doughty narrates the daily raillery among the rest of the tribe regarding the scandal. He reveals the basis of their dispute: Hirfa desires a child and Zeyd is infertile. Soon Zeyd's second wife returns and heightens the quarrel. Thus Doughty begins an analysis of the status of women in Bedouin society.

No women of any significance appear in any of Lawrence's works, and to take notice of a household quarrel is beneath his dignity. There are no domestic details which reveal, for instance, Feisal's or Nasir's character, no relationships established between them and others except heightened ones of public consequence (e.g., Feisal's antagonism toward his father). All characters appear curiously isolated. Lawrence can neither establish for himself nor recognize in others intimate relationships—even in *The Mint*, which is wholly devoted to his private self. In *Seven Pillars* he declares that he could never "open myself friendly to another" (563).

Doughty is "never morbid, never introspective" and he "refused to be the hero of his story."[34] He does not imitate the Arabs; indeed, he despises them. Yet to Lawrence he represents the complete Englishman abroad. Doughty is like the Bedouin in his bluntness, his superstition, his unquestioned belief in his own customs, his black and white image of the world[35]—much more like them than Lawrence, who possesses none of the Bedouin simplicity and yet aspires toward them as thesis to antithesis. Doughty can create characters because he "really believed that the English were better than the Arabs: that this thing was better than that thing: in fact, he did really believe in something. That's what I call an absolute. Doughty, somewhere, if only in the supremacy of Spenser, had a fixed point in his universe, and from one fixed point a moralist will, like a paleontologist, build up the whole scheme of creation. Consequently Doughty's whole book is rooted: definitive; assured. That makes his outline as hard as iron, as sharp as photographs: as amateur's photographs."[36] Doughty had an "uncharitable narrowness of mind."[37]

There is also a formal reason why Doughty's characters live and Lawrence's do not. According to Ian Watt, the more organized the plot, the less vivid and living are the characters who are controlled by it.[38] Lawrence believes that Doughty has no concern for structure; the book is "a brick yard rather than a building."[39] Doughty "had no sense of design. *Arabia Deserta* remains wonderful, because there his weak imagination had only to select from an array of thronging facts; . . . his sense of design could express itself only in the aimlessness of his wanderings . . . " (*L* 534). Lawrence sacrifices character to form, for the interests of truth and form differ.

Lawrence directly contrasts his work to Doughty's: "Search my book through, and you will hardly find an assertion which is not . . . eventually qualified. It's due to an absence of the fixed point from which Doughty radiated. My views are like my photographs of Jidda: the edges, even of the sharpest, are just modulated off, so that you can't put a pin point on them. Drawn, not in line, but in tone. Atmospheric. It's the difference between impressionism and the classical."[40] The self is the only absolute which Lawrence recognizes, his only fixed point; he posits as real only that which can be absorbed or dominated.

He condemns Doughty's power to judge other men and to believe in the existence of things outside the self:

> Who are we to judge? I don't believe even God can. Learning only teaches us the resemblances, the ultimate sameness of things. I fancy if we knew all we would know only one thing, but that would comprehend mind and matter, energy, soul and spirit. If we could reach

far enough across space we would find every ray emanating from a central sun. The divisions we make are pictures only, meant to help us grasp the final unity: for our finite minds can get nearest to infinity by envisaging it as an infinite series; a staircase set up from earth to heaven: whereas there is only one step. . . . But it's all wrong to imagine that there are any differences. There is only one element, which is the same as the sole source of energy. If there were Gods there might be men. But there aren't. It's a picture we have put on: our shapes I mean.[41]

Men are "puppets—but not . . . my puppets—God's, whatever every person means by the word God."[42] The Romantic conception to which Lawrence adheres is that the world originates in and reflects the self. Then the self is God, the central sun or final unity. Other characters are illusions or aspects of that self and are controlled or determined by it, though the self can never be determined or fixed.

The presentation of self and others in the war narrative of *Seven Pillars* is representative of the first stage in the development of the Romantic hero. A passage in *The Mint* summarizes the stage concisely and clearly. A minister lecturing the airmen, who are Lawrence's postwar successors to the Bedouin, cannot "convict our party of sin. They are yet happy, being innocent of the reflection which creates a sense of sin. . . . [The men] don't chop up their meat into mince for easy digestion by the mind: and . . . are therefore intact as we are thereby diseased. Man . . . was born as one . . ." (*M* 178-79). The introspective self is excluded by definition. The passage describes a period of health, of absorption of others into the self, of creation of the world out of one's will. In *Seven Pillars* this is dramatized by the optimistic war narrator. As Wordsworth writes, "The mind is lord and master—outward sense/The obedient servant of her will."[43] All power is in the will and the will is the self. The hero, like Napoleon, Faust, Manfred, Ahab, Zarathustra, seeks the infinite, asserts the unlimited power of mind over matter, displays the will to conquer and explore. Man becomes divine. "But did not the being believed by many make for a distorted righteousness?" Lawrence asks. "The mounting together of the devoted hopes of years from near-sighted multitudes, might endow even an unwilling idol with Godhead, and strengthen It whenever men prayed silently to Him" (549).

The war narrator attributes to his will a god-like power to determine events and transmute matter: "when we let our will shine out the flesh melted like a mist" (MS 315). Materials are "always apt to serve a purpose, and Will a sure guide. . . . There was no flesh." Lawrence believes that he has extraordinary powers: "Always I grew to dominate those things into which I had drifted. . . . I saw myself a danger to ordinary men, with such capacity yawing rudderless at their disposal" (564). He seeks an absolute of the will as he is later to seek an absolute of the body.

Lawrence's will wins "redemption, perhaps for all a race." He absorbs others in his role as redeemer: "Such false investiture bred a hot though transient satisfaction, in that we felt we had cheated ourselves of ourselves, assumed another's pain or experience, his personality. It was triumph, and a mood of enlargement; we had avoided ourselves, conquered our geometrical completeness, and snatched a momentary 'change of mind' " (MS 355; cf. text 550). Lawrence's attitude in the war narrative is clear: "To suffer in simplicity for another gave a sense of greatness, of super-humanity. There was no such loftiness as a cross from which to contemplate the world. The pride and exhilaration of it were beyond conceit" (MS 356; cf. text 551). The only way he can relate to society is to assimilate it, to incorporate it into himself. Indeed, for "one to be comfortably surrendered [to an idea], the others must surrender too" (MS 355).

The check must come; man cannot absorb the whole. In the second stage man, born as one, "breaks into little prisms when he thinks" (M 179). "Contact with natural man," Lawrence says, "leads me to deplore the vanity in which we thinking people subinfeudate ourselves. I watch, detachedly, my fingers twitching when I'm frightened . . . judging myself now carried away by instinct, now ruling a course by reason, now deciding intuitively: always restlessly cataloguing each aspect of my unity" (M 178). The experience is that of Coleridge, Carlyle, and Mill, for the "habit of analysis has a tendency to wear away the feelings."[44] The expansion of the self, the absorption of others, ceases. The self contracts its boundaries, the will atrophies, and the oceanic sense is lost.

Will is no longer able to create and control. The self or identity is threatened, then withdraws to a last stronghold and removes itself from society. In Lawrence's confessions, the omnipotent will of the war narrator of *Seven Pillars* is reduced to the small, trembling, naked body with which *The Mint* begins. The central theme of all Lawrence's introspection is the use and restraint of the will. All introspection in *Seven Pillars* is written from the viewpoint of the shattered Romantic hero, whether it appears early or late in the work.

But there are advantages to this second stage. The hero now seeks to define the self by isolating it from its social role.[45] He desires "the purer distillation of self that comes about when the values of the other are rejected."[46] In *The Byronic Hero: Types and Prototypes*, Peter Thorslev argues that the process of self-definition can take "the form of a lust for violent emotional experience, even for suffering—any psychic activity which will heighten . . . a sense of self-awareness and self-identity."[47] In describing the sado-masochism of his bodyguard, Lawrence remarks that the punishment is welcomed "as a means of self-knowledge, by which to explore themselves, to learn how far beyond the bounds of daily fortitude their bodies could endure" (MS 393). After Deraa, as *Seven Pillars* demonstrates, the frequency of tests of endurance increases, and the first two sections of *The Mint* record the course and consequences of a single, sustained test. Identity is what you have left when you take everything else away; the real self can emerge only when the will is denied and the boundaries of self precisely determined. Lawrence writes: "We might have found free-will, if we had constantly not done what lay within our power to do: by choosing nothing as we had a choice we might have isolated ourselves clear of circumstance, and so arrived at self-knowledge, which, unlike other human knowledge, did not expire with its sister smell, the body" (MS 356). The end of this process is extinction of personality, and Lawrence both desires and fears this loss of self.[48]

There is an escape, a third stage for the Romantic hero. If Carlyle and Mill can go beyond the annihilation of self and achieve affirmation, "The Everlasting Yea," so too can

Lawrence—by assertion if not by dramatization. If a man "passes through thought into despair, or comprehension, he again achieves some momentary onenesses with himself. And not only that. He can achieve a oneness of himself with his fellows: and of them with the stocks and stones of his universe: and of all the universes with the illusory everything (if he be positive) or with the illusory nothing (if he be nihilist) according as the digestive complexion of his soul be dark or fair" (*M* 179). To escape the prison of the self and recover spiritual health he seeks now to be absorbed rather than absorb: "But can I be an egotist, if my self rejects the reality of my self and assimilates it in the cloud of matter?"[49] The hero can pass beyond the stage of annihilation and again achieve harmony after extinguishing the self and the will.

The public voice of the war narrative remains in the expansive stage throughout *Seven Pillars*. The latter two stages of the Romantic hero, as Lawrence modifies and dramatizes them, are discussed in Chapters VI and VII below. Here I have explored his triumph only. If character is revealed by what a man chooses or avoids, if it is what a man's acts make him, Lawrence, as he presents himself in the war narrative, dominates other men, grasps and uses ideas, has extraordinary confidence in his power to act, and exhibits little remorse for the blood he sheds or little doubt of the purpose for which it is shed. He expresses indirectly a love for mastery and seems confused neither about his motives nor his power. He is proud, confident, healthy, triumphant. The boundaries of the self are at their outermost limits and include even an alien society. The war narrator can assume another's personality, become a redeemer of a race, and seek a spiritual absolute which denies flesh. He is the amoral Romantic hero using his will to earn freedom for an enslaved people.

NOTES TO CHAPTER III

1. Richards, *Portrait*, p. 187.
2. Erving Goffman, *The Presentation of Self in Everyday Life* (Garden City,

N.Y.: Doubleday, 1959), p. 19, argues that "the role we are striving to live up to—this mask is our truer self."

3. *The Phenomenology of Mind*, trans. J. B. Baillie (London: Allen and Unwin, 1949), pp. 349-50.

4. Gertrude Himmelfarb, *Victorian Minds* (New York: Knopf, 1968), pp. 206-10, discusses the common Victorian emphasis on endurance sports and concludes, "Certainly there is no other country where both the spirit of sportsmanship and the physical activity of sports have penetrated so deeply into society as to determine the character of its intellectuals." For Lawrence's youthful expression of this concern for endurance, see, for example, *Letters*, p. 54; *The Home Letters of T. E. Lawrence and His Brothers*, ed. Montagu R. Lawrence (New York: Macmillan, 1954), p. 59; and *The Diary of a Journey Across the Euphrates*, in *Oriental Assembly*, pp. 5-62.

5. Letter to Charlotte Shaw, 20 March 1928.

6. Letter to Charlotte Shaw, 14 April 1927.

7. Foreword to *Cavalleria Rusticana* by Giovanni Verga, in *Phoenix: The Posthumous Papers of D. H. Lawrence*, ed. Edward D. McDonald (New York: Viking Press, 1972), p. 248.

8. Letter to Harley Granville-Barker, 18 May 1924, in *Eight Letters from T. E. Lawrence* (London: privately printed, 1939).

9. Said of *Seven Pillars*, pp. 286-87. For comment on this passage see Gordon Mills, "T. E. Lawrence as a Writer," *Texas Quarterly*, V (Autumn, 1962), 39.

10. Letter to Charlotte Shaw, 20 March 1928. Laing, *The Divided Self*, p. 83, writes of the schizoid personality that external events "no longer affect him in the same way as they do others: it is not that they affect him less; on the contrary, frequently they affect him more."

11. *Oriental Assembly*, p. 152.

12. Lawrence is aware that the public would find offensive the massacre of Turkish officers after the earlier train mining (370); he suppresses this detail in *Revolt in the Desert* (London: Jonathan Cape, 1927).

13. For a discussion of this passage, see D. H. Lawrence, *Phoenix*, p. 351.

14. Letter to W. F. Stirling, 25 September 1917, quoted by Phillip Knightley and Colin Simpson, *The Secret Lives of Lawrence of Arabia* (New York: Bantam Books, 1971), p. 85.

15. Introduction to Charles M. Doughty, *Travels in Arabia Deserta* (New York: Random House, 1936), I, 26.

16. Letter to Charlotte Shaw, 21 December 1927.

17. The field report is in the *Arab Bulletin*, 26 January 1918; rpt. in *Secret Despatches from Arabia* (London: Golden Cockerel Press, 1939).

18. In *T. E. Lawrence to His Biographers*, II, 104-05, Lawrence's pleasure in the battle is apparent.

19. Hubert Young, *The Independent Arab* (London: John Murray, 1933), p. 245, confirms the aggressiveness of Lawrence at this moment in the campaign.

20. Similar assertions are deleted from the text: e.g., "my will, the worn instrument which had so long forged our path, broke suddenly in my hand and felt useless" (MS 411).

21. *The Home Letters*, pp. 334, 336-37, 338, 339, 349.

22. Letter to Charlotte Shaw, 14 April 1927.

23. *Shaw-Ede*, p. 26.

24. Letter to Charlotte Shaw, 30 April 1924.

25. Letter to Charlotte Shaw, 17 June 1926.

26. Letter to Charlotte Shaw, 25 February 1928.

27. Laing, p. 162.

28. Cf. Jeffrey Meyers, *The Wounded Spirit*, p. 105, who writes, Lawrence "is annealed into knowledge and achieves his most acute intellectual and psychological perceptions when he suffers pain most acutely."

29. Trans. Robert Baldick (Baltimore: Penguin, 1959), p. 36.

30. For a description of Lawrence's physical qualities which shows him similar to Ali, see Robert Graves, *Lawrence and the Arabian Adventure* (New York: Doubleday, 1928), p. 27.

31. "Prose and Minds: A Psychoanalytic Approach to Non-Fiction," in *The Art of Victorian Prose*, eds. George Levine and William Madden (New York: Oxford University Press, 1968), p. 314.

32. Foreword to Bertram Thomas, *Arabia Felix: Across the Empty Quarter of Arabia* (London: Jonathan Cape, 1932), p. xvi.

33. *Arabia Deserta*, I, 272. These scenes ("the picture of Zeyd's tent") are among those particularly admired by Lawrence in his Introduction, p. xxv.

34. Introduction to Doughty, *Arabia Deserta*, I, 19.

35. *Ibid.*, I, 20-21.

36. Letter to Charlotte Shaw, 10 June 1927.

37. Letter to Charlotte Shaw, 4 May 1927.

38. *The Rise of the Novel* (Berkeley: University of California Press, 1957), pp. 279-80.

39. Letter to Charlotte Shaw, 4 May 1927.

40. Letter to Charlotte Shaw, 10 June 1927.

41. *Ibid.*

42. Letter to Charlotte Shaw, 14 April 1927.

43. *The Prelude*, xii, 222-23, in *Poetical Works*, eds. Thomas Hutchinson and Ernest de Selincourt (London: Oxford University Press, 1969).

44. John Stuart Mill, *Autobiography and Other Writings*, ed. Jack Stillinger (Boston: Houghton Mifflin, 1969), p. 83. See also Coleridge, "Dejection: An Ode," and Carlyle, *Sartor Resartus*.

45. Morse Peckham, *Beyond the Tragic Vision: The Quest for Identity in the Nineteenth Century* (New York: George Braziller, 1962), p. 210; see also p. 159.

46. Frederick Garber, "Self, Society, Value, and the Romantic Hero," in *The Hero in Literature*, ed. Victor Brombert (Greenwich, Conn.: Fawcett, 1969), p. 215; rpt. from *Comparative Literature*, XIX (Fall, 1967), 321-33.

47. Minneapolis: University of Minnesota Press, 1962, p. 89.

48. Letter to Charlotte Shaw, 20 March 1928.

49. Letter to Charlotte Shaw, 11 January 1928.

IV

Civilization Disease:
"Europe Is Not a Thing Easily Digested"

LAWRENCE ARGUES THAT DURING THE WAR "EUROPE CAME bodily to Western Asia." The disease the West brings "is physical, material, moral, mental, all you will. It is the civilisation-disease, the inevitable effect of too close contact with the West. The aborigines of Australia got it when they met us, and they died of it. . . . Asia is tougher, older, more numerous, and will not die of us—but indubitably we have made her very ill. Europe is not a thing easily digested."[1] The imaginative pattern Lawrence makes of the West's impact is complex and his attitude toward its effect on Arabia ambivalent. In *Seven Pillars* the consequences of the civilization disease are dramatized, but seldom overtly stated. Sometimes proudly, sometimes guiltily, Lawrence portrays himself as the principal carrier of the contagion.

Lawrence, echoing a line from Swinburne, declares that nationalism has become the modern creed: "Not the Galilean but the politician had conquered."[2] Lawrence is marching "all the pilgrim road up to Damascus, making in arms the return journey" of the Muslims from Mecca.[3] His ambitions are immense, for he will "quicken history in the East, as the great adventurers of old had done" (MS 415). "I had dreamed . . . ," Lawrence proclaims extravagantly in the final sentences of *Seven Pillars*, "of hustling into form, while I lived, the new Asia which time was inexorably bringing upon us. Mecca was to lead to Damascus; Damascus to Anatolia, and afterwards to Bagdad; and then there was Yemen. Fantasies, these will seem, to such as are able to call my beginning an ordinary effort" (661). It is, as Conrad writes of the dying gesture of Lord Jim, "a last flicker of superb egoism."[4]

Lawrence begins *Seven Pillars* by appropriating the

Bedouins as thoroughly as he did Homer in his Translator's Note. But unlike Homer, whose perfection represents a triumph of technique over spirit parallel to the triumph of West over East, the Bedouins embody an ideal toward which he aspires. He defines them against the West; in fact they are to be both an accusation of the values of Europe and a spiritual reflection of Lawrence. The basic difference between the Bedouin and the European is inherent in his analysis of the Arab cycle of migration (Chapters II-III). The Arabs engage in a gradual and perpetual movement from the coastal towns under pressure of overpopulation to increasingly less fertile agricultural land until they are "flung out of the furthest crazy oasis into the untrodden wilderness as nomads." Every year they wander "a little further north or a little further east as chance has sent them down one or other of the well-roads of the wilderness, till finally this pressure drives them from the desert again into the sown, with the like unwillingness of their first shrinking experiment in nomad life." The oases in the desert contain "the true centre of Arabia, the preserve of its native spirit, and its most conscious individuality. The desert lapped it round and kept it pure of contact." The Bedouin keeps "vigour in the Semitic body. There were few, if indeed there was a single northern Semite, whose ancestors had not at some dark age passed through the desert. The mark of nomadism, that most deep and biting social discipline, was on each of them in his degree."

Lawrence commends the migratory cycle even while engaged in subverting it by giving the Bedouin a history and a desire for progress. He promulgates the religion of nationalism, reverses the natural East-West pattern of prophecy, makes the Arabs self-conscious, and drives them from the Garden of Eden (*L* 372). He has a degree of contempt for what he has done: "As pools shrink they stench."[5] Lawrence is the Satanic figure who brings to the Bedouins the knowledge of good and evil which precipitates their fall. Indeed, at the end of the Revolt he "felt like Lucifer just after his forced landing."[6] Their fall in the garden is paralleled by his fall.

The Bedouins are considered ideal because they are outside history. This is not Lawrence's argument but his *image* of them. They are a "cold" society as opposed to the "hot" societies of the West. Claude Lévi-Strauss writes that "the clumsy distinction between 'peoples without history' and others could with advantage be replaced by a distinction between . . . 'cold' and 'hot' societies: the former seeking, by the institutions they give themselves, to annul the possible effects of historical factors on their equilibrium and continuity in a quasi-automatic fashion; the latter resolutely internalizing the historical process and making it the moving power of their development."[7] Early in *Seven Pillars* in the march on Wejh a native looks out over the army "saying half-sadly, 'We are no longer Arabs but a People' . . . . to him the joys of life were a fast camel, the best weapons, and a short sharp raid against his neighbour's herd: and the gradual achievement of Feisal's ambition was making such joys less and less easy for the responsible" (152). The Bedouin's sadness defines his concrete recognition of the change from a synchronic to a diachronic society, from cold to hot.

Late in *Seven Pillars* Lawrence describes the horrifying pace at which Arabs would accumulate property: "Parties of peasants flowed in on our advance. At first there were five or six to a weapon: then one would win a bayonet, another a sword, a third a pistol. An hour later those who had been on foot would be on donkeys. Afterwards every man had a rifle, and a captured horse. By nightfall the horses were laden . . ." (632). The war accelerates the historical process, precisely reversing Lawrence's ascetic motives for going into the desert. It resembles the long cycle of the nomads moving back into the sown speeded up a thousandfold. "What seems to me noteworthy, today," he writes, "is the shortness of our generations, the rapid tempo of life. We seem to accelerate in geometrical progressions" (*L* 811).

Lawrence's destruction of the cycle of migration that gives vigor to the Semites, his quickening of history in the East (or thinking he does so), ravages and uproots his ideal, attacks a source from which value flows into him. What Lawrence

condemns in his own society is precisely what he brings to
the Bedouins'. With reason he declares that "the mere
wishing to be an Arabian betrays the roots of a quirk."[8]
Instead of his becoming like them, the Arabs become like
him; he imitates their acts and they imitate his thought. He
wants to submit and instead dominates and shapes. Unable
to accept the norms of his own society, he transforms theirs
into an image of the one he has rejected. *Seven Pillars*
narrates Lawrence's failure to conform to traditional
Bedouin ideals and his triumph in introducing new ones.
His sojourn among the Bedouins is, in the phrase of Lévi-
Strauss, an "exploration of the deserts of memory."[9]

Lawrence clearly describes his alienation at the end of the
first chapter: "I could not sincerely take on the Arab skin; it
was an affectation only." He insists that "the evil of my tale
may have been inherent in our circumstances. For years we
lived anyhow with one another in the naked desert, under the
indifferent heaven." Yet in the next two chapters the naked
desert is seen as a moral force which preserves uncon-
taminated the true Arabian spirit (34). Now Lawrence
describes the skin he desired to assume and portrays the
idealized life of the Bedouin to which he aspires. He envies
the circumstances and the psychology he deplored a page or
two earlier. These chapters present the narrator's initial
idealistic view of the Arab; they possess the order, beliefs, and
clarity of his war narrative. Their subjects—the geography
of the Arabian peninsula and the character of its
inhabitants—have no direct bearing on specific events and
ostensibly contain no insight into Lawrence. Seemingly the
narrator of Chapters II and III, unlike that of I, is unaware
that he will end in Damascus listening to Arab prayers after
victory: "While my fancy, in the overwhelming pause,
showed me my loneliness and lack of reason in their
movement: since only for me, of all the hearers, was the event
sorrowful and the phrase meaningless" (652). That prayer
and dejection are to be "the philosophic climax of the
narrative" (*L* 494); nonetheless the attitudes he acknowledges in Chapter I are not different from those with which
he ends the book.[10]

In a letter of 1918 Lawrence presents a more balanced view of the Arabs than the deprecatory attitude of the first chapter or the glorification of them in the two following ones, perhaps because he is not distorting for purposes of dramatization.

> You guessed rightly that the Arab appealed to my imagination. It is the old, old civilization, which has refined itself clear of household gods, and half the trappings which ours hastens to assume. The gospel of bareness in materials is a good one, and it involves apparently a sort of moral bareness too. They think for the moment, and endeavor to slip through life without turning corners or climbing hills. In part it is a mental and moral fatigue, a race trained out, and to avoid difficulties they have to jettison so much that we think honourable and grave: and yet without in any way sharing their point of view, I think I can understand it enough to look at myself and other foreigners from their direction, and without condemning it. I know I'm a stranger to them, and always will be; but I cannot believe them worse, any more than I could change to their ways. (*L* 244)

Arabia is an old, refined civilization, possessing an estimable material and moral bareness. The Arabs are mentally and morally exhausted. Lawrence confuses aesthetic and genetic decadence in his description of the Bedouin. The English "were a broad-faced, low-browed people, blunt-featured beside the *decadent* Arabs whom generations of in-breeding had sharpened to a radiance ages older than these *primitive*, blotched, honest Englishmen" (MS 354; cf. text 544; italics added). The Arabs are the "race of the individual genius" (39). Decadence is viewed with approbation, as among *fin de siècle* writers. The qualities Lawrence admires in the Arabs—overrefined physical beauty, devotion to ritual and gesture for its own sake, and a decaying mode of life—are characteristics praised by these writers. The Bedouin whom Lawrence seeks to emulate is the perfect Decadent hero.

Nowhere in *Seven Pillars* does he approach the letter's clarity in analyzing his relationship to the Arab (or, rather, the Bedouin, for the nomad is the only Arab who embodies these ideals). In his Preface to Eric Kennington's catalogue of Arab portraits, Lawrence declares that the "Arab townsman or villager is like us and our villagers, with our notion of property, our sense of gain and our appetite for material success. He has our premises as well as our processes. The Beduin, on the other hand, while his sense is as human and his mind as logical as ours, begins with principles quite other than our own, and gets further from us as his character strengthens. He has a creed and practice of not-possessing, which is tough armour against our modern wiles. It defends him against all sentiment."[11]

Most of the elements he considers in letter and Preface as ideal, or at least superior to Western practice, are presented without qualification, as if sociological fact, in the opening pages of *Seven Pillars*. Chapters II-III emphasize that a paucity of materials in the desert generates intellectual, moral, and social bareness. The desert produces "a universal clearness or hardness of belief, almost mathematical in its limitation." Semites were "a dogmatic people, despising doubt, our modern crown of thorns. They did not understand our metaphysical difficulties, our introspective questionings" (38). Lawrence reveals his admiration for these Arabian qualities by contrasting them to Western doubt, the crown of thorns he himself wears in some introspective chapters of *Seven Pillars*. Unlike the English, who "had an instinct so strong for compromise that it would be called a passion if its object were not the mean" (MS 378), the Arabs "were at ease only in extremes. They inhabited superlatives by choice" (38). In Chapter I he writes that living continually "on the crest or in the trough of waves of feeling" (29) produces evil. Now he expresses approval of the pattern. Arab vacillation between extremes is central to his admiration of the Bedouin, for "the petty, incarnate Semite . . . reached heights and depths beyond our reach, though not beyond our sight. They realized our absolute in their unrestrained capacity for good and evil . . ." (MS 378).

He fashions the Bedouin in his own image. Licentious in the towns, ascetic in the desert, the "Semite hovered between lust and self-denial." The sterile experience of the Bedouin "robbed him of compassion and perverted his human kindness to the image of the waste in which he hid. Accordingly he hurt himself, not merely to be free, but to please himself. There followed a delight in pain, a cruelty which was more to him than goods. The desert Arab found no joy like the joy of voluntarily holding back. He found luxury in abnegation, renunciation, self restraint" (41). The masochism is immediately understood as a general delight in pain, whether in subject or object. The Bedouins are given the masochism which he attributes to himself in letters of the early 1920's written at the time he was revising *Seven Pillars*. In fact he deletes from the published text several instances of the Bedouin delight in pain, perhaps because these would reveal too clearly his own obsession.

Lawrence is also indirectly writing about himself when he describes the pattern of Eastern prophets: "None of them had been of the wilderness. . . . Their birth set them in crowded places. An unintelligible passionate yearning drove them out into the desert. There they lived a greater or lesser time in meditation and physical abandonment; and thence they returned with their imagined message articulate, to preach it to their old, and now doubting, associates. . . . To the thinkers of the town the impulse into Nitria had ever been irresistible, not probably that they found God dwelling there, but that in its solitude they heard more certainly the living word they brought with them" (39). Nonetheless he cannot avoid the directly personal; in the final sentences of Chapter III, he overtly identifies himself with the prophet: "Since the dawn of life, in successive waves they had been dashing themselves against the coasts of flesh. . . . One such wave (and not the least) I raised and rolled before the breath of an idea, till it reached its crest, and toppled over and fell at Damascus" (43). But the political prophecy Lawrence preaches is taken into the desert, not acquired and made articulate there. It is Western in every respect. Yet he loses his creed by acting it out, weakens rather than strengthens his political motive by making the pilgrimage.

Ironically, the actual creed he acquires and preaches in *Seven Pillars* itself, as opposed to his preaching of nationalism in the Arab Revolt, is nihilism, "a chilly creed:

whose first article is 'Thou shalt not convert.' "[12] Lawrence's personal creed is an assertion, not an argument. Like the prophet, this full vision in the desert makes "him uncouth, a man apart." Nihilism is his unintelligible, passionate yearning made articulate after his physical abandonment in the desert; it is clearly the basis for his exposition of the Arab religion: "The common base of all Semitic creeds, winners or losers, was the ever present idea of world-worthlessness. Their profound reaction from matter led them to preach bareness, renunciation, poverty; and the atmosphere of this invention stifled the minds of the desert pitilessly." Far from being circumstances and attitudes productive of evil, he finds the "purity of rarefaction" in this reaction against matter. Once Lawrence is led through the ruins of a palace in which each room smells of a different perfume. At last he smells the sweetest scent of all, the "effortless, empty, eddyless wind of the desert." This, he is told by his Arab guide, "is the best: it has no taste" (40). But Lawrence had long felt this; even in 1908 before seeing Arabia, he prefers the empty plains of France to its mountains, for the "purifying influence is the paramount one in a plain, there one can sit down quietly and think. . . ."[13]

Ideally the Arabs and Lawrence reject matter and society "to choose the things in which mankind had had no share or part." To reject matter, the productions of man, and the fecundity of nature is to become pure and "to achieve a personal liberty which haunted starvation and death." Lawrence's concept of purity or "cleanness" is peculiar. Theoretically purity is a quality possessed by those entities which contain no admixture of material or flesh.[14] But Lawrence becomes a materialist in the Revolt; he no longer believes in the antithesis of body and soul. He comes to think that "our bodies, the universe, our thoughts and tactilities were conceived in and of the molecular sludge of matter . . ." (468; cf. *L* 453). If being pure or clean means no contamination by matter, and if Lawrence is a materialist, then the purity of rarefaction means death, achieving a nihilistic oneness "with the illusory nothing" rather than the Bedouin's oneness "with the illusory everything" (*M*

179), the immanent God. Death is directly associated with purity in such phrases as the cover motto of *Seven Pillars*: "the sword also means clean-ness and death."

Lawrence's exposition of Arab society declares in part what he thought he was, in part what he sought to become. He finds his journey into the desert imitative of their archetypal pattern of prophecy: literal in the war narrative, ironic in introspection. Whether the Arabs actually possess the characteristics Lawrence gives them is questionable. The movement is always in toward Lawrence, not out toward the Bedouin. They become him, not he them. There is, for instance, no way to prove that the Arab people vacillate between extremes. These assertions have more validity applied to Lawrence than to the Arabs, and the pattern he gives them was first imposed on himself. In technique, the Bedouin characterization is similar to his sketches of individuals. Lawrence exhibits a dominance over the Arab character which admits of no qualification. It corresponds to his personal power and control in battle. His psychological imperialism, his attribution of his own desires and qualities to the Bedouin, is thoroughgoing. As G. B. Shaw writes hyperbolically, "you have already used the whole Arab race and the New Testament and the entire armies of all the countries engaged in the war to advertize yourself. . . ."[15]

Lawrence's characterization of the Bedouin is not unique among those actively engaged in advancing the bounds of Empire. The qualities Lawrence attributes to the nomads are typical of representations of natives by colonialists and imperialists. The use of others to define the self is at the heart of psychological imperialism. While Lawrence refuses to impose his image of self on the English, he gives the Arabs no character except what he lends them from himself. O. Mannoni writes in *Prospero and Caliban: The Psychology of Colonization*: "What the colonial in common with Prospero lacks is awareness of the world of Others, a world in which Others have to be respected. . . . Rejection of that world is combined with an urge to dominate. . . ." The more remote people are, "the more they seem to attract our projections. . . . it is himself a man is looking for when he goes far away; near at hand he is liable to come up against Others."[16] Lévi-Strauss warns against such projections. Never can the anthropologist or outsider act in the name of the native, "for their otherness prevents him from thinking or willing in their place: to do so would be tantamount to identifying himself with them." The effects of imitation are pernicious for both imitator and imitated: "our own society is the only one which we can transform and yet not destroy, since the changes which we should introduce would come from within."[17]

The colonialist's view of the native Algerian as described by Frantz Fanon in his anti-imperialist tract, *The Wretched of the Earth*, is remarkably similar to Lawrence's concept of the Bedouin: "The North African likes extremes, so we can never entirely trust him. Today he is the best of friends, tomorrow the worst of enemies. He is insensible to shades of meaning, and Cartesianism is fundamentally foreign to him; the sense of balance, the weighing and pondering of an opinion or action clashes with his most intimate nature." The native does not commit suicide because "it means practicing introspection. . . . There is no inner life where the North African is concerned." He displays "mental puerility, without the spirit of curiosity found in the Western child. . . . The questions he asks himself always concern the details and exclude all synthesis." The native is, in short, a "lobotomized European."[18]

Similarly Lawrence finds the Bedouins at ease only in extremes, hovering always between lust and self-denial. They sit "to the eyes in a cloaca, but with their brows touching Heaven."[19] They are "absolute slaves of their appetite, with no stamina of mind" (219). Their "inert intellects lay fallow in incurious resignation." The Bedouins "did not understand our metaphysical difficulties, our introspective questionings." The least morbid of peoples, "they had accepted the gift of life unquestioningly, as axiomatic. . . . Suicide was a thing impossible." Their powers of synthesis are limited, for they are capable of "no organizations of mind or body. . . . no systems of philosophy, no complex mythologies" (38-39). Lawrence

instructs his English comrades to "beat the Arabs at their
own game, for we have stronger motives for our action, and
put more heart into it than they."[20] The colonialist Fanon
describes in his polemic is, of course, not similar to
Lawrence in every respect. Yet neither does Lawrence escape
the stain of imperialism simply because he professes to work
for a reformulation of its doctrines and would remake the
Arab nations into client states of Britain rather than
unwilling subjects of the Ottoman Empire (MS 415). In
accepting these goals for the Arab peoples Lawrence
identifies with the Europeans in substance, if not detail.

The savage imperialism that Joseph Conrad documents
and condemns at the turn of the century in *An Outpost of
Progress* and *Heart of Darkness* is not Lawrence's sort. In
Conrad's novels value is in civilization and its restraints, in
society, tradition—the fragments that man shores against his
ruin. The banal heroes of *An Outpost of Progress* and Kurtz
are destroyed by the savagery which absorbs them and which
they come to imitate. Conrad conceives of the native as
primitive in the crudest and most literal sense: primitive is
the antonym of civilized. Kurtz's reversion to the horrors of
savagery defines the primitive. If Marlow indicts imperialism by showing how European values become debased
and corrupted in Africa, he nevertheless assumes the
psychology of the imperialist in defining the savage.

Lawrence's struggle is precisely the opposite. Kurtz resists
becoming savage and loses value as he moves toward
primitive darkness; Lawrence finds a source of value in the
Bedouins and seeks to emulate them as he moves toward the
blinding light of the desert. He is dismayed by his failure to
become like them. Lawrence also reverses the pattern of *An
Outpost of Progress*. Conrad's heroes, before they come to
imitate native savagery, are sheltered by a society which
forbade "them all independent thought, all initiative, all
departure from routine; and forbidding it under pain of
death. They could only live on condition of being
machines."[21] Lawrence ends where they begin, extolling the
machine that he has become.

The contrast between Conrad and Lawrence can be seen

most clearly in an image both use to symbolize the obscuring of moral values. After the farcical murder of Carlier in *An Outpost of Progress,* Kayerts is oppressed by a heavy mist, "the mist penetrating, enveloping, and silent; the morning mist of tropical lands; the mist that clings and kills; the mist white and deadly, immaculate and poisonous."[22] In *Seven Pillars* the narrator watches a desert sunset, "fierce, stimulant, barbaric; reviving the colours of the desert like a draught—as indeed it did each evening, in a new miracle of strength and heat—while my longings were for weakness, chills and grey mistiness, that I might not be so crystalline clear, so sure of the wrong which I was doing" (MS 353a; cf. text 544). By Lawrence's own admission it is he who perverts and makes more savage the traditional Arab conduct of war. Though he regrets his return to the crowded world before him and asserts that he is broken by his effort at the peace talks, Lawrence chooses the immaculate and poisonous mist of the West. His moral jungle is Europe.

In writing about his postwar life in *The Mint* Lawrence recreates in microcosm the situation which led to his imperialism in Arabia. As with the Bedouin, he frequently refers to the soldiers in the ranks as children.[23] He declares that, unlike him, they are "mask-less," that is, "transparently unhesitant to declare their inmost or their whole purpose, practising the sinless honesty of all things clearly done" (*M* 113). He finds that the "good soldier is inconsequential as a child" (*M* 155). The soldiers, like the Arabs, have an identity he envies: "the Definiteness of British troops in uniform" (559). His leadership from the ranks recalls Arabia where the Bedouin chief has no formal position of authority, is equal to his men, yet appears better in himself. Yet Lawrence is the only fallen one in the ranks, the only one with self-consciousness, a sense of sin. The men are beasts, animals among whom Nebuchadnezzar lives (*L* 410); he transcends their intellect and will and becomes their consciousness.

The role of English armies in the Arab theater becomes a major part of the war narrative of *Seven Pillars,* particularly in Book IX. *Seven Pillars* assumes a circular pattern as the Bedouins he leads link up with the English armies toward the war's end. Lawrence begins in a wholly English world, escapes to take up the role of an adventurer, and then is returned to his initial condition by the very success of his efforts. He lives out his own migratory pattern, but it can never be repeated, as can the Bedouins'. The escape comes to appear only illusory and is soon exploited by the English. The rebellion he has led is, after all, within the purview of the English. Indeed, from the English viewpoint the rebellion is *only* personal, not political—a "personal essay in Rebellion." Lawrence rejects the values of his own society only within its accepted imperial pattern.

Lawrence is a rebel away, a conformist at home.[24] He first enters Bedouin society with the hope of conforming to it. In reality he has all along been attached to English values, confirming them and entrenching himself in England's political and military establishment. "I've crashed my life and self and gone hopelessly wrong," he writes in 1925 after dining with a high British official, "and hopelessly it is, for I'm never coming back, and I want to. . . ."[25] To Lawrence, isolation from society is weak, evil, despite his yearning to escape its strictures. He is weak to need to isolate himself, weaker still to fail in the attempt. In the beginning he praises Arab society because it is the antithesis of English values, but he comes to know that his action subverts the Bedouins, Westernizes them. His conscious feelings appear to run counter to his acts. Yet he cannot repudiate either acts or feelings, though he doubts both the efficacy of his deeds and the honesty of his professed emotions. At first Lawrence's efforts to identify with the Bedouin provide an opportunity for him to express contempt for English culture and values. He is antagonistic towards his own society and, as Lévi-Strauss says of the anthropologist, compares its "image with that of other societies, in the hope that they would either display the same shortcomings or help the West to explain how these defects could have come into being."[26]

The attempt to identify soon ends in failure, a failure implicit in his seeking an absolute in the Bedouin: spirit independent of body. Stimulated by increased contact with English troops, in the final book of *Seven Pillars* Lawrence expresses nostalgia for his homeland. At night he would walk among the men, "an unconsidered Arab: and this finding myself among, but cut off from, my own kin made me strangely alone" (641). He now praises the English passion for compromise and says he is "tired to death of these Arabs, and of my unlikeness to them" (MS 378). England is now the land of heart's delight, and he longs for its moody skies (544). Lawrence attributes his sense of alienation from the English to his attempt to identify with the Arabs, though he shows that he has always felt an outsider in England. In reality events in Arabia do not generate his alienation; rather, his alienation generates events in Arabia. He has not become like the Bedouin: they have become like him as he leads them out of the desert into the historical process and toward the Western creed of nationalism. As *Crusader Castles*, his Oxford undergraduate thesis, asserts of medieval architecture in Arabia, the West influences the East.

The machine in the desert is the most extreme symbol of the triumph of Western values in Arabia. Lawrence's use of the machine in *Seven Pillars* and *The Mint* reflects the characteristic view of it in much nineteenth-century literature. In *The Machine in the Garden* Leo Marx describes the symbolic effect of the machine as a "sudden, shocking intruder upon a fantasy of idyllic satisfaction. It invariably is associated with crude, masculine aggressiveness in contrast with the tender, feminine, and submissive attitudes traditionally attached to the landscape."[27] The desert is the garden of the nihilist, the pure pastoral situation outside of history. The occasional gardens or oases Lawrence encounters are perceived as forces of corruption, and he is always relieved to ride out into the desert beyond them. Value is not in the fecundity of the oasis but in the sterility of the desert. The desert has the unifying force of Henry Adams' Virgin, "plainly One, embracing all human activity."[28] Upon this desert intrudes the railroad connecting Damascus and Medina, putting an end to the great traditional pilgrimages by road.[29] The railroad begins the destruction of the medieval unity of the desert: "Asia has in thirty years leaped across a stage which took us hundreds. . . . some of us, the mediaevalists, lament it. However, that is just a pose."[30]

Lawrence spends much of the war literally attacking the railroad, but his hostility toward the machine and his defense of the desert's purity are compromised as *Seven Pillars* progresses. With his cooperation, the war is removed increasingly "from the sphere of joyous adventure" (507). His Arabian sideshow is linked with plans for a final thrust against the Turks by the British Army in Palestine. Lawrence mocks the English when they first enter the desert. He parodies their dehumanized war: "Tenders 1 and 3 would then demolish bridges A and B on the operations' plan (scale 1/250,000) at zero 1.30 hours . . ." (521). The edge of his contempt is sometimes blunted in the text; for example, he writes in the manuscript that Sherif Hazaa "had acquired such ascendancy over those feeble Arabs as to discipline them like troops" (MS 331; struck from text 519). And his contempt for the Turks is meant for the British as well, for if the occupying power in Arabia had been British, the issue of the campaign would have been more quickly achieved: "We'd have gone through them like brown paper."[31]

The British army not only uses the machine, it is one. The wills of its members are extinguished through discipline, and each becomes an element in its vast apparatus. The function of military discipline in both Arab and English troops is to "obliterate the humanity of the individual" (510). Lawrence's contrast of Bedouin and English emphasizes the distinction between individual and machine. The uniform of the English soldier makes the troops impersonal, gives them "the singleness and tautness of an upstanding man. This death's livery which walled its bearers from ordinary life, was sign that they had sold their wills and bodies to the State: and contracted themselves into a service not the less abject for that its beginning was voluntary. Some of them had obeyed the instinct of lawlessness: some were hungry: others thirsted for glamour, for the supposed colour of a military life: but, of them all, those only received satisfaction who had sought to degrade themselves, for to the peace-eye they were below humanity" (641).[32] Lawrence dramatizes the inhumanity of the soldiers by smelling them as he walks among them at night (642).

However contradictory it may seem, he also exults in the supremacy of the machine. In his description of the castle at Amruh, he acknowledges the feelings of superiority the machine gives to its English possessors and the contempt it

casts on ancient ways of life.[33] Lawrence could tell vague
tales of its inhabitants, "their poetry, and cruel wars: but my
memories were not sharp enough to draw themselves and
their life. It was so distant and tinselled an age: and I was not
sure whether all our knowledge, had I had it, would have
helped me much" (MS 369; cf. text 573). Despite his years as
an archaeologist, he cannot escape the present: "I felt guilty
at introducing the throbbing car, and its trim crew of khaki-
clad northerners, into the remoteness of this most hidden
legendary place; but my anticipation went astray, for it was
the men who looked real and the background which became
scene-painting" (559). The crowd "destroyed my pleasure in
Azrak" (586). Amruh is irrevocably dead, a myth to which he
can only give strained literary tributes. The machine easily
dominates the desert, and each mechanically organized
Englishman "would out-ride, out-fight and out-suffer any
forty men in Feisal's army" (569).

The full implications of Lawrence's apostrophe to the
machine are apparent only in *The Mint*. He exults in his
motorcycle: "A skittish motor-bike with a touch of blood in
it is better than all the riding animals on earth, because of its
logical extension of our faculties, and the hint, the
provocation, to excess conferred by its honeyed untiring
smoothness" (*M* 244-45). He perceives the "lustfulness of
moving swiftly" and calls speed "the second oldest animal
craving in our nature." At high speeds he becomes identified
with the machine: "I feel the earth moulding herself under
me. It is *me* piling up this hill, hollowing this valley,
stretching out this level place."[34] The contrast between
riding animal and machine epitomizes the distinction
between the organic ideal of the first half of *Seven Pillars*
and the mechanical ideal of the last half of *The Mint*. Eventually he comes to believe that motorbike and airplane are
superior to camel, English troops to Bedouin. The training
of troops in *The Mint* delineates the spiritual exercises by
which Lawrence seeks to annihilate the self and become a
machine. The person dies "that to the company might be
born a soul" (*M* 191). He equates discipline and mechanism
with spiritual death: "Uniformity is my bed fellow. . . .
Chaos breeds life: whereas by habit and regularity comes
death, quickly" (*L* 529).

The apotheosis of the machine, prevalent among Lawrence's contemporaries, is given radical expression in F. T. Marinetti's influential *Futurist Manifesto* (1909), which anticipates Lawrence's attitude in *The Mint* and links the glorifying of war and aggressive action to praise of the machine. Marinetti writes:

> We will sing of great crowds excited by work, by pleasure, and by riot; we will sing of the multicolored, polyphonic tides of revolution in the modern capitals; we will sing of the vibrant mighty fervor of arsenals and shipyards blazing with violent electric moons; greedy railway stations that devour smoke-plumed serpents; factories hung on clouds by the crooked lines of their smoke; bridges that stride the rivers like giant gymnasts, flashing in the sun with a glitter of knives; adventurous steamers that sniff the horizon; deep-chested locomotives whose wheels paw the tracks like the hooves of enormous steel horses bridled by tubing; and the sleek flight of planes whose propellers chatter in the wind like banners and seem to cheer like an enthusiastic crowd.[35]

In a late, brilliant letter Lawrence, echoing Carlyle a hundred years before, describes this as "the mechanical age." He has entered "the RAF to serve a mechanical purpose, not as leader, but as a cog in the machine. The key-word, I think, is machine." The air force is "the nearest modern equivalent of going into a monastery in the Middle Ages. . . . Being a mechanic cuts one off from all real communication with women. There are no women in the machines, in any machine" (*L* 852-53). "Woman" is Lawrence's euphemism for heterosexuality. At one point in the manuscript he writes of "our British conception of sex, or rather of woman" and strikes the reference to sex (MS 322; cf. text 508). The machine, in the terminology of Henry Adams, is the Dynamo as opposed to the Virgin.

Lawrence admired art he deemed mechanical. According to a friend, he liked "to look at the Brancusi I had in my room; it had almost a mechanical cleanness."[36] T. E. Hulme a decade earlier had predicted that sculptors would come to prefer to natural forms "the hard, clean surface of a piston rod."[37] To the notions "cleanness" and "machine," separately or in combination, Lawrence attributes great value. Reacting against his own Romantic individualism, he comes to realize, in phrases that sum up his whole experience in Arabia and at the peace table in Paris, that "progress today is made not by the single genius, but by the common effort." He applies this conviction directly to himself in an elegant apothegm: "The genius raids, but the common people occupy and possess" (*L* 852).

Lawrence's letter on machines concludes, "All this reads like a paragraph of D. H. L., my step-namesake" (*L* 853). Not quite, though his comparison is intriguing, for D. H. Lawrence also felt Marinetti's influence. T. E. read all of D. H. Lawrence's work, wrote about some of it, and admired much of it, sometimes extravagantly, particularly the later works which express the power urge (e.g., *The Plumed Serpent*).[38] The novelist's most complete use and explication of the machine symbol is in "The Industrial Magnate" chapter of *Women in Love*.[39] The polarities D. H. Lawrence establishes are similar to T. E.'s, though the novelist's values and conclusions are antithetical. D. H. Lawrence argues that giving oneself to the machine is "the substitution of the mechanical principle for the organic, the destruction of the organic purpose, the organic unity, and the subordination of every organic unit to the great mechanical purpose." Gerald Crich turns the machine upon "the earth and coal it enclosed. This was the sole idea, to turn upon the inanimate matter of the underground, and reduce it to his will." The machine literally devours the pastoral world of the Midlands, makes it dead fecal matter. The machine is the "godlike medium between himself and the matter he had to subjugate." It is "the very expression of his will, the incarnation of his power." The will to domination and power is the essence of the machine to both writers. In an earlier chapter, "Coal-Dust," D. H. Lawrence describes the will's sadistic nature in the domination of the horse, the organic, by Gerald, the God of the machine. With a "mechanical relentlessness, keen as a sword pressing into her," Gerald makes the horse stand before the train it sought to flee. Gudrun Brangwen understands the domination sexually and, as she watches the blood flow while the man presses his spurs into the horse, the "world reeled and passed into nothingness." To both writers the machine is the incarnation of the will to power, and the man who uses his will in this way becomes identified with the machine. He becomes the machine which dominates nature and which represents an inhuman will sexually toned, a sadistic will.

Man's will is the only absolute, and the inhuman perfection of that will is the machine.

Both Lawrences reflect Carlyle's assertion that this is "the Age of Machinery, in every outward and inward sense of that word." Men "are grown mechanical in head and in heart, as well as in hand."[40] But T. E. Lawrence honors in the breach his affinity with Carlyle. Understanding fully the significance of his choice, in *The Mint* he struggles to become a machine. Early in *Seven Pillars* he insists "that in all my life objects had been gladder to me than persons, and ideas than objects" (114). He ends declaring that he loves "objects before life or ideas" (549). The change is significant. The idea driving the Romantic hero's quest, and the domination of things through that idea, has given way to the desire to become a thing. By the end of his account of the Revolt Lawrence has become identified with the object of his horror, the antithetical symbol to the organic, migratory cycle. Lawrence himself becomes not only the perpetrator but the victim of Western imperialism. The machine is the image of the sadist becoming masochist, for it is the instrument of power to which he humbles the self, or the individual will, but which acts out the domination of the mass will. The self becomes the machine in the garden.

NOTES TO CHAPTER IV

1. "The Changing East," in *Oriental Assembly*, pp. 82, 72.

2. *Ibid.*, p. 84.

3. Introduction to Doughty, *Arabia Deserta*, I, 27.

4. *Lord Jim* (Boston: Houghton Mifflin, 1958), Ch. XLV.

5. Foreword to Thomas, *Arabia Felix*, p. xvi.

6. Letter to Charlotte Shaw, 18 August 1927.

7. *The Savage Mind*, trans. George Weidenfeld (Chicago: University of Chicago Press, 1966), pp. 233-34.

8. Foreword to Thomas, *Arabia Felix*, p. xvi.

9. *Tristes Tropiques*, trans. John Russell (New York: Atheneum, 1969), pp. 392, 376.

10. Lawrence unified the material of the three opening chapters in his Introduction to Doughty's *Arabia Deserta*. Based on an early draft of *Seven Pillars*, the Introduction first, like Chapter I, discusses the clean and foul ways a foreigner may live among Arabs and then, like II and III, abstractly characterizes the peoples of Arabia.

11. "On Eric Kennington's Arab Portraits," in *Oriental Assembly*, pp. 153-54.

12. *T. E. Lawrence to His Biographers*, I, 78.

13. *Home Letters*, p. 66.

14. Richard Aldington believes that Lawrence associates the word "clean" with homosexual relations, as opposed to "foul" heterosexual relations; see *Lawrence of Arabia: A Biographical Enquiry* (London: Collins, 1955), p. 335.

15. *Letters to T. E. Lawrence*, p. 170.

16. Trans. Pamela Powesland (London: Methuen, 1956), pp. 108, 111.

17. *Tristes Tropiques*, pp. 385, 392.

18. Trans. Constance Farrington (New York: Grove Press, 1963), pp. 298-302.

19. Introduction to Doughty, *Arabia Deserta*, I, 21. This is a paraphrased quotation from Doughty, I, 95.

20. *Secret Despatches*, p. 130.

21. *The Portable Conrad*, ed. Morton Dauwen Zabel (New York: Viking Press, 1947), pp. 463-64.

22. *Ibid.*, p. 487.

23. See, for example, letter to Charlotte Shaw, 11 January 1928.

24. On the conformity induced by the experience of a new society, see Lévi-Strauss, *Tristes Tropiques*, pp. 381-82.

25. Letter to Charlotte Shaw, 28 September 1925.

26. *Tristes Tropiques*, p. 388.

27. New York: Oxford University Press, 1964, p. 29. For a Marxist view of Lawrence's embrace of the machine, see Christopher St. John Sprigg (pseud. Caudwell), "T. E. Lawrence: A Study in Heroism," in *Studies in a Dying Culture* (London: The Bodley Head, 1938), pp. 38-39. The intensity of Lawrence's literal attacks on the machine has been described in Chapter III above.

28. *The Education*, p. 468.

29. Introduction to Doughty, *Arabia Deserta*, I, 26.

30. *Oriental Assembly*, pp. 73-74.

31. Letter to Charlotte Shaw, 14 April 1927.

32. Similar descriptions of Englishmen in the ranks occur earlier, e.g., "outcasts, low fellows cut off from life by contempt" (MS 224; cf. text 339).

33. Herbert L. Sussman, *Victorians and the Machine* (Cambridge, Mass.: Harvard University Press, 1968), p. 4, discusses this notion.

34. *T. E. Lawrence to His Biographers*, I, 121, and II, 160.

35. *Marinetti: Selected Writings*, ed. R. W. Flint, trans. R. W. Flint and Arthur A. Coppotelli (New York: Farrar, Straus and Giroux, 1971), p. 42.

36. *Shaw-Ede*, p. 50.

37. "Modern Art and Its Philosophy," in *Speculations*, ed. Herbert Read (London: Kegan Paul, Trench, Trubner, 1936), p. 97. This essay was first delivered as a lecture in January 1914.

38. See a review of *Novels by D. H. Lawrence*, *The Spectator*, 6 August 1927; rpt. in T. E. Lawrence, *Men in Print: Essays in Literary Criticism* (London: Golden Cockerel Press, 1940).

39. New York: Viking Press, 1960, Ch. XVII.

40. "Signs of the Times," in *Sartor Resartus and Selected Prose*, ed. Herbert L. Sussman (New York: Holt, Rinehart and Winston, 1970), pp. 6, 10.

V

Deraa: "Pain for Me and Pain for You"

That is the "bad" book, with the Deraa chapter. Working on it always makes me sick. The two impulses fight so upon it. Self-respect would close it: self-expression seeks to open it. It's a case in which you can't let yourself write as well as you could.[1]

THE HERO OF A CONFESSION, PARTICULARLY A MODERN confession, is deeply wounded in his sex. Medieval Abélard is castrated in bed as he awakens; he writes with incongruous delicacy of the brutal act: "they cut off those parts of my body with which I had done that which was the cause of their sorrow."[2] Sex for the modern hero is more complex, though the end is no less destructive. Abelard's offense appears physical, with punishment of the body precise, so precise as to cut out the source of guilt. Castration is not the cause of his greatest misfortunes; more important is persecution for his theological convictions. Abélard is primarily interested in his public self and character; from his own point of view his sexual condition becomes irrelevant. Wilde's *De Profundis*, on the other hand, has as its center a homosexual liaison with its disastrous aftermath. Wilde is persecuted for his sexual indiscretions, and his perverse passion is the core of his confession. In *The Thief's Journal* Genet unabashedly inverts the moral order on the pivot of his own homosexuality.

Frequently the sexual wound is sadomasochistic. The opposing symbols of Lucrece and Judith, wounded and wounding women, give order to Leiris' confession: *Manhood* is "an account of my life from an erotic point of view (a preferential one, since sexuality then seemed to me the cornerstone in the structure of the personality). . . ."[3] The masochism of Arthur Adamov's "The Endless Humiliation," as well as his sadistic hostility toward women, is explicit: "The taste for the fall is endless.

106

At the bottom of the world, I must discover somewhere lower still, some subsoil in which to work myself deeper, beneath woman herself. I must be lower than that which is low."[4] In Rousseau the confession has a major precedent for expressing sadomasochistic themes. Lawrence likes "the *Confessions*: or at least I am interested in them. What a queer fish R[ousseau] was."[5] Rousseau establishes the paradigm for the modern secular confession, as Augustine for the religious one. Beaten in childhood by an attractive woman, Rousseau discovers "in the shame and pain of the punishment an admixture of sensuality which had left me rather eager than otherwise for a repetition by the same hand." The physical act has great psychological and moral consequences: "Who could have supposed that this childish punishment, received at the age of eight at the hands of a woman of thirty, would determine my tastes and desires, my passions, my very self for the rest of my life. . . ."[6] Similarly, Lawrence believes that the flagellation he endures at Deraa determines the rest of his life. He would have the reader believe that his tastes, sexual desires, his very self are governed by a need for painful moral and physical stimuli which arose out of this traumatic experience. His humiliation at Deraa by no means provides the only motive in his life, but it is the center of his confessions. Deraa, which occurs in the penultimate chapter of Book VI, is Lawrence's only important attempt to dramatize the course of the introspective self, to show rather than to assert the link between act and self. It is meant to serve as a formal bridge between war narrative and reflection. The flagellation is intended to explain the change in emphasis that Lawrence believes takes place in *Seven Pillars*. It is to be the climax of the work, the turning point in the hero's fortunes.

Book VI, "The Failure of the Bridges," narrates the first important military defeat in the Arab campaign, an abortive raid on the Yarmuk bridges. After the raid Lawrence and his followers wait out the winter in Azrak gathering intelligence and converting tribes to their cause. He writes that in Azrak's fortress on "these slow nights we were secure against the world" (438). Lawrence decides to explore the country around Deraa and leaves the fortress to gather intelligence. He boldly enters the city in disguise and is arrested as a Circassian deserter. On the evening of his capture he is brought before the Bey, who wants to bugger him. Lawrence struggles defiantly and knees the Bey in the testicles. The Bey has him bound, slaps him, and, as in a ritual, cuts a fold of flesh over his ribs. The Bey remarks cryptically, "You must understand that I know: and it will be easier if you do as I wish" (433). Lawrence at first fears the remark refers to his military role, but it may also hint at his sexual proclivities. Eventually the Bey orders him whipped to compel his acquiescence. He is physically and spiritually broken by the beating and cries out for mercy.

Yet he is also sexually aroused: "I remembered smiling idly at him, for a delicious warmth, probably sexual, was swelling through me: and then that he flung up his arm and hacked with the full length of his whip into my groin." Whether he does yield to the Bey or his tormentors after such persuasion is uncertain, though the published account clearly says he willed to submit, but sodomy was not attempted. He is "sobbing for mercy," but is "now rejected as a thing too torn and bloody for his bed" (445). Later he is permitted to escape and make his way back to Azrak. But the moral effect of the flagellation is said to be absolute. Henceforth he is "gentling a broken will" (13). He now must "carry the burden, whose certainty the passing days confirmed: how in Deraa that night the citadel of my integrity had been irrevocably lost" (447).

The authenticity of the Deraa torture is much disputed.[7] In his letters Lawrence insists that the Bey, or his men, did not in fact reject him: "I wanted to put it plain in the book, and wrestled for days with my self-respect . . . which wouldn't, hasn't, let me. For fear of being hurt, or rather to earn five minutes' respite from a pain which drove me mad, I gave away the only possession we are born into the world with—our bodily integrity."[8] In a letter to Robert Graves regarding the longer Oxford Text of *Seven Pillars,* Lawrence finds its sincerity "absolute, except once where I funked the distinct truth, and wrote it obliquely. I was afraid of saying something, even to myself. The thing was not written for anyone to read. Only as I get further from the strain of that moment, confession seems a relief rather than a risk" (*L* 463).

The style of the Deraa episode is that of the war narrative, yet the helpless, ambivalent figure it portrays is found primarily in introspective chapters. Deraa has the clarity and control of descriptions of battles and train minings, and Lawrence seemingly narrates the event without intrusive afterthoughts. He indulges in none of the obscurantism of his introspection. Yet Lawrence's handwriting in the manuscript shows every sign of the tension characteristic of introspection: pages closely written to the margin, minute script, extraordinarily elaborate revisions and insertions. For the Deraa chapter, this "is about its ninth revise. Not that the many revises have changed its essence: they add a little, to make it richer, or plane off a little, to make it swifter. . . . my prose in it gets nearer to Style than elsewhere in the book. But then quite a lot happens there . . . which is one of the desiderata for Style."9 Since the manner of the chapter is unbroken, there must be some emotion in the scene which resembles his war narratives, something which enables him to see himself as object, to present himself here as coldly as he narrates a train mining.

Freud writes that "real situations are in fact only a kind of make-believe performance of the [masochistic] phantasies— the manifest content is of being pinioned, bound, beaten painfully, whipped, in some way mishandled, forced to obey unconditionally, defiled, degraded. . . . the subject is placed in a situation characteristic of womanhood, i.e. . . . he is being castrated, is playing the passive part in coitus, or is giving birth."10 To a remarkable degree the conventions of flagellation literature are found in Deraa: the instrument of punishment is described in great detail; the victim is bound to a piece of furniture; his attitude changes from defiance to supplication; pain is succeeded by pleasure; and sexual differences blur.11 The beating is a prelude to its repetition, in desire if not in fact, or (in Lawrence's case) if not in the book, in the life.

As in sadomasochistic fantasies or pornographic literature, Lawrence records the progress of his beating with unnatural detachment and extraordinary detail: "Always for the first of every new series, my head would be pulled round, to see how a hard white ridge, like a railway, darkening slowly into crimson, leaped over my skin at the instant of each stroke, with a bead of blood where two ridges crossed. As the punishment proceeded the whip fell more and more upon existing weals, biting blacker or more wet . . ." (444). The description of his weals is inordinately precise. He notes that the railway which he sought to destroy is being reconstructed on his back. The bead of blood is a masterful detail. It is physically impossible for Lawrence to perceive these effects or to be looking "at the instant of each stroke." He is both observer and victim.

In revising this chapter Lawrence modified his revealing preoccupation with detail. The passages italicized below were excised from the published text. The Bey slaps Lawrence with a *"black, soft"* slipper. He is fascinated by the instrument of his punishment. The corporal beats him with "a Circassian *riding* whip, *of the sort which gendarmes carried.* They were a *single* thong of supple black hide, rounded, and tapering from the thickness of a thumb at the grip (which was wrapped in silver, *with a knob inlaid in black designs*), down to a hard point *much* finer than a pencil" (MS 284-85; cf. text 443-44). His description of the whip is an unwitting parody of pornographic conventions, particularly in its grip, which ends in a phallic knob, the appropriate sadistic instrument for a male to wield.[12] This interest continues in *The Mint*. A drill instructor symbolically deflowers new recruits under his authority. Sergeant Poulton would "pick on first one and then another of the flight, playing with them for an hour, twisting the point of his contempt slowly into their tenderness" (126). Lawrence is similarly fascinated with his drill instructor's stick: "It was brass-pointed, split lengthwise, and hinged like a pair of callipers, to measure the infantry-pace. 'See that point? It's going up your fucking guts till it's full of blood. I mean to have three rings on it a day' " (142).

Deraa and other beatings provide Lawrence with his expressed, conscious model for most sexual behavior. Lawrence fantasizes that even normal copulation is aggression, rape, violation. In an apparent reference to Deraa Lawrence writes to the virginal Mrs. G. B. Shaw: "Perhaps the possibility of a child relieves sometimes what otherwise might seem an unbearable humiliation to the woman:—for I presume it's unbearable. However here I'm trenching on dangerous ground, with my own ache coming to life again."[13] He conceives of the sexual act, in the words of Freud, "as an attempt to overpower the woman, as a combat, the sadistic misconception of coitus."[14]

Immediately before the Deraa episode Lawrence shows love as aggression in his idyllic description of the play of the homosexual lovers Farraj and Daud. Daud hurls Farraj into a pool and the latter hides under a rock. Fearing his friend is drowning, Daud leaps in to save him. When he becomes aware of being duped, Daud begins "a wild struggle in the sand beside the water hole. Each sustained hurt, and they returned to my fire dripping wet, in rags, bleeding, with their hair and faces, legs, arms and bodies covered with mud and thorns, more like the devils of a whirlwind than their usual suave delicate presences. They said they had been dancing, and had tripped over a bush . . ." (410). Lawrence finds this manner of expressing affection among homosexuals appealing, perhaps because pain has veiled the sexual desires of the pair. Periodically the pair are threatened with beating. Once Lawrence promises to thrash the two as punishment for another prank, painting a Sheik's camels, but deletes from the text a highly ambiguous description of the beating: "I took the opportunity of the enforced rest to liquidate on Farraj and Daud (not painfully) my promise to Sheikh Yusuf in the matter of his illuminated camels" (MS 280).

As with the Bedouin, play among the airmen in *The Mint* frequently has a homosexual cast: Dickson "shifted his other hand to that fatal 'bollock-hold' of our impolite wrestling code. You bunch the things tightly and knead them" (*M* 168;

v M 174). Richard Meinertzhagen, once an English officer on the Palestine front, tells of an incident which links Lawrence's aggression and his homosexuality: "I remember an occasion in the Majestic Hotel in Paris when he ran off with my knobkerrie; I chased him, caught him, and holding him tight gave him a spanking on the bottom. He made no attempt to resist and told me later that he could easily understand a woman submitting to a rape once a strong man hugged her." Meinertzhagen gives this interlude a simple homosexual explanation: "He had no use for women, his sexual inclination being big strong men. He had little use for small men such as he was himself."[15] Whether Lawrence was overtly homosexual is uncertain, but he was fascinated by the knobkerrie, a short club with a knotted end used by African tribes as a weapon. Lawrence uses it effectively in his sketch of Meinertzhagen, one of the most vivid in *Seven Pillars.* For once Lawrence gives life and conviction to a man who is the introspective Ali's antithesis. Meinertzhagen's "hot immoral hatred of the enemy expressed itself as readily in trickery as in violence. . . . He was a strategist, a geographer, and a silent laughing masterful man; who took as blithe a pleasure in deceiving his enemy (or his friend) by some unscrupulous jest, as in spattering the brains of a cornered mob of Germans one by one with his African knobkerri. His instincts were abetted by an immensely powerful body and a savage brain, which chose the best way to its purpose, unhampered by doubt or habit" (384). By emphasizing the homosexuality implicitly revealed by the Paris incident, Meinertzhagen neglects the explicit: the desire to be beaten, or to beat, as an end in itself. To be spanked by Meinertzhagen is a fine thing indeed, and his knobkerrie is the perfect sadist's weapon, a symbolic phallus.

All sadomasochism is, according to Wilhelm Stekel in *Sadism and Masochism,* "a surrogate, a substitute for homosexuality." Stekel's analysis summarizes the nature of the dichotomy in Lawrence's confessions: "the sadomasochist stands between man and woman and cannot decide which direction to take." He "mistreats the woman in himself and wants to gain the victory over her."[16] Homosexuality is, as Deraa shows, inextricable from sadomasochism for Lawrence. In *The Other Victorians* Steven Marcus concludes that the literature of flagellation, "along with fantasies it embodied and the practices it depicted, represents a kind of last-ditch compromise with and defense against homosexuality."[17] In Chapter I masochism is clearly presented as both a substitute and a punishment for homosexuality. Immediately after praising "intimate hot limbs in supreme embrace" (30), Lawrence writes that several men, "thirsting to punish appetites they could not wholly prevent, took a savage pride in degrading the body, and offered themselves fiercely in any habit which promised physical pain or filth" (30). In his narrative of Deraa he joins crime and punishment in his homosexual rape and flagellation. Lawrence presents a beating which serves as an ideal defense against and persuasion for homosexuality; he is not beaten to prevent the act or as punishment for it, but to submit to it. Yet in the published version he is flagellated so severely he is too fouled and bloody for sodomy. The means of persuasion effectively prevents consummation. Lawrence portrays himself as the victim of a symbolic defloration, merging the crucifixion motif with the virginal: "I thought he was going to kill me, and was sorry: but he only pulled up a fold of the flesh over my ribs, worked the point through, after considerable trouble, and gave the blade a half-turn. This hurt, and I winced, while the blood wavered down my side, and dripped to the front of my thigh. He looked pleased and dabbled it over my stomach with his finger tips" (443). Here Lawrence seems to identify with the female, reinforcing within the homosexual nature of the attack from without.

An extraordinary number of beatings are described in the latter half of *Seven Pillars*, particularly in the manuscript version. Twenty pages after Deraa, Lawrence narrates a beating subsequently suppressed in the text; in its essentials it recalls Deraa. The beating is administered both to atone for homosexuality and to prevent it. An English soldier and an Arab boy commit sodomy and are found *in flagrante delicto*; the boy is immediately whipped by the Arabs. After a debate the English take matters into their own hands and whip their soldier too rather than proceed with more restrained disciplinary measures. The beating is clearly a defense against interracial homosexuality: "we heard of no second case of British being mixed up with Arabs: which was a good thing, for many reasons other than the sanitary" (MS Chapter XCII).

In this suppressed chapter Lawrence discusses the sexual proclivities of the Arab; he is tolerant of homosexuality among them, intolerant of it among the English. Of Arab homosexuality he writes: "While these were voluntary and affectionate, they were winked at; for they seemed amateurish. . . ." In the published text he displays this tolerance in his descriptions of love couples such as Farraj and Daud, Ali and Turki. Such homosexual behavior either is a direct consequence of Arab loss of inhibition in the war or reveals deficiencies in their character. The Arabs conform to a less rigid standard of sexual morality than the English, and he fears the English may be contaminated: "The real danger, to my mind, was lest the contagion of example (and with it that still more dreaded physical contagion) spread to the British units." Lawrence's puritanical view of heterosexual acts and interracial intercourse seems to be responsible for the deprived sexual state of English soldiers: "I had put my own guard over the three prostitutes in Akaba because they were so beastly that I could not stand the thought of their being touched by the British; even though deprivation drove the men into irregularities." Lawrence justly remarks to the English pederast that "he was not being condemned by me morally, since neither my impulses nor my convictions were strong enough to make me a judge of conduct. . . ."

Book VI ends with the triumphal entry into Jerusalem of Allenby, the English commander of the Egyptian Expeditionary Force. Lawrence joins the parade; the entry is his "supreme moment of the war" (453) and contrasts vividly with his degradation at Deraa: "It was strange to stand before the tower with the Chief, listening to his proclamation, and to think how few days before I had stood before Hajim [the Bey], listening to his words" (MS 289). The ironic equation of Hajim with Allenby also has homosexual overtones. As Edward Garnett writes, Lawrence wants to submit to strong, simple men ("to be very great a man must be pretty stupid")[18]—Allenby and, later, Trenchard, the commander of the R.A.F.—for his "feminine side has a passion for being under these heavy military men."[19]

The classic psychoanalytic expositions of sadomasochism provide a basis for understanding Lawrence's presentation of self in his confessions and his analysis of painful experiences in his letters.[20] Algolagnia denotes the connection between sexuality and violence or pain; sadism is active algolagnia, masochism passive.[21] In Lawrence's words, there is "no pain or joy, only sensation" (*L* 421). Sadism may be transformed into masochism. The dynamics of the perversion were summarized by Freud in 1915:

> (a) Sadism consists in the exercise of violence or power upon some other person as its object.
> (b) This object is abandoned and replaced by the subject's self. Together with the turning round upon the self the change from an active to a passive aim in the instinct is also brought about.
> (c) Again another person is sought as object; this person, in consequence of the alteration which has taken place in the aim of the instinct, has to take over the original role of the subject.
> Case (c) is the condition commonly termed masochism. Satisfaction follows in this case also by way of the original sadism, the passive ego placing itself in fantasy back in its former situation, which, however, has now been given up to another subject outside the self.[22]

This continuum can be reversed: "Where once the suffering of pain has been experienced as a masochistic aim, it can be carried back into the sadistic situation and result in a sadistic aim of *inflicting pain*, which will then be masochistically enjoyed by the subject while inflicting pain upon others, through his identification of himself with the suffering object. Of course, in either case it is not the pain itself which is enjoyed, but the accompanying sexual excitement. . . . "[23] Thus where either sadism or masochism exists, the other is present. For instance, Lawrence's description of his scars at Deraa is sadistic in character; only a subject could properly assume this viewpoint. Wilhelm

Stekel describes the perversion less technically than Freud: the sadist is gratified by his "sense of power in overcoming the resistance of another and from his feeling himself into the humiliation of his partner; in the masochist, from the overcoming of his own resistances (power over himself!) and the feeling of himself into the partner who humbles him. . . ."[24]

Freud and his followers, though retaining the basis of his original definition of sadomasochism, extend its application beyond physical pain and direct sexual stimulation. The names of the polarities in the perversion suggest this broader interpretation. "Masochism," of course, is derived from the works of Leopold von Sacher-Masoch, "sadism" from those of the Marquis de Sade. The cruelties the two men describe in their novels are not always directly related to sexuality; they describe many kinds of suffering, humiliation, and abuses of power. Erich Fromm and Karen Horney have developed theories which define the masochistic character or moral masochism.[25] Horney writes: "the term masochism originally referred to sexual perversions and fantasies in which sexual satisfaction is obtained through suffering, through being beaten, tortured, raped, enslaved, humiliated. Freud has recognized that these sexual perversions and fantasies are akin to the general tendencies toward suffering, that is, those which have no apparent sexual foundations; these latter tendencies have been classified as 'moral masochism.' "[26]

Stekel's portrait of the sadomasochistic character in *Sadism and Masochism* parallels at numerous points that of Lawrence's confessional hero. The secret of "masochism is the fear of pain."[27] Lawrence says that "Pain of the slightest had been my obsession and secret terror, from a boy" (446). The sadomasochist, Stekel finds, "hates woman—often with a single exception. This hatred drives him to homosexuality." His "primary attitude of hatred [is] toward the mother."[28] Lawrence's mother has given him "a terror of families and inquisitions. . . . Knowledge of her will prevent my ever making any woman a mother, and the cause of children."[29] The sadomasochist frequently prefers "very old women . . . to younger women."[30] Perhaps Lawrence's most intimate correspondence is with the aged and chaste Charlotte Shaw. He also is a devotee of several other older women (Florence Hardy, for example, the wife of Thomas Hardy) and seems most comfortable with them. On the other hand, one of Lawrence's most vicious attacks on anyone is directed against a friend's mistress, whose appeal is "carnal only" and who is "passionate, and lustful, and strong and cruel." He concludes his analysis of her character by remarking that he "cannot have patience with people who tickle up their sex until it seems to fill all their lives and bodies."[31]

According to psychoanalytic theory, the sadomasochist is exceptionally clean and, like Lawrence, is disgusted by, but fascinated with, dirt and filth. Lawrence professes inordinate disgust for the body and its reproductive and excremental functions, but his confessions deal extensively with feces, decay, and the beauty and ugliness of the dead (e.g., 308). In *The Mint* an account of an airman's first intercourse ends with his exclamation, "I can't ever do it the first time again: but Christ, it was bloody wonnerful. I say, what've I got to do now? Wash it, I s'pose. Got any dope?" (*M* 224).[32] The vagina is constantly presented as if it were unclean and feared. For example, Lawrence quotes extensively from a song about a whore: "And in one corner of her cunt, she'd stowed the cutter's crew!" (*M* 66).[33] By contrast, in the opening pages of *Seven Pillars* the anus becomes the desirable sexual organ: "our youths began indifferently to slake one another's few needs in their own clean bodies—a cold convenience that, by comparison, seemed sexless and even pure" (30). Men "quivering together in the yielding sand" are hardly sexless; rather Lawrence describes them so as a defense against his own fears of sexuality. For Lawrence, to be clean is to reject sexuality, accept death. After discussing the carnality of the soldiers in the Tank Corps, Lawrence writes Lionel Curtis that "surely the world would be more clean if we were dead or mindless" (*L* 414). The Damascus charnel house where living and dead become shit, "liquescent with decay," the whole of *The Mint*, the fragments of "Leaves in the Wind"[34]—all constitute an anal romp generated by what

Lawrence aptly terms "the attraction of unlikeness" (*M* 35).
Fromm argues that "the anal character is attracted by feces as
he is attracted by everything that is useless for life, such as
dirt, death, decay."[35] Lawrence's sadomasochistic motto for
Seven Pillars is "the sword also means clean-ness and
death." It is his attraction to that which is dead which
explains his interest in the machine, the simulacrum of the
organic. The self has become dead: "there is nothing in
oneself unknown, or producing a fresh joy."[36]

Stekel believes the sadomasochist is religious.[37] He is "the
blasphemer and atheist *par excellence* inasmuch as his inner
religiousness manifests itself outwardly in a pathological
asceticism which renounces the highest goal, the possession
of a woman. Masochists conceal their religious nature only
in rare exceptional cases. A certain amount of penitence and
religious feeling is mixed in their paraphilia, which
sometimes assumes a direct religious character (flagellation,
asceticism, self-torture, withdrawal from every pleasure out
of religious motives)."[38] Fromm finds that the "religious
experience . . . of absolute dependence is the definition of
the masochistic experience in general."[39] Lawrence is, of
course, an ascetic and compares his retreat into the ranks of
the R.A.F. to that of a cenobite monk, his sufferings in
Arabia to those of Christ: "Saint and sinner touch" (*M* 179).

According to Fromm, "The different forms which the
masochistic strivings assume have one aim: *to get rid of the
individual self, to lose oneself.*"[40] Lawrence's attempt to
annihilate the self is the subject of *The Mint.* As Horney
explains, this desire need not be pathological: "By dissolv-
ing the self in something greater, by becoming part of a
greater entity, the individual overcomes to a certain extent
his limitations. . . . This seems to be the great consolation
and gratification which religion has to offer human beings;
by losing themselves they can become at one with God or
nature."[41] Lawrence does not want a small and still voice as a
guide to wisdom or truth: "Mine will be an overwhelming
guide: so very great and powerful that all my thinking and
seeing and speaking and hearing are only parts of
it. . . . 'comprehension' should be the answer of the world

to the creed of 'morcellation': the dividing and subdividing subtleties of mind. . . ."[42] But Horney argues that "our culture serves to reinforce the anxiety connected with the drives toward oblivion. In Western civilization there are but few, if any, cultural patterns in which these drives, even regardless of their neurotic character, can be satisfied. Religion . . . has lost its power and appeal for the majority."[43]

The expression of the dynamics of sadomasochism in Lawrence's confessions is most clear in a suppressed scene from the manuscript version of Book X. As punishment for his bodyguards' failure to respond to commands, the leaders batter the men "till the pain overmastered their endurance." Each man had gotten "his standard of pain and danger and the longing for it; . . . [I knew] that these vigorous fellows needed more than ordinary weaklings, to satisfy their health and strength: but today I was a Benthamite, shrinking from anything which hurt, and accordingly I saw something bestial in their deliberate search after abnormality, their breeding for it. After wrong-doing they would expect, almost claim, their punishment, as an honor due, welcoming it as a means of self-knowledge, by which to explore themselves, to learn how far beyond the bounds of daily fortitude their bodies could endure." This actual pain then becomes not a memory but a fantasy so its original strength may constantly be experienced anew. Lawrence soon identifies with the Bedouin and writes a hymn to pain: "Afterwards, since memory of pain was so short, they made a fantasy of it, toying with it, running its risk that in passionate excitement they might ride the neck of this unknown force so much stronger than themselves, thrilling with joy of surf-bathers who snatch life like a cork between elemental powers. Pain became an allurement like danger of which the best that was and the worst that was remained secret, brooded upon and colouring them inwardly. What was this hoarding of extremes, this laying up of the highest and lowest, as the prime mental food?" Lawrence's confusion is evident: all is bestial and abnormal, yet some part of that whole is the highest, the best that is, some part the lowest, the worst that

is. All is secret and colors the entire inner life and all these
fantasies are *mental* food. At the end of the passage Lawrence
draws back appalled as he describes the sadism which ·this
masochism produces in observers and victims: "The effect
for the moment was to disgust me with them, and to make
them useless for my purpose. Such cruel punishment was
preceded by fear: but the memory of its infliction provoked
only wilder lawlessness among the stronger victims, and a
greater likelihood of as violent offenses among the witnesses.
Accordingly after so general a stimulus as that of today, the
wisest thing was to leave them alone a while to calm down.
They would have been dangerous to me, to themselves; or to
the enemy as the whim and opportunity provided, had we
gone into action together tonight" (MS 393).

Lawrence's letters and confessions demonstrate his
awareness of the pathology of sadomasochism. In an
unpublished letter he briefly and perceptively compares
Jung and Freud.[44] He knows well the works of major writers
influenced by psychoanalytic theories—D. H. Lawrence and
James Joyce among others. Though he cannot speak from
heterosexual experience, Lawrence does have feelings about
sexual intercourse, and his customary evaluation is not
enthusiastic: "if the perfect partnership, indulgence with a
living body, is as brief as the solitary act, then the climax is
indeed no more than a convulsion, a razor-edge of time,
which palls so on return that the temptation flickers out into
the indifference of tired disgust once a blue moon, when
nature compels it" (*M* 128). Yet he vividly portrays his
erection during the Deraa torture and says his kindest words
about the erotic feeling in all his work here, calling it "a
delicious warmth." And in *Seven Pillars* Lawrence describes
a masochistic religious ceremony which his bodyguard joins
gratuitously: "The Ageyl stared open-mouthed at the
ceremony, but before it ended swung themselves monkey-
like down, grinning lewdly, and stabbed in their thorns
where they would be most painful" (530). Lawrence's
masochism in *The Mint* is concentrated in one vivid sexual
image which he uses to express his feelings when other
airmen sympathize with his pain: "It was like hot fingers
stroking my shame" (*M* 184).

Lawrence admits to masochism and implies recognition of the dynamics of sadomasochism in letters to Lionel Curtis in 1923. In the ranks of the Tank Corps, he writes, you may "abuse yourself in any way. I cried out against it, partly in self-pity because I've condemned myself to grow like them, and partly in premonition of failure, for *my masochism remains and will remain, only moral.* Physically I can't do it: indeed I get in denial the gratification they get in indulgence. I react against their example into an abstention even more rigorous than of old. . . . It's terrible to hold myself voluntarily here: and yet I want to stay here till it no longer hurts me: till the burnt child no longer feels the fire" (*L* 415-16, italics added). Lawrence believes that pleasure or pain is relative, a matter of judgment, and he does not repeat the experience if he thinks it unpleasant to his judgment.[45] The pain of the purgative or minting process is a means to an end: "the burning out of freewill and self-respect and delicacy from a nature as violent as mine is bound to hurt a bit" (*L* 419).

Despite his assertion above, Lawrence's masochism does not remain moral or ideal, independent of direct sexual expression; rather it is acted out repeatedly in the postwar years in rituals which recall both the beating at Deraa and early childhood beatings by his mother. We now know that, at his own request, Lawrence was periodically flagellated from 1923 until his death. In addition to other less direct and more elaborate humiliations, he constructed a fantasy in which an old man, an uncle, insisted that Lawrence be punished by a soldier in the ranks. Like a recalcitrant child, he was beaten on his bared buttocks, at times until he ejaculated. Lawrence played both the part of the sadistic old uncle demanding that his nephew be punished and of the nephew who was flagellated. The fantasy is virtually a schematic presentation of the sadomasochistic continuum, the old man feeling his way into the humiliation of the nephew by detailed written questions asked of the soldier who administered the beatings.[46] Lawrence was compelled to act out his masochism, as earlier he acted out his impulse for mastery. The strength of his masochism indicates the power of his sadistic urge, for the former serves to restrain the

latter. The masochistic impulse connects the themes of
Seven Pillars with those of *The Mint*. The former records his
test in the deserts of mastery and the use of Romantic will,
the latter in the deserts of submission and self-abnegation.

In masochism the superego assumes the role of sadistic
aggressor against the ego and id. Lawrence clearly identifies
his will with conscience or superego: "Conscience in healthy
men is a balanced sadism, the bitter sauce which makes more
tasteful the ordinary sweets of life: and in sick stomachs the
desire of condiment becomes a craving, till what is hateful
feels therefore wholesome, and what is repugnant to the
moral sense becomes (to the mind) therefore pure and
righteous and to be pursued. So because my senses hate it, my
will forces me to it . . . and a comfortable life would seem
now to me sinful" (*L* 417-18). Freud explains "the origin of
human conscience by some such 'turning inward' of the
aggressive impulse."[47] In *Civilization and Its Discontents*
Freud argues that "conscience is formed in the beginning
from the suppression of an aggressive impulse and
strengthened as time goes on by each fresh suppression of the
kind."[48] The destructive component has "entrenched itself
in the superego and turned against the ego. . . . It is
remarkable that the more a man checks his aggressive
tendencies toward others, the more tyrannical, that is
aggressive, he becomes in his ego-ideal."[49] *The Mint*
dramatizes a similar process: "my will has apparently turned
against self" (*M* 105).

Deraa is the most prominent instance of Lawrence's overt
recognition of the sexual component in his masochism. A
discussion of Shaw's *Saint Joan* with Mrs. Shaw soon leads
to Deraa: "Poor Joan, I was thinking of her as a person, not
as a moral lesson. The pain meant more to her than the
example. You instance my night in Deraa. Well, I'm always
afraid of being hurt: and to me, while I live, the force of that
night will lie in the agony which broke me, and made me
surrender." The burning scene should have been staged, for
"if the play was to be not a morality but life itself, he would
have given the physical its place above the moral."[50] While
Lawrence finds that the degradation he endures paradoxical-

ly purifies by fire, burns out "freewill and self-respect and delicacy," it is also an end in itself:

> From henceforward my way will lie with these fellows here, degrading myself (for in their eyes and your eyes and Winterton's eyes I see that it is a degradation) in the hope that some day I will really feel degraded, be degraded, to their level. I long for people to look down upon me and despise me, and I'm too shy to take the filthy steps which would publicly shame me, and put me into their contempt. I want to dirty myself outwardly, so that my person may properly reflect the dirtiness which it conceals. . . . and I shrink from dirtying the outside, while I've eaten, avidly eaten, every filthy morsel which chance threw in my way.[51]

Lawrence contrasts what he is to others to what he is to himself. To perceive the extent of his own fantasied degradation he must look through the eyes of others, must cease to be a subject and become an object, must look at himself from outside, as a sadist would, to feel fully his humiliation.

In a very real sense Lawrence's suffering and renunciation are attacks on society. Karen Horney writes, "Suffering has finally the function of expressing accusations against others in a disguised but effective way."[52] Hostility against others is present in both masochism and sadism, though in the former its expression is indirect and generally unconscious.[53] The masochist kills himself on the offender's doorstep.[54] Even the gaze which Lawrence turns upon himself in chapters of introspection is aggressive, an attack. As Laing remarks, ". . . how charged with hostility is the self-scrutiny to which the schizoid subjects himself. . . . The schizoid individual exists under the black sun, the evil eye, of his own scrutiny. The glare of his awareness kills his spontaneity, his freshness; it destroys all joy."[55] Indeed, Lawrence's ostentatious withdrawal into the ranks of the R.A.F. is frequently interpreted as a bitter attack by an idealist on the postwar settlement in Arabia and on the old men who "came out again and took from us our victory" (MS 10). Lawrence himself at times denies, at times encourages this view. Certainly after 1922 he refused to give pleasure to other men and to his society by virtue of public acts and the constructive use of his unquestioned intelligence and his power to lead.

Even his important literary works were written with great
hesitation and circulated privately, as if he were reluctant to
provide this pleasure too, as if the creative and reproductive
acts were one, and shameful. Lawrence always demonstrated
that he had the power to perform great deeds and then
refused to apply that power in any way consistent with his
abilities. Not surprisingly, such withholding produced
frustration and hostility in many people who knew him
personally as well as in others who had only read of his
achievements.

Lawrence's preoccupation with Deraa is evinced struc-
turally in *Seven Pillars*; it is also revealed in veiled references
to the event throughout *The Mint*. But if only Lawrence's
bodily integrity is involved, the effect of Deraa is incommensurate with his avowed contempt for the flesh; he observes
bodies with "hostility, with a contemptuous sense that they
reached their highest purpose, not as vehicles of the spirit,
but when, dissolved, their elements served to manure a field"
(468). But perhaps Lawrence has discovered at Deraa that his
morbid desire is sadistic as well as masochistic. He writes
elsewhere that "our character was what we were not aware of
ourselves, and any conscious quality presupposed the
presence of its opposite" (MS 357). According to Fromm,
sadism is "usually less conscious and more rationalized than
the socially more harmless masochistic trends."[56] The
confessions could be said to be about the transformation of a
sadist into a masochist by increasing conscious or unconscious grasp of the relation between pain and sexuality.
But Lawrence either is unable to perceive fully this pattern
or is not so neat or dishonest as to impose it on the
confessions. Even after Deraa he vividly portrays his
acceptance of Arab cruelty, approving, for instance, of the
maltreatment of Turkish prisoners: "They were driving
them mercilessly, the bruises of their urging blue across the
ivory backs: but I left them to it, for these were Turks of the
police battalion of Deraa, beneath whose iniquities the
peasant-faces of the neighborhood had run with tears and
blood, innumerable times" (630). In the manuscript he adds
that "a taste of such bitterness as their customary own would

not kill them, but might make them thoughtful for the future, less docile instruments of tyranny. With some of them I had my own account" (MS 402). He repays the sadism of Deraa in kind.

Lawrence narrates other sadistic acts with the same degree of attention to melodramatic details which he gave to his own beating. After one of his bodyguards shoots a wounded Turk, he watches the blood come out "with his heart beats, throb, throb, throb, slower and slower." On the same day he witnesses the results of a Turkish massacre at Tafas: "In a madness born of the horror of Tafas we killed and killed, even blowing in the heads of the fallen and of the animals; as though their death and running blood could slake our agony." By Lawrence's order no prisoners were to be taken. In ignorance of his decree, an Arab unit captures two hundred prisoners: "They said nothing in the moments before we opened fire. At last their heap ceased moving . . ." (631-33). Unlike the earlier slaughter of prisoners after a train mining, Lawrence participates in and is directly responsible for the atrocity. Of course Lawrence's torture alone does not produce these reprisals nor is it ever used to justify them, but it is constantly recalled. He refuses to sleep in Deraa after its capture: "I had felt man's iniquity here: and so hated Deraa that I lay each night with my men upon the old aerodrome" (638).

Despite his maimed will, Lawrence still exhibits his mastery of others. It is not what he does publicly that betrays his loss of will, but what he writes in chapters of introspection. Lawrence reveals, explicitly in the manuscript, implicitly in the text, that the damage to self which appears to come from without is only a catalyst which activates a principle within:

> I was feeling very ill, as though some part of me had gone dead that night in Deraa, and leaving me maimed, imperfect, only half-myself. It could not have been the defilement, for no one ever held the body in less honour than I did myself: probably it had been the breaking of the spirit by that frenzied nerve-shattering pain which had degraded me to beast level, when it made me grovel to it, and which had journeyed with me since, a fascination and terror and morbid desire, lascivious and vicious perhaps, but like the striving of a moth towards its flame. (MS 285)

He is to have this masochistic desire again, but does not believe that what happened imposed the desire on him. The inner self must have cooperated in his maiming: "Collapse rose always from a moral weakness eating into the body, which of itself, without traitors from within, had no power over the will" (468). Yet Lawrence vacillates; others, untainted before, are affected as he is: "Incidents like these made the thought of military service in the Turkish army a living death for wholesome Arab peasants, and the consequences pursued the miserable victims all their afterlife, in revolting forms of sexual desire" (MS 284).

Lawrence believes that the Deraa experience "penetrated to his innermost nature."[57] Deraa's significance is not simply that his will is broken by an outside power, but that he is forced to acknowledge for the first time the strength of his perverse desires. The flagellation is the moment when the external world begins to impinge on the freedom and expansive power of the Romantic hero. Lawrence admits he will now be only "half-myself," presumably the masochistic, passive, introspective self rather than the sadistic self, for it is the former he intends to concentrate on in the next books. Perhaps to become half-himself is to become more himself, or more the inner self, to achieve a harmony by extinguishing one of the antithetical principles within him. Clearly Deraa portrays the birth of a new self or the death of an old one: "the core of life seemed to heave slowly up through the rending nerves, expelled from its body by this last indescribable pang" (445).[58]

At times Lawrence argues that it is only the defilement of Deraa which determined his future degradation in the ranks: "It's an unforgivable matter, an irreconcilable position: and it's that which has made me foreswear decent living, and the exercise of my not-contemptible wits and talents. You may call this morbid: but think of the offense, and the intensity of my brooding over it for these years. It will hang about me while I live, and afterwards if our personality survives. Consider wandering among the decent ghosts hereafter, crying 'Unclean! Unclean!' "[59] In writing about Deraa Lawrence imposes a Byronic pattern on his experience;

Deraa is his inner demon, a torturing memory of an enormous though incomprehensible guilt. He convinces many of his friends, biographers, and readers that his torture and its aftermath are the deepest truths about him. The assertion that Deraa determines his tastes and desires for life is psychologically untenable, even if supported by the whole argument of *Seven Pillars*, which it is not. Like Rousseau's childhood beating, Deraa confirms a taste already developed; Lawrence is betrayed by "traitors from within." Deraa is seized as a way to dramatize his masochism. In his published confessions Lawrence asserts that Deraa is a cause at the same time he demonstrates that it is a symptom.

From Lawrence's point of view choosing to be masochistic is choosing not to be sadistic. He learns that his masochism controls his love for power and mastery. After a meeting with some of his comrades during the Arabian campaign, Lawrence writes:

> Do you know what it is when you see, suddenly, that your life is all a ruin? . . . Thinking drives me mad, because of the invisible ties about me which limit my moving, my wishing, my imagining. All these bonds I have tied myself, deliberately, wishing to tie myself down beyond the hope or power of movement. And this deliberation, this intention, rests. It is stronger than anything else in me, than everything else put together. So long as there is breath in my body my strength will be exerted to keep my soul in prison, since no where else can it exist in safety. The terror of being run away with, in the liberty of power, lies at the back of these many renunciations of my later life. I am afraid, of myself. Is this madness?[60]

Lawrence's original masochism, as in the classic psychoanalytic view, is reinforced by the renunciation of aggressive urges. He alone is strong enough to protect others from himself. His humiliating position is less expiation than restraint: "Seven years of this [life in the ranks] will make me impossible for anyone to suggest for a responsible position, and that self-degradation is my aim. I haven't the impulse and conviction to fit what I know to be my power of moulding men and things" (*L* 411).

Deraa is a consequence of the impulse for mastery which precedes it, the wages of sin. It is "the earned wages of rebellion" (13), and the phrase echoes the ambiguity of the original subtitle of *Seven Pillars*, a "personal essay in Rebellion." Freud argues that "a sense of guilt is invariably the factor that transforms sadism into masochism."[61] In the "manifest content of the masochistic phantasies a feeling of guilt comes to expression, it being assumed that the subject has committed some crime (the nature of which is left uncertain) which is to be expiated by his undergoing the pain and torture."[62] But Lawrence himself never sees his transformation this clearly. He divides himself into two people, "one wanting to go on, the other wanting to go back. That is not right. Normally the very strong one, saying 'No,' the Puritan, is in firm charge, and the other poor little vicious fellow can't get a word in, for fear of him."[63] The dichotomy seems to be between the Puritan (the public self, the superego, the active, the strong, the masterful, the father, the sometime sadist) and the vicious fellow (the private self, the id, the passive, the weak, the mother, the masochist). But the division is confusing, not unlike the polar extremes of the sadomasochistic continuum. Why is the little fellow vicious? Why does the Puritan produce fear in the vicious fellow? Is not the Puritan the principle of restraint, the vicious fellow release? But then why is it the Puritan who wants to go on, or is it he who so desires? It is Michael versus Lucifer, but who is Michael and who Lucifer is difficult to determine.[64] From Lawrence's point of view the roles are interchangeable.

Lawrence states his love of power most clearly in the epilogue: "We took Damascus, and I feared. More than three arbitrary days would have quickened in me a root of authority" (661) or "vice of authority" (MS 415). In the epilogue he intends, as he writes Charlotte Shaw, "to leave people who get so far in the book with a harsh taste in their mouths. You will say that . . . the bitterness is sensible all through; but remember that no one will ever again read the book as carefully as you have done. . . . Casual readers require direct statement to reinforce the impression which their fleeting acquaintance may have missed."[65] Lawrence generally shuns such direct statement of his desire for mastery as ends his book. He can express his masochism without fear of social condemnation, especially since it can be made to fit religious preconceptions. His sadism hardly would be so received; even the part that shines through the published text is frequently condemned by readers and biographers.

If the love of power produces renunciation and guilt, Deraa is designed both to reveal and to disguise this causality. The strength of his reaction to Deraa, his despair and nihilism, can be accounted for only by an inner desire which he recognizes to be at once sadistic and masochistic and which destroys the active half of the self. In Deraa Lawrence claims that an outside event drastically affects his private self. Significantly, the style of Deraa is that of the war narrative, rather than introspection. Lawrence has a fixed identity to be broken at Deraa. If he has been an actor in the Revolt, he now gets real pains and a real breaking of body and spirit. To paraphrase Emily Dickinson, Lawrence likes a look of agony because he knows it's true. He belatedly acknowledges that the private self has been present throughout the action of the Revolt.

The explanatory function of Deraa is not convincing. Lawrence's mentor, D. G. Hogarth, "had no knowledge of evil: because everything to him was fit to be looked at, or to touch."[66] Lawrence, on the other hand, tries "never to dwell on what was interesting" (563) and proceeds only so far in his analysis: "Into the sources of my energy of will I dared not probe" (468). Why, for instance, is pain Lawrence's secret obsession? What is the etiology of this symptom?[67] The disproportion between event and analysis is great, and the reasons Lawrence can go no further in his confessions are inconclusive. In only one or two brief passages does he reflect on his childhood, and rarely does he do so in his letters. He knows that "man's emotions, like water-plants, sprout far-rooted from his basic clay pushfully into the light. If very luxuriant they dam life's current. . . . Whereas to root out one of my thoughts—what upstirring of mud, what rending of fibre in the darkness!" (*M* 125). But the deepest he can fathom the Deraa episode is to say that he has renounced his future use of power because of a "collapse of will"—an explanation so vague it becomes a barrier to understanding. In a discussion of Rousseau's *Confessions*, Karen Horney suggests that his "frankness in sexual matters helps to keep him from seeing how little he actually faces his other problems." In introspection there is "a tendency to harp always on the 'bad' sides. . . . Confessing and condemning can then take the place of understanding. This is done partly in a spirit of hostile self-recrimination but also with a secret belief that confession alone is enough to harvest a reward."[68]

I have shown only that Deraa is not the adequate explanation that Lawrence presents it as, indicated only what is missing. Like Lord Jim's explanation of his leap from the *Patna*, *Seven Pillars* and *The Mint* are as much about what Lawrence does not understand as what he does. As is common in the confessional genre, the ordering myth of self is subject to internal question and revision. The reader is like Marlow, who cannot get to the heart of the mystery of Lord Jim's motivation but to whom the hero confesses hopefully. Lawrence writes of his mother, "I have a terror of her knowing anything about my feelings, or convictions, or way of life. If she knew they would be damaged: violated: no longer mine. You see, she would not hesitate to understand them, and I do not understand them, and do not want to."[69]

If the means of acting out his impulses are provided by imperial England, by the training he has received in its service, and by the War, the source of Lawrence's sadomasochistic character must be in his childhood. He contrasts his father ("large scale, vibrant, experienced, grand, rash, humoursome, skilled to speak, and naturally lord-like") with his mother ("brought up as a child of sin in the Island of Skye by a bible-thinking Presbyterian, . . . then 'guilty'—in her own judgement—of taking my father from his wife"). Lawrence believes that "the inner conflict, which makes me a standing civil war, is the inevitable issue of the discordant natures of herself and my father, and the inflammation of strength and weakness which followed the uprooting of their lives and principles."[70] In truth, the confessional hero stands between man and woman, strength and weakness, and cannot decide which direction to take.

NOTES TO CHAPTER V

1. Letter to Charlotte Shaw, 26 December 1925. The quoted phrase in the chapter title is from Wilhelm Stekel, *Sadism and Masochism: The Psychology of Hatred and Cruelty* (New York: Washington Square Press, 1968), I, 27; pagination is the same as that of the original Liveright edition of 1929.

2. Peter Abélard, *The Story of My Misfortunes*, trans. Henry Adams Bellows (New York: Macmillan, 1927), p. 30.

3. Leiris, p. 159.

4. Adamov, p. 70.

5. Letter to G. Wren Howard, 23 October 1928, Texas Collection; italics added.

6. *The Confessions of Jean-Jacques Rousseau*, trans. J. M. Cohen (Baltimore: Penguin Books, 1954), pp. 25-26.

7. For a detailed discussion, see Knightley and Simpson, *Secret Lives*, pp. 241-46.

8. Letter to Charlotte Shaw, 26 March 1924.

9. Letter to Charlotte Shaw, 30 July 1925.

10. "The Economic Problem in Masochism," in *Collected Papers*, trans. Joan Riviere (London: Hogarth Press, 1933), II, 258.

11. Steven Marcus, *The Other Victorians: A Study of Sexuality and Pornography in Mid-Nineteenth Century England* (New York: Bantam Books, 1966), pp. 255-68.

12. See the discussion of the instrument of his punishment in Knightley and Simpson, pp. 249-50.

13. Letter to Charlotte Shaw, 10 June 1924. Like Lawrence, Charlotte Shaw supposedly never had sexual intercourse.

14. *A General Introduction to Psychoanalysis*, trans. Joan Riviere (New York: Washington Square Press, 1960), p. 327.

15. *Middle East Diary: 1917-1956* (New York: Cresset Press, 1960), p. 42.

16. Stekel, I, 146, 156, 232.

17. Marcus, p. 263. Lawrence controls and directs his masochism into socially accepted forms by institutionalizing it. Similarly his homosexual proclivity binds him to the ranks. In Arabia homosexual lovers "found there hidden in the darkness a sensual co-efficient of the mental passion which was welding our souls and spirits in one flaming effort" (30). Women in the East were accorded all the physical world: "Yet by this same agreement all the things men valued, love, companionship, friendliness, became impossible heterosexually, for where there was no equality there could be no mutual affection. Women became a machine for muscular exercise, satisfying the physical appetite of men: but his psychic side could be slaked only among his peers . . . by spiritual union, a fierce homosexual partnership which satisfied all that yearning of human nature for more than the attraction of flesh to flesh. Whence arose these bonds between man and man, at once so intense, so obvious, and so simple" (MS 322; cf. text 508-09). He understands the dynamics of leadership as clearly as Freud, who writes in the Postscript to *Group Psychology and the Analysis of the Ego* (1921) that "homosexual love is far more compatible with group ties [than heterosexual], even when it takes the shape of uninhibited sexual tendencies. . . ." For an analysis of Lawrence's homosexuality as evinced in the Deraa episode, see Jeffrey Meyers. *The Wounded Spirit: A Study of Seven Pillars of Wisdom*, pp. 121-24.

18. Letter to Charlotte Shaw, 3 May 1925.

19. *Letters to T. E. Lawrence*, p. 99.

20. For a general discussion of sadomasochism in Lawrence, see G. Wilson

Knight, "T. E. Lawrence," in *Neglected Powers: Essays on Nineteenth and Twentieth Century Literature* (London: Routledge and Kegan Paul, 1971), pp. 322-28. See also Desmond Stewart, *T. E. Lawrence* (London: Hamish Hamilton, 1977); Stewart explores aspects of Lawrence's sexual proclivities in portions of Books Four and Five of his biography.

21. Sigmund Freud, *Three Essays on the Theory of Sexuality*, trans. and ed. James Strachey (New York: Avon, 1965), pp. 47-48.

22. "Instincts and Their Vicissitudes," in *A General Selection from the Works of Sigmund Freud*, ed. John Rickman (Garden City, N.Y.: Doubleday, 1957), p. 78.

23. *Ibid.*, p. 79.

24. Stekel, I, 57.

25. Erich Fromm, *Escape from Freedom* (New York: Avon Books, 1965), p. 170. Cf. Freud, "The Economic Problem in Masochism," in *Collected Papers*, II, 262: moral masochism has "loosened its connection with what we recognize to be sexuality."

26. *The Neurotic Personality of Our Time* (New York: Norton, 1937), pp. 259-60.

27. Stekel, I, 99; italicized in the original.

28. *Ibid.*, I, 154, 174.

29. Letter to Charlotte Shaw, 14 April 1927. In *A Prince of Our Disorder: The Life of T. E. Lawrence* (Boston: Little, Brown, 1976), pp. 26-34, 417-19, John E. Mack discusses Lawrence's ambivalence toward his parents, emphasizing particularly his intense fear of his mother.

30. Stekel, I, 202.

31. Letter to David Garnett, 4 May 1929, Texas Collection.

32. Forster, *Letters to T. E. Lawrence*, p. 68, finds this scene "so charming, so pretty." For a discussion of the relationship between Forster and Lawrence, see Jeffrey Meyers, "E. M. Forster and T. E. Lawrence: A Friendship," *The South Atlantic Quarterly*, LXIX (Spring, 1970), 205-16.

33. Gershon Legman, *Rationale of the Dirty Joke: An Analysis of Sexual Humor* (New York: Grove Press, 1968), p. 114, catalogs this as an instance of homosexual humor.

34. British Museum Additional Manuscript 46355. Much of this manuscript appears in Garnett's edition of *Letters*; see especially pp. 502-3.

35. *The Anatomy of Human Destructiveness* (New York: Holt, Rinehart and Winston, 1973), p. 462.

36. Letter to Charlotte Shaw, 11 January 1928.

37. Stekel, II, 459.

38. *Ibid.*, I, 51.

39. *Escape from Freedom*, p. 193.

40. *Ibid.*, p. 173.

41. *Neurotic Personality*, p. 273.

42. Letter to Charlotte Shaw, 21 May 1928.

43. *Neurotic Personality*, p. 278.

44. Letter to Charlotte Shaw, 25 February 1928.

45. *T. E. Lawrence to His Biographers*, II, 163.

46. See Philip Knightley and Colin Simpson, *The Secret Lives of Lawrence of Arabia* (New York: Bantam, 1971), pp. 192-98, 215-19, and John E. Mack, "T. E. Lawrence: A Study of Heroism and Conflict," pp. 1086-87. In *A Prince of Our Disorder*, Ch. 33, Mack discusses these beatings in some detail.

47. Sigmund Freud and Albert Einstein, *Why War?* (Dijon, France: League of Nations, 1933), p. 46.

48.   Trans. Joan Riviere (Garden City, N.Y.: Doubleday Anchor Books, n.d.), p. 85.

49.   *The Ego and the Id*, in *General Selection*, p. 231. Freud later modified his view of sadomasochism in developing the idea of the death instinct: "we are led to the view that masochism is older than sadism, and that sadism is the destructive instinct directed outwards, thus acquiring the characteristic of aggressiveness." See *New Introductory Lectures on Psychoanalysis*, trans. and ed. James Strachey (New York: Norton, 1965), p. 105.

50.   Letter to Charlotte Shaw, 26 March 1924.

51.   Letter to Charlotte Shaw, 28 September 1925.

52.   *Neurotic Personality*, p. 264.

53.   Fromm, *Escape from Freedom*, p. 181.

54.   *New Ways in Psychoanalysis* (New York: Norton, 1939), p. 262. For an opposing view, see Hannah Arendt, *Origins of Totalitarianism* (New York: Harcourt, Brace, 1951), pp. 218-21, who views Lawrence's renunciation of personal power as a direct consequence of the war and the political settlement made by the old men who "took from us our victory."

55.   *The Divided Self*, p. 112.

56.   *Escape from Freedom*, pp. 165-66.

57.   Quoted in Meinertzhagen, *Middle East Diary*, p. 32.

58.   The confessions and the act of writing itself are described by Lawrence in the imagery of childbirth. The creation of the book parallels Deraa: Lawrence believes "that no one should write except out of necessity; until he had matter so imperious within him that it burst him to come forth. I would have the bearing of books an agony, like child-birth." Letter to R. M. Gouldby, 18 May 1934, Bodleian MS. English Letters e.91, fols. 71-76.

59.   Letter to Charlotte Shaw, 26 March 1924.

60.   Letter to Charlotte Shaw, 28 September 1925.

61.   " 'A Child Is Being Beaten,' " in *Collected Papers*, II, 184; see also Stekel, I, 58.

62.   "The Economic Problem in Masochism," *Collected Papers*, II, 259.

63.   Letter to Charlotte Shaw, 28 September 1925.

64.   See letter from H. M. Tomlinson, *Letters to T. E. Lawrence*, p. 189.

65.   Letter to Charlotte Shaw, 17 November 1925.

66.   Letter to Charlotte Shaw, 10 November 1927.

67.   In "Fetishism and Sadomasochism," *Science and Psychoanalysis*, XV (1969), 71-80, Paul H. Gebhard is still puzzled by the etiology of sadomasochism. Certainly the genesis of Lawrence's illness is by no means clear. Gebhard argues that only complex, civilized man is affected by sadomasochism and remarks the highly symbolic nature of its symptoms and manifestations. In *Perversion: The Erotic Form of Hatred* (New York: Delta, 1976) psychiatrist R. J. Stoller presents an incisive, brilliant revision of Freud's theory of perversion. Stoller defines perversion as "a fantasy, usually acted out but occasionally restricted to a daydream. . . . It is a habitual, preferred aberration necessary for one's full satisfaction, primarily motivated by hostility. . . . The hostility in perversion takes form in a fantasy of revenge hidden in the actions that make up the perversion and serves to convert childhood trauma to adult triumph." (p. 4). For example, at Deraa Lawrence's sexual arousal in the face of his pain and fear reveals the difficulty and psychological expense in any expression of his sexuality, but he does express it and this is a triumph.

68.   *Self-Analysis* (New York: Norton, 1942), pp. 295-97.

69.   Letter to Charlotte Shaw, 14 April 1927.

70.   *Ibid.* In "The Economic Problem in Masochism," *Collected Papers*, II, 264,

Freud writes that the "super-ego is in fact just as much a representative of the *id* as of the outer world. It originated through the introjection into the ego of the first objects of the libidinal impulses in the *id*, namely, the two parents. . . . Now the super-ego has retained essential features of the introjected persons, namely, their power, their severity, their tendency to watch over and to punish." See also the discussion in Mack, "T. E. Lawrence: A Study of Heroism and Conflict," pp. 1088-91.

VI

Introspective Hero: "Passing Through Thought into Despair"

For if any be a hearer of the word, and not a doer, he is like unto a man beholding his natural face in a glass:
For he beholdeth himself, and goeth his way, and straightway forgetteth what manner of man he was. (James I: 23-24)

THE TYPICAL ROMANTIC HERO AT FIRST PERCEIVES THE centrality of the self.[1] The mind or will is the source of order in the universe and is independent of material and social limits; it assumes the creative powers formerly attributed to God[2] and even rewards and punishes. Coleridge writes that the malignant Romantic "will becomes Satanic pride and rebellious self-idolatry in the relations of the spirit to itself, and remorseless despotism relatively to others; the more hopeless as the more obdurate by its subjugation of sensual impulses, by its superiority to toil and pain and pleasure; in short, by the fearful resolve to find in itself alone the one absolute motive of action, under which all other motives from within and from without must be either subordinated or crushed."[3] Expansion of self is natural at this period, and the hero may, according to Frederick Garber, "include the values of the other and thus . . . draw them in to the components of his own being." He exhibits an "insistence on personal freedom, an expansiveness of self so total as to be almost without bounds." Consciously and arrogantly the hero attempts to complete the self by entering a society and assuming its habits.[4] He conceives of his role as that of a spiritual and political redeemer.[5] Thus Lawrence chooses a society which he imagines corresponds to his private self. Originally he acknowledges no conflicts between self and the Bedouin community because he feels it either is the image of the self or can be shaped into that image by his will. But if society and the outside world can be absorbed into the self by will, they can also be expelled by it. The Romantic hero has both a desire to lose himself in an absolute and an opposing desire to assert his individuality so strongly as to threaten such a commitment.[6]

After Deraa Lawrence says his will is broken and his integrity lost. Theoretically, the first stage of the Romantic hero's development, the war narrator's relentless expansion of the boundaries of self, the power to assume another's pain and experience, has ended. He becomes "half-myself." The Romantic hero's second stage, contraction and annihilation of self, is the subject of all introspection in *Seven Pillars* and *The Mint*, wherever it occurs in these books, and is rigid and consistent in its presentation of self. Part Three of *The Mint* appears to be an exception to this rule (though in fact it is not) and will be discussed in Chapter VII below. In analyzing the qualities of the introspective hero I shall focus on Chapter I, the suppressed introduction to *Seven Pillars*, and Chapters XCIX-CIII. I shall emphasize the stylistic differences between the war narrative and introspection and isolate in the early introspection the themes of self-division and contraction of self. Here these themes are undeveloped and are not put into a larger context until the later introspection, though they suggest the elaboration to come in the final books of *Seven Pillars*. In the later introspection I shall consider, first, the direct personal analysis of the hero's loss of will and, second, the larger Romantic pattern under which this loss of will is subsumed.

The dedicatory poem and first chapters of *Seven Pillars* emphasize introspective themes to an extent not seen again until the Deraa beating and sodomy of Chapter LXXX. Perhaps this is because they have more the qualities of epilogue than preface. The reader looks for introspection in the war narrative which follows, but this is sparse indeed in the first four books. The highly emotional beginning of the work and its motifs of alienation and perversion seem unrelated to the tone suddenly assumed by the narrator in Chapter IV and continued throughout the next several books.

The first chapter of *Seven Pillars* neither presents action nor considers its consequences. Rather it seeks psychological causes for the "evil of my tale" (29) and ignores military and political ones. The reader is forced to ask how Lawrence reached this nihilistic state, rather than contemplate what he achieved in the Revolt. Chapter I is characteristic of Lawrence's introspection in its style, pretensions, and disorganization. It is to such introspection Lawrence refers when he finds the book hysterical, a case study in the abnormal, and "redhot with passion. . . . Never was so shamelessly emotional a book" (*L* 542). The introspective chapters have a very different style from the narrative. As in MS Chapter LXXXVII, the Deraa beating, Lawrence's handwriting changes when he is composing introspective passages; the dimensions of the words on the unruled paper contract and each sheet of his account book is crowded to its edges, as if he had much to tell and could not condense. Interlinear revisions greatly increase. Graves observes a similar change in the letters he receives from Lawrence: "This letter and the one that follows are in minute handwriting. . . . When Lawrence was feeling low his handwriting shrank; when he was pleased it sometimes grew enormous." Handwriting evinces his dichotomy in style and the desire to write the introspection in cypher, to veil or disguise it. Of the style of Chapter I in particular, Lawrence says its "rhythm is unlike the rest."[7] At least the rhythm is unlike most chapters until the introspective ones in the final third of *Seven Pillars*.

E. M. Forster finds that *Seven Pillars* has "very rightly several styles, one for R. E. 8s [airplanes], and that sort of thing, another for normal narrative, another for reflections, another for crises of emotion or beauty. The criticism I'd offer is that your reflective style is not properly under control. Almost at once, when you describe your thoughts, you become obscure, and the slightly strained sense which you then (not habitually) lend words, does not bring your sentence the richness you intended, imparts not colour but gumminess." He concludes that "reflection does instantly have an effect on your writing of English."[8] The four styles categorized by Forster can easily be reduced to two; the technical and narrative constitute one, the reflective and the emotional another. Of course the latter style is that of Chapter I, and it is strongly condemned, privately by Forster, publicly by such critics as Herbert Read, Bernard Bergonzi, and R. P. Blackmur. In *English Prose Style* Read quotes a long passage from Chapter I of *Seven Pillars* and tersely instructs the reader: "Analyze for all the common faults of pretentious writing; above all for literary clichés."[9] Bergonzi, in *Heroes' Twilight: A Study of the Literature of the Great War*, agrees with Read, noting two styles: "As a writer of narrative, Lawrence undoubtedly had great gifts, and the scenes of action in his book are superb; but he was almost uncontrollably given to turgid reflections of an insufferably pretentious kind, which had a very corrupting effect on the quality of his prose."[10] Blackmur, concentrating on the introspective chapters but mistakenly projecting their qualities onto the whole of *Seven Pillars*, says that it "was forced writing, seldom discovered writing, never the writing of momentum."[11]

Lawrence frequently admits his pretensions and would readily agree with these critics. Whenever he writes about himself he becomes self-consciously literary. In a real sense the agnostic Lawrence turns to literature and art as his missionary mother and brother turn to religion. In introspection he frequently uses Romantic literary models to present the private self, though he can present action or military plans without these patterns. He begins the manuscript of *Seven Pillars* by apologizing for its literary atmosphere: "As a great reader of books, my own language has been made up of choosing from the black heap of words those which much-loved men have stooped to, and charged with rich meaning, and made our living possession" (MS 8). He insists that he dwelt on each paragraph of *Seven Pillars* until it contained one sentence which pleased him, and that this generally was a quotation. He documents this by asserting that the first three paragraphs of Chapter LXXVI (419) contain successively an echo of Gray's "Elegy,"

Arnold's "Dover Beach," and Robert Vansittart's *Singing Caravan*.[12] However, these references are difficult to perceive without Lawrence's annotation and are irrelevant to the meaning of the passages.

Lawrence's standard for introspective prose is that of the *fin de siècle* writers he admires, for "prose depends on a music in one's head which involuntarily chooses and balances the possible words to *keep tune* with the thought. The best passages in English prose all deal with death or the vanity of things, since that is a tune we all know, and the mind is set quite free to think while writing about it. Only it can't be kept up very long, because of mortal weakness and the wear and tear of things . . ." (*L* 318). An illustration of both subject and style occurs after the battle of Aba el Lissan. Lawrence goes out at night alone to look at the dead Turks stripped naked by the victorious Arabs. The dead men "looked wonderfully beautiful" in the moonlight and he straightens their corpses so that "they would be comfortable at last." He contrasts the dead with the "restless, noisy, aching mob up the valley, quarreling over the plunder, boasting of their speed and strength to endure God knew how many toils and pains of this sort; with death, whether we won or lost, waiting to end the history" (308). The one specimen page he saves from an early manuscript of *Seven Pillars* is a similar reflection on the "strange empty subject of victory," and his contempt for continued life (MS 415; cf. text 314). The Decadent emphasis on decaying or dying things is evident in these passages and in the poems on failure which bracket the manuscript. In introspection Lawrence displays most of the qualities associated with the Decadents. He writes in a style that constantly calls attention to itself; he considers art superior to nature, finds the greatest beauty in death and dissolution, is obsessively self-conscious, overrefines his feelings, attacks accepted moral standards, and praises homosexual relations at the expense of heterosexual. *Seven Pillars*, Lawrence declares, is "a study in disillusionment, in failure, in complaint. They [the writings] lack courage: they dissuade from activity (a balm to

the young is activity, purging their bodies of evil humors)
and preach defeat."[13] Of his works the reader might exclaim,
like Wilde's Dorian Gray, "One hardly knew at times
whether one was reading the spiritual ecstasies of some
medieval saint or the morbid confessions of a modern
sinner."[14]

The style of Chapter I contrasts strongly with the
understated passages of the war narrative. In an extreme
instance of a common melodramatic quality found in
introspection, Lawrence writes: "We had ropes about our
necks, and on our heads prices which showed that the enemy
intended hideous tortures for us if we were caught. Each day
some of us passed; and the living knew themselves just
sentient puppets on God's stage: indeed, our taskmaster was
merciless, merciless, so long as our bruised feet could stagger
forward on the road" (29). The effect of such intense passages
is contrary to that sought in narratives, where direct
emotional statement is eschewed in order to make "the book
unearthly in feel" (*L* 380). The war narrator stresses his
physical control in the face of danger by a commensurate
control of narrative. Reflection generates emotions independent of any action, while action ostensibly produces no
emotion except coldness, calculation. This psychological
difference is more apparent than real. In Stekel's *Sadism and
Masochism*, a patient remarks, "I cannot yield to emotion,
for I—apparently totally without feeling for those nearest
me—am too full of feeling, and it so permeates me that I
always overreach my goal. . . ."[15] Lawrence declares of *The
Mint* that the "tightness you particularly feel, everywhere, is
my guard against the hysteria which is the prime instinct of
my nature. I'd like to choke out everything: hence that guard
over my lips."[16] This is the unearthly feeling, the tension,
that Lawrence's narrative communicates. The self who acts
seems totally alien to the yielding self who reflects on a
vague, merciless taskmaster.

Perhaps thinking of his own narratives of battle,
Lawrence condemns a style which "is too smooth, too sure,
too unfaltering to hold much mind."[17] He argues that excess
of emotion "always ends in a carelessness of style."[18] He
defends his introspective cypher:

'Clean and clear, hard and cold and BALD.' . . . In writing nearly everybody tries for hardness and clearness: but the unconscious drag all the while is to cover up. A negro might make quite uncovered things, if he and his people had never thought of clothes: but for a clothed race to be deliberately naked in art intention is to be ever so un-natural. . . . We should not, in thought, pass the bounds we set ourselves in deed: or our ideas will not ring true. And to live bald and hard and clean: ah; that's beyond a fellow's power, except he be solitary. (*L* 591)

There can be no clarity in manner "while the ever-lasting doubt, the questioning, bound up my mind in a giddy spiral, and left me never space for thought" (545). Concomitantly, the clarity of style in his war narrative indicates that these uncertainties of motive do not touch it and gives stylistic evidence that act and introspection are independent, expressed not only in a different manner, but operating on wholly different matter.

Chapter I presents in microcosm all the themes and confusions of the introspection which permeate the later chapters: alienation, sadomasochism, self-division. He first tries to find "the evil of my tale . . . inherent in our circumstances" (29). The word evil has a strength and clarity which both chapter and book deny by their end. Lawrence lists several circumstances which produced this "evil." He commences with climate and geography. But immediately he veers from external conditions, for which the men had no remedy or control, toward psychological circumstances, for which he is primarily responsible: "We were a self-centered army . . . devoted to freedom, the second of man's creeds. . . . We had sold ourselves into its slavery. . . ." Suddenly he moves from consideration of circumstances to consequences: "By our own act we were drained of morality, of volition, of responsibility, like dead leaves in the wind." But after the dedicatory poem, which emphasizes the will of the speaker, even if it is the will to shatter the unfinished house of wisdom, the reader is properly suspicious of the assertion that he was drained of volition.

Lawrence uses "we" throughout the book's opening paragraphs, but the Bedouins are not a part of this "we" who sense and appraise the evil of the tale, who are drained of morality. Of course all were subject in Arabia to extremes of feeling and this "was bitter to us" (29). But he argues elsewhere that the Bedouins preferred this mode of life, that their "thoughts lived easiest among extremes."[19] In fact, the "we" is reduced to "I" as the chapter proceeds. Halfway through the chapter as halfway through the book, Lawrence indicates division between himself and the Arabs and shows the speciousness of the "we." Later in the chapter he again assumes the plural only to drop it finally, but the loftiness and certainty of his generalizations are clearly reduced to his own case. He "was sent to these Arabs as a stranger, unable to think their thoughts or subscribe their beliefs . . ." (30). The attempt to identify with the Arabs ends in failure in the midst of Chapter I as in the midst of the Revolt. Lawrence implies that the ultimate crime, the primary source of evil, is that of alienation from all society as a consequence of prostituting himself and his talents in serving another race.

The effort to imitate the Arabs' "mental foundation . . . quitted me of my English self, and let me look at the West and its conventions with new eyes: they destroyed it all for me." Lawrence believes he has "dropped one form and not taken on the other." The behavior of an alien among Arabs is one of three types. The first and "cleaner class," of which he finds C. M. Doughty a prime example, may "do a thing of himself . . . a thing so clean as to be his own (without thought of conversion), letting them take what action or reaction they please from the silent example." Its members represent "the foreigner intact" and "reinforce their character by memories of the life they have left. . . . they take refuge in the England that was theirs. They assert their aloofness, their immunity, the more vividly for their loneliness and weakness." In short, their identity is reinforced by contact with the foreign. The second class also recognizes no challenge to its identity. These Englishmen stand against the Arabs, "batter and twist them into something which they, of their own accord, would not have been." The third class, "after my model, . . . may imitate them so well that they spuriously imitate him back again. Then he is giving away his own environment: pretending to theirs; and pretences are hollow, worthless things" (31-32).

Imitation robs both the Englishman and his Arab followers of individual will; it is a "parody" (347) and generates "strange, unnatural courses."[20]

Seven Pillars intentionally disguises the pre-Arabian causes of Lawrence's alienation. His alienation from English culture had already been accomplished. Before Arabia "I cherished my independence almost as did a Beduin" (563). Nonetheless he knows that in his behavior in Arabia "his own nature lay hid, unnoticed" (346). From Lawrence's viewpoint what he does in Arabia cannot be an image of his hidden nature. This hidden nature, the "I" who is overtly independent of a social existence (though secretly attached to it, for he needs it to define his rebellion), is portrayed in chapters of introspection. Lawrence ends Chapter I emphasizing his self-division in the strongest and most direct manner he is to use for the next eighty chapters. He writes of the detachment he felt seeing "through the veils at once of two customs, two educations, two environments" (32). Lawrence's body "plodded on mechanically, while his reasonable mind left him, and from without looked down critically on him, wondering what that futile lumber did and why." The social "we" has become "I"; the latter is subdivided into the self who acts and the self who observes or is.

Another consequence of circumstances in Arabia is the succession of sensual crimes, primarily sadomasochistic, to which the "we" is given. All became reckless of "what spite we inflicted or endured, since physical sensation showed itself meanly transient. Gusts of cruelty, perversions, lusts ran lightly over the surface without troubling us; for the moral laws which had seemed to hedge about these silly accidents must be yet fainter words" (29). The body, which engages in these crimes, is not identified with the ideal self, which acts to earn redemption for a race, for the body is "too coarse to feel the utmost of our sorrows and of our joys. Therefore, we abandoned it as rubbish: we left it below us to march forward, a breathing simulacrum . . ." (30). Already Lawrence expresses the division between the private acts of the body and the public acts of the self. But here the narrator identifies with the public self, the ideal self which transcends and dominates the body.

By the end of *Seven Pillars* and the beginning of *The Mint* Lawrence, while retaining the image of a true self beneath the mask of flesh and act, reverses his earlier judgment, deciding that he is body rather than spirit or will. Only a few chapters after Deraa he writes, surprisingly, that the "conception of antithetical mind and matter, which was basic in the Arab self-surrender, helped me not at all. I achieved surrender (so far as I did achieve it) by the very opposite road, through my notion that mental and physical were inseparably one . . ." (468). Lawrence is dismayed over his inability to reconcile his motives, feelings, and values—what he calls the "my self" which restrains the beast of will—and his acknowledged power of action. He cannot join what he is to himself to what he is to others. His will, which he tells us can only be expressed in action, is the anti-self.

The opening chapter of the manuscript, suppressed in 1926 and published in a revised version in 1939, contrasts subtly with the present Chapter I (the original Chapter II). Close analysis belies its initial appearance of unity with the introspective side of the dichotomy. The manuscript's first chapter "was cut out because G. B. [Shaw] called it very inferior to the rest" (*L* 546). Lawrence notes in the Preface to *Seven Pillars*, "My best critic told me it was much inferior to the rest" (23). A. W. Lawrence, in writing an introduction to this chapter in *Oriental Assembly*, a posthumous collection of his brother's miscellaneous writings, seems to challenge the professed literary motive; he suggests that it was "suppressed" for political reasons. In 1940 Shaw says only that he had cut out the libelous passages in Lawrence's book.[21] In letters to Lawrence, Shaw warns repeatedly against publishing passages "which would force certain people either to take an action against you or throw up their jobs."[22] At any rate some of the stronger passages of the chapter are reintroduced in Book IV (275-76). If the chapter is "suppressed," the suppression is certainly haphazard.

Shaw's influence upon *Seven Pillars* has been exaggerated,

particularly in Stanley Weintraub's generally excellent
Private Shaw and Public Shaw. Lawrence, while replete
with contradictory statements, insists that he seldom acted
on the advice he received from Shaw regarding the revision
of *Seven Pillars.*[23] There seems little evidence that, as
Blackmur asserts, "Lawrence was docile, in the very measure
of his scrupulousness, and in imagination as well as act, to
those whom he admired."[24] Lawrence did ask Shaw's help in
the revision, as he did Forster's and Edward Garnett's, but,
except for the first chapter's excision, Weintraub can point to
no specific passages which were changed by Shaw or by his
wife. Weintraub admits, "What specific stylistic changes
were effected by each one is impossible to tell. . . ."[25] The
direction of these changes as a whole is hardly one with
which Shaw would sympathize, the aestheticism evident in
the final version. Even less does Weintraub demonstrate that
Shaw influenced the extensive excision of introspection in
the final books of the manuscript of *Seven Pillars.* Lawrence
must be given the credit or blame for these suppressions.

If we believe Lawrence and assume that the first chapter of
the manuscript was removed for aesthetic considerations, the
specific motive for excision is at first difficult to perceive.
Most critics feel the chapter should have been retained.
David Garnett writes that it is "one of the most moving
things Lawrence ever wrote" (*L* 262). Forster considered it "a
helpful piece of writing and propelled the reader easily into
the action."[26] Even Weintraub, who, unlike most readers,
finds the text superior to the manuscript and believes we owe
Shaw a "Not inconsiderable debt" for the text's revision,
argues that a new edition of *Seven Pillars* "should restore the
major cut G. B. S. insisted on and in which the author
acquiesced—the eloquently wrong-headed introductory
chapter."[27]

Perhaps Lawrence felt the suppressed chapter was not
introspective in the same way as the poem and Chapter I and
believed it would contradict and dilute their emphasis. The
MS chapter analyzes the narrator's political convictions
rather than his psychological state. It represents the active
Lawrence, not the introspective, and its main argument is

that political factors determine the narrator's personal sense of tragedy and guilt. In short, the chapter implies that the action in which he engages does affect the self. Thus he writes: "The Cabinet raised the Arabs to fight for us by definite promises of self-government afterwards. Arabs believe in persons, not in institutions. . . . So I had to join the conspiracy, and, for what my word was worth, assured the men of their reward. . . . In this hope they performed some fine things, but, of course, instead of being proud of what they did together, I was continually and bitterly ashamed."[28] Frequently this political conception of the process of deterioration presented in *Seven Pillars* is used by critics to explain Lawrence's increasing alienation and his subsequent penitential course: Lawrence is the idealistic victim of forces beyond his control. *Seven Pillars* does on occasion present this simple view of the cause of the narrator's disillusionment, but ultimately the book rejects it as firmly as its first statement is expelled from a place of prominence.

In the suppressed chapter, Lawrence repeatedly emphasizes his sense of the fraud perpetrated by the British and uses the "we" and "our" in professing to identify with the Arabs: "when we achieved and the new world dawned, the old men came out again and took our victory to remake in the likeness of the former world they knew. Youth would win, but had not learned to keep: and was pitiably weak against age. We stammered that we had worked for a new heaven and a new earth, and they thanked us kindly and made their peace." But Lawrence was not this pure-minded idealist caught in an Oedipal situation. Rather he was, as Knightley and Simpson's *The Secret Lives of Lawrence of Arabia* relentlessly demonstrates, very much a part of the English Establishment; he was not a naïve scholar, but an intelligence agent in the Middle East before and during the war. *Seven Pillars* well represents this unscrupulous, opportunistic aspect of his life. But the suppressed chapter resembles the propaganda Lawrence disseminated to obtain a popular hearing for the Arab cause in the immediate postwar years. The rhetoric is extravagant, mocking the complex vision of Chapter I and the whole of *Seven Pillars*: "new world dawned"; "new heaven and a new earth." The narrator is intentionally exaggerating his naïveté.

The style radically differs from that of Chapter I. It is not involuted, heavy, a cypher; thoughts are fleshed out by references to names, places, and events. The suppressed chapter is well organized, giving a sense of control. The emotion is cold, clear, fixed, and the narrator detached, ironic, like the narrator of battle. It is the style of a man of action, a politician: blunt, certain, consistent, righteous. The "I" never becomes alienated from the Arab "we." The narrator clearly perceives and defines his identity. The clarity and rhetoric of the chapter resemble the series of letters to editors in which Lawrence attacks British foreign policy in Mesopotamia. In one letter he comments ironically on methods of Arab pacification: "It is odd that we do not use poison gas on these occasions. Bombing the house is a patchy way of getting the women and children. . . . By gas attacks the whole population of offending districts could be wiped out neatly. . . ."[29] The MS chapter's narrator is this public Lawrence, the purveyor of propaganda for the Arab cause. The evil circumstances of naked desert, alienation, death in life, which are emphasized in the published Chapter I, do not appear in the suppressed chapter. He writes "partly for the pleasure it gave me to recall the fellowship of the revolt. We were fond together, because of the sweep of the open places, the taste of wide winds, the sunlight, and the hopes in which we worked. The morning freshness of the world-to-be intoxicated us. We were wrought up with ideas inexpressible and vaporous, but to be fought for." Nothing could be further from the spirit of Chapter I and the other introspective chapters, or closer to the spirit with which he sends a trainload of wounded Turks skyward. In eliminating the suppressed chapter, Lawrence is implicitly denying that what the narrator did and what was done to him and to the Arabs militarily and politically account primarily for his guilt and nihilism.

In all introspection in his confessions Lawrence condemns his use of will during the war, though after Deraa he greatly intensifies his censure. A common soldier in 1923, he reads "chapters 113 to 118 [text XCIX-CIII], and saw implicit in them my late course" (*L* 411). If Lawrence is working out his past course as he writes *Seven Pillars* (*L* 692), so too is he determining his future one and is announcing steps to control will. These late chapters are the heart of the introspection of *Seven Pillars* and explore the motives for Lawrence's subsequent renunciations and withdrawal. Lawrence acknowledges his failure to absorb and dominate others, appraises the pain he has received and generated in trying to do so, and plans his withdrawal. He seeks to define the "invisible self" disoriented by his effort to expand.

Lawrence's analysis commences as the boundaries of self begin to contract. Only now does he make clear the pattern in which the opening chapter is to be integrated.[30] He scrupulously examines his conscience, judging himself without appeal to any absolute standard; thoroughly secular, he rejects the concept of a God or any absolute outside the self. If he were Christian, this would be the moment of recognition of sin and the vow of penance and expiation. Schopenhauer writes that "the doctrine of original sin (assertion of the will) and of salvation (denial of the will) is the great truth which constitutes the essence of Christianity."[31] In Freudian terminology, Lawrence's private self now becomes the passive victim of his aggressive drive. The death instinct, earlier projected outward in the desire for mastery, is introjected; the superego forms an alliance with the id and punishes the ego or self. Lawrence explains it as precisely, though less technically. If the power of army discipline can take away his freedom of choice, it will be curious "after the willful life in which I seemed so set. Now my will has apparently turned against self. . . ." The ultimate goal of this process is extinction of self: "How welcome is death . . . to them that have nothing to do but to die" (*M* 105-06).

Chapter CIII approaches the self directly, seemingly without any intervening pattern, subject, or idea. The synopsis of Chapter CIII reads: "My birthday, by good fortune, is peaceful." The external circumstances are calm; internally he is to savage himself. His explanation of his intention reveals the hostility inherent in this act: "On this birthday in Bair, to satisfy my sense of sincerity, I began to dissect my beliefs and motives, groping about in my own pitchy darkness. This self-distrusting shyness held a mask, often a mask of indifference or flippancy, before my face, and puzzled me. My thoughts clawed, wondering, at this apparent peace, knowing that it was only a mask; because, despite my trying never to dwell on what was interesting, there were moments too strong for control when my appetite burst out . . ." (563). The mask is "full of the wailing of the underworld" (MS 364). Carlyle, to whom Lawrence has important affinities, writes that his Romantic hero, Teufelsdröckh, exhibits "the strangest Dualism: light dancing, with guitar-music, will be going on in the fore-court, while by fits from within comes the faint whimpering of woe and wail."[32] From Lawrence's mask come similar cries.

The appetite which frightens him is by imagery associated with the Romantic will he has theoretically resolved in Chapters XCIX-C should be restrained and foregone. At the very center of CIII he writes: "True there lurked always that Will uneasily waiting to burst out. My brain was sudden and silent as a wild cat, my senses like mud clogging its feet, and my self (conscious always of itself and its shyness) telling the beast it was bad form to spring and vulgar to feed upon the kill. So meshed in nerves and hesitation, it could not be a thing to be afraid of; yet it was a real beast . . ." (564). Both appetite and will "burst out"; both seem to be allied, the former indirectly, the latter directly, to the beast within. The beast is a wild cat, an image expressive of the sadist's concept of self. It is associated first with the thoughts that claw at the mask of self (and are therefore outside the self) and second (as organ rather than function) with the brain.

Will dominates materials and flesh, has its source in the beast, but can only be shown by action. It is behavior, not experience of self, to which will belongs. Will excludes introspection and is inaccessible to it. Steven Marcus asserts that "although the will is a form of consciousness and is consciously employed, its energies have historically been directed against consciousness itself—against intellect, introspection, self-examination, curiosity. Will is, in other words, a controlled consciousness which often contains within itself a fear of consciousness."[33] Lawrence himself writes that into "the sources of my energy of will I dared not probe" (468). Marcus and the war narrator of *Seven Pillars* seem to accept Nietzsche's notion that "will is precisely that which treats cravings as their master and appoints to them their way and measure."[34] Will in this sense must be directed against emotions, for if "very luxuriant they dam life's current" (*M* 125).

But there are two contradictory concepts of will in Lawrence's confessions. Marcus and Nietzsche define only one—that the will is the power to master self and others and is perceived by the individual who exerts it as good. It is in this sense of the word that Lawrence speaks of his "maimed will" (447) and of "gentling a broken will" (13) after Deraa and laments his loss of mastery. Schopenhauer, whose worldview in many respects corresponds to Lawrence's, presents an antithetical definition. Will is desire, craving, instinct, the unconscious, a beast; it is not the master of such cravings, but identified with them. According to Schopenhauer, every

> individual act, and also its condition, the whole body itself which accomplishes it, and therefore also the process through which and in which it exists, are nothing but the manifestation of the will, the becoming visible, *the objectification of the will.* . . . The parts of the body must, therefore, completely correspond to the principal desires through which the will manifests itself; they must be the visible expression of these desires. Teeth, throat, and bowels are objectified hunger; the organs of generation are objectified sexual desire; the grasping hand, the hurrying feet, correspond to the more indirect desires of the will which they express.[35]

Ideally one should deny and extinguish the will. Like Schopenhauer, Lawrence exalts reason and declares that "it was an idiosyncrasy with me to distrust instinct, which had its roots in our animality. Reason seemed to give men something deliberately more precious . . ." (511). Instead

of extinguishing or absorbing the will of others as he did in
Arabia, Lawrence sets out after the war to extinguish his own
will. His desire, his will now, is to extinguish all his other
drives, to put an end to the endless striving which is the
manifestation of will. The will to power becomes exclusively
the will to power over the self's desires. Schopenhauer writes:

> His will turns round, no longer asserts its own nature, which is reflected
> in the phenomenon, but denies it. The phenomenon by which this
> change is marked is the transition from virtue to asceticism. . . .
> Essentially nothing else but a manifestation of will, he ceases to will
> anything, guards against attaching his will to anything, and seeks to
> confirm in himself the greatest indifference to everything. His body,
> healthy and strong, expresses through the genitals the sexual impulse;
> but he denies the will and gives the lie to the body; he desires no sensual
> gratification under any condition. Voluntary and complete chastity
> is the first step in asceticism or the denial of the will to live.[36]

Certainly this is the project of self-annihilation Lawrence
commences in *The Mint*. Schopenhauer provides theoretical
support for the denial of the Nietzschean will, a denial which
Lawrence found masochistically attractive at Deraa.

Schopenhauer's denial of the will produces the truly
rational man previously obscured by the activity of willing.
Reason triumphs over instinct. T. E. Lawrence cannot
accept Schopenhauer's conclusions, though he does affirm
his process. To T. E. as well as to Carlyle and D. H.
Lawrence, denial of the will means a rejection of the
overdeveloped intellect, a cultivation of feeling. It constitutes a simple recognition of the true animal nature of
man behind the mask of the angel who imagines he can treat
"cravings as their master." T. E. Lawrence discovers that all
along he was a brute. But he does not consider the
recognition as a sign of his growth into a higher moral state;
in fact Lawrence would prefer to use the dominant,
Nietzschean will he praised earlier. But he is thwarted now
that he has come to know the bestial source of all willing.
Thus both use and denial of will are products of the animal,
of instinct. The war narrator affirms Nietzsche, the
introspective self Schopenhauer, but in the end Lawrence
accepts the latter's concept of will and finds the former's
illusory. Lawrence ultimately rejects the optimism and

activity of Nietzsche for the pessimism and passivity of
Schopenhauer. Nonetheless the sympathy of the introspective narrator is with the Nietzschean will; to it he gives vital
metaphors. Despite what he says, he feels that loss of mastery
is destructive to his integrity.

In Chapter CIII "my self," which orders the beast of will
not to spring, is not the brain (and the will which merges
with it and issues from it) nor the senses which provide
material limits. Lawrence's notion of self is difficult to
determine, for definition is by exclusion and absence. In *The
Divided Self* Laing describes the schizoid personality in
terms similar to Lawrence's. Laing believes that some men
"come to experience themselves as primarily split into a
mind and a body. Usually they feel most closely identified
with the 'mind.' " The body

> is felt more as one object among other objects in the world than as the
> core of the individual's own being. Instead of being the core of his true
> self, the body is felt as the core of a *false self*, which a detached,
> disembodied, 'inner,' 'true' self looks on at with tenderness, amuse-
> ment, or hatred. . . . The unembodied self, as onlooker at all the body
> does, engages in nothing directly. Its functions come to be observation,
> control and criticism *vis-a-vis* what the body is experiencing and doing,
> and those operations which are usually spoken of as purely 'mental.'

The self, according to Laing, "wishes to be complex,
indeterminate, and unique. . . . 'He,' his 'self,' is endless
possibility, capacity, intention. The act is always the
product of a false self."[37]

The schizoid is preoccupied with being seen. The divided
man for his "whole life has been torn between his desire to
reveal himself and his desire to conceal himself." The
anxiety that he see himself and be seen indicates fear that he
is invisible. Laing believes that, where there is a "primary
inadequacy in the reality of his own experience of himself as
embodied[,] . . . his preoccupation with his body-for-
others arose, i.e., his body as seeable, hearable, smellable,
touchable by the other." Where feeling of temporal
continuity is lacking, "there is a tendency to rely on spatial
means of identifying oneself." This assures him of his
existence. Laing finds that to "the schizophrenic, liking

someone equals *being like* that person: being like a person is equated with being the same as that person, hence with losing identity." The schizoid's "view of human nature in general, based on his own experience of himself, was that everyone was an actor."[38]

The divided man may not wish to be touched, partially because of his feeling of destructiveness: "His isolation is not entirely for his own self's sake. It is also out of concern for others. . . . In the last resort he sets about murdering his 'self,' and this is not as easy as cutting one's throat. He descends into a vortex of non-being in order to avoid being, but also to preserve being from himself." He gives himself to an "intentional project of self-annihilation." The "schizoid individual characteristically seeks to make his awareness of himself as intensive and extensive as possible. . . . he turns the living spontaneity of his being into something dead and lifeless by inspecting it. This he does to others as well, and fears their doing it to him. . . ."[39] Indeed, Lawrence argues that his confessions destroy his will.

Several passages in Chapter CIII reinforce positions Lawrence takes throughout the introspection of his confessions. Lawrence is "insanely rational," and does not know if his "distrust of emotion is justifiable: it is not rational."[40] While very "ready to hire my body out on petty service, I hesitated to throw my mind frivolously away" (63). He implies that he *is* the mind, not the body. As in Laing's description of the schizoid, divisions of self are rife. The "man of action" is eyed by a "detached self"; "my choice" is overruled by the tyrannous head; the self longs to be "as superficial, as perfected" as "women and animals," but "my jailer held me back." This is the division between "man-instinctive" and "man-rational" (548) he presents earlier. His choice or desire is restrained by an internal force which is conscious and comprehensible and thus not from his deepest nature, perhaps his reason: "Always feelings and illusion were at war within me, reason strong enough to win, but not strong enough to annihilate the vanquished, or refrain from liking them better; and perhaps the truest knowledge of love might be to love what self despised" (563-64). He ends the chapter declaring that "the truth was I did not like the 'myself' I could see and hear" (566). The statement implies that there is another self, an "invisible self," which he likes and which is, perhaps, to be identified with the vanquished feelings.

Lawrence can scarcely turn his attention from flesh, yet repeatedly expresses his contempt for it. His will triumphs over flesh, denies it: "There was no flesh" (564). He is "ashamed of my awkwardness, of my physical envelope" (562). Men "talked of food and illness, games and pleasures, with me, who felt that to recognize our possession of bodies was degradation enough, without enlarging upon their failings and attributes" (566). He hates touching or being touched:

> The lower creation I avoided, as a reflection upon our failure to attain real intellectuality. If they forced themselves on me I hated them. To put my hand on a living thing was defilement; and it made me tremble if they touched me or took too quick an interest in me. This was an atomic repulsion, like the intact course of a snowflake. The opposite would have been my choice if my head had not been tyrannous. I had a longing for the absolutism of women and animals, and lamented myself most when I saw a soldier with a girl, or a man fondling a dog, because my wish was to be as superficial, as perfected; and my jailer held me back. (563)

Confusion of feeling is rampant in the passage. The "I," the feeling of identity, avoids and hates the lower creation (i.e., women and animals). One touch by a man "discharges all the virtue you have stored up," he writes elsewhere.[41] Nonetheless his choice is to be like woman and soldier. Head or intellect or jailer (the "I") restrains him, prevents his making "the choice," fulfilling his wish. Yet the hatred of flesh is "atomic repulsion," feeling not intellect.

In Chapter CIII he desires to see himself as passive object: "my impotence of vision showed me my shape best in painted pictures, and the oblique overheard remarks of others best taught me my created impression. The eagerness to overhear and oversee myself was my assault upon my own inviolate citadel" (563). He must constantly make the self at every moment, for it has no essence, no fixed qualities, no core from which a feeling of identity can arise. An invisible self independent of what he does exists, but it is either always changing or can never be discovered once and for all. Thus he is fascinated by art, which fixes this evanescent self. Later he expresses a similar motive for his behavior, but here he is active, creating an impression or staging it: "Much of my doing was from this egoistic curiosity."

> There was a special attraction in beginnings, which drove me into everlasting endeavour to free my personality from accretions and project it on a fresh medium, that my curiosity to see its naked shadow might be fed. The invisible self appeared to be reflected clearest in the still water of another man's yet incurious mind. Considered judgments, which had in them of the past and future, were worthless compared with the revealing first sight, the instinctive opening or closing of a man as he met the stranger.

Lawrence asserts his identity by eccentricity, embarking "on little wanton problems of conduct, observing the impact of this or that approach on my hearers, treating fellow-men as so many targets for intellectual ingenuity . . ." (566). In part this parallels his attempt to make himself visible in his style. In his stylistic individualism and the degree of self-consciousness it betrays, he asserts the existence he doubts. Lawrence's conception of others is that they should be modelled after himself: "There was my craving to be liked—so strong and nervous that never could I open myself friendly to another. The terror of failure in an effort so important made me shrink from trying; besides, there was the standard; for intimacy seemed shameful unless the other could make the perfect reply, in the same language, after the same method, for the same reasons." In short, the other must *be* the self to be loved. This solipsism recalls Lawrence's idealized characterization of Ali, his Arab double. Erich Fromm defines narcissism as a state "in which only the person himself, *his* body, *his* needs, *his* feelings, *his* thoughts, *his* property, everything and everybody pertaining to *him* are experienced as fully real, while everybody and everything that does not form part of the person or is not an object of his needs is not interesting, is not fully real, is perceived only by intellectual recognition, while *affectively* without weight and color."[42] Narcissism is characteristic of Lawrence, even in his war narrative.

Lawrence's analysis of his destructive use of will corresponds remarkably with Romantic theory. The Romantic pattern he expounds in Chapters XCIX-C (543-52) is clear, even if the style is overwrought and repetitious— "gummy," Forster calls it appropriately enough. In the manuscript it constitutes a single chapter and displays the unity of argument it actually possesses. The context is a "last preaching," an attempt by Lawrence and Feisal to convert Arab tribes to the nationalist ideals of the Revolt. The narrative of these preachings becomes increasingly abstract and intellectual: He then begins a long, repetitive, involuted reflection on the ethics of sacrifice for this or any other cause. These reflections are interwoven with fragments of Lawrence's confession so the reader seems to move abruptly from the general to the specific until he recognizes that all of this is intensely subjective and personal. Though Lawrence again vacillates unpredictably from "I" to "we" (e.g., 549), it reflects his case and no other (at least from his viewpoint, if not that of the Romantic theorist). The pattern is, in any event, philosophical and literary, not political.

The subject of these chapters is the abstract causes of the phenomenon observed in *The Mint* that man "breaks into little prisms when he thinks." Lawrence argues that a redeemer—so he designates himself, no less—must not will for others, must not let the redeemed mistake "the deed for the will." Not only is life "so deliberately private that no circumstances could justify one man in laying violent hands upon another's" (548), but nothing can validate the imposition of one's will upon another. This precludes the possibility of political activity. The dedicatory poem to S. A. can now clearly be perceived as ironic: no one can write his "will across the sky in stars/To earn you Freedom." If S. A. "is rather an idea than a person,"[43] the fate of Lawrence parallels that of S. A.; he asserts that his motive has died in the Revolt, his power to act or will in any society has been destroyed. In the epilogue Lawrence clearly indicates this by a pronoun: "It [i.e., 'the strongest motive throughout'] was dead, before we reached Damascus."

The reasons Lawrence gives for his declaration damning

the use of will are multiple and complex. No pride and "few pleasures in the world were so joyful, so rich as this choosing voluntarily another's evil to perfect the self" (550). It gave "a sense of greatness, of super-humanity" (MS 356). "The virtue of sacrifice lay within the victim's soul" (551). This use of will prevents the others from using theirs, and it is only through personal use of will that the self can be realized and redeemed. To the Romantic, value must come from the self, not others, and the only spiritual (as opposed to political) redemption possible is the inculcation of that principle and the self's acceptance of moral responsibility: "To each opportunity there could be only one vicar, and the snatching of it robbed the fellows of their due hurt. Their vicar rejoiced, while his brethren were wounded in their manhood. To accept humbly so rich a release was imperfection in them: their gladness at the saving of its cost was sinful in that it made them accessory, part-guilty of inflicting it upon their mediator" (550-51).

The act also shames the redeemed, "it being many times harder to offer than to endure sacrifice" (467). If the redeemed understood the ethics of sacrifice, he "might feel the shame which was the manly disciple's lot: or might fail to feel it, and incur the double punishment of ignorance." Thus self-conscious modern man can only pretend to altruism: "we had borne the vicarious for our own sakes, or at least because it was pointed for our benefit: and could escape from this knowledge only by a make-belief in sense as well as in motive." In Nietzsche's words, "He who humbles himself wills to be exalted." Lawrence's ethics of sacrifice transforms his aggression into masochism at one stroke. The ideal redeemer must be "free and child-minded. When the expiator was conscious of the under-motives and the after-glory of his act, both were wasted on him. So the introspective altruist appropriated a share worthless, indeed harmful, to himself, for had he remained passive, his cross might have been granted to an innocent. To rescue simple ones from such evil by paying for them his complicated self would be avaricious in the modern man" (550-51).

The other possibility is "to stand among the crowd, to

watch another win the cleanness of a redeemer's name. By the one road lay self-perfection, by the other self-immolation, and a making perfect of the neighbour." Both active and passive approaches may be pernicious: "we seemed like the cells of a bee-comb, of which one might change, or swell itself, only at the cost of all" (551). So far is the leader from altruism that he is actively destructive of others. At the end of *The Mint* the bee-comb image expresses his ideal; troops are to be as "like and close-fitting as bee cells" (*M* 239). But in both confessions the bee-comb is empty, whether the void is alive and swelling or mechanically dead. At the center of the image is the empty cell, not the fertile, pulsating queen bee, who dwarfs others.

One can neither be vicar nor watch another sacrificed. The paralysis of the potential Romantic redeemer is vividly emphasized: "Complex men who knew how self-sacrifice uplifted the redeemer and cast down the bought, and who held back in his knowledge, might so let a foolish brother take the place of false nobility and its later awakened due of heavier sentence. There seemed no straight walking for us leaders in this crooked lane of conduct, ring within ring of unknown, shamefaced motives cancelling or double-charging their precedents" (551-52). The self, the man of action, is shut up in a prison of its own construction. The theory of self-redemption, and thus social redemption, is fine if you are Shelley's Prometheus, but if you are called to take political action you are in a dilemma you cannot resolve. If, as Conrad believes of imperialism, what redeems political action "is the idea only,"[44] Lawrence attacks the idea of Arab nationalism with Romantic notions; he can only imitate Arab "bondage to the idea" (548). Lawrence states the thesis succinctly: "Crucifixion doesn't concern the sinner. It benefits the saint only."[45] Thus what he suffered, he suffered for himself, or perhaps for none, if he is a sinner. Needless to say, the war narrative is not assimilated to these convictions, and Lawrence can and does define as well as anyone the political and material benefits which did accrue or should have accrued to the Arabs from the Revolt.

Lawrence's ethic of sacrifice is similar to that of the hero of Conrad's *Lord Jim* (1900). Presumably Lawrence read *Lord*

Jim at the time he was writing the first draft of *Seven Pillars*; he initials his copy "T. E. L., Paris, 1919."[46] The similarities are strongest in the Patusan episode of *Lord Jim*. Jim at the beginning of the adventure is offensively optimistic: "He was voluble like a youngster on the eve of a long holiday with a prospect of delightful scrapes, and such an attitude of mind in a grown man and in this connection had in it something phenomenal, a little mad, dangerous, unsafe." Like Lawrence, Jim leads natives in a rebellion against their masters and triumphs. Jim too withholds certain of his motives from the natives. He accepts complete responsibility for the motives, becomes their redeemer: " 'His word decided everything. . . . An awful responsibility.' . . . Thus he illustrated the moral effect of his victory in war. It was in truth immense. It had led him from strife to peace, and through death into the innermost life of the people. . . ." From his race he is totally and utterly isolated, but "this isolation seems only the effect of his power."[47]

Jim alone knows the motives which contaminate his act. He redeems himself rather than society; it is impossible to satisfy both self and other. His primary motive is personal rather than political, not altruistic but fulfilling a psychological need: he has to compensate for his cowardice in abandoning, in belief if not fact, a shipload of drowning pilgrims. As the narrator Marlow puts it, "Now and then, though, a word, a sentence, would escape him that showed how deeply, how solemnly, he felt about that work which had given him the certitude of rehabilitation. That is why he seemed to love the land and the people with a sort of fierce egoism, with a contemptuous tenderness." In Novalis' epigraph to *Lord Jim*, the hero's need for the approval of the natives is expressed: "It is certain my Conviction gains infinitely, the moment another soul will believe it." Jim tells Marlow, "I must stick to their belief in me to feel safe."[48] Similarly an astonished Lawrence says that "Even I, the stranger, the godless fraud inspiring an alien nationality, felt a delivery from the hatred and eternal questioning of self . . . [;] for one to be comfortably surrendered, the others must surrender too" (MS 355; cf. text 548).

Jim's complex personal motives and needs negate his

good acts and eventually bring disaster upon the Patusans.
Only a simple hero like Achilles would serve Lawrence and
Conrad. Jim and Lawrence resemble more Philoctetes.[49] The
redemption is not ambiguous, only the motive. As Feisal
declares, either "forced good or forced evil will make a
people cry with pain. Does the ore admire the flame which
transforms it?" (100). What a man does may be good or bad;
what he *is* is otherwise and incommensurate with his act.
Like Lawrence, Jim conducts a life-long inquiry into his
motives, but never finds the answer. Jim's inquiry seems
designed to redeem rather than damn, to relieve rather than
convict. He cannot accept his act as final or even his own
responsibility: "It had happened somehow." He is more
than the act, other than the act. Crew members had leaped
from the *Patna*, but he "was not one of them; he was
altogether of another sort." Marlow concludes that "no man
ever understands quite his own artful dodges to escape from
the grim shadow of self-knowledge."[50] Similarly Lawrence's
so-called metaphysic, his Pepysian cypher, escapes the
simplicity of his acts.

Both Jim and Lawrence explicitly deny finding in
themselves the common effects of imperialism yet display its
most subtle and deleterious qualities. The egoism of both
heroes is unrestrained and grows in direct proportion to
their misfortunes. Neither would cut throats for a bag of
pepper, like the straw imperialists they knock over. But the
heart of imperialism is the "conquest of love, honour, men's
confidence—the pride of it, the power of it."[51] Holbrook
Jackson argues that the Decadents demand "wider ranges,
newer emotional and spiritual territories, fresh woods and
pastures new for the soul. If you will, it is a form of
imperialism of the spirit, ambitious, arrogant, aggressive,
waving the flag of human power over an ever wider and
wider territory. And it is interesting to recollect that decadent
art periods have often coincided with such waves of imperial
patriotism as passed over the British Empire and various
European countries during the Eighteen Nineties."[52]

Conrad writes that " 'giving your life up to them' (*them*
meaning all mankind with skins brown, yellow, or black in

colour) 'was like selling your soul to a brute.' " Lawrence
echoes this passage: "A man who gives himself to be a
possession of aliens leads a Yahoo life, having bartered his
soul to a brute-master" (31). The solution, for Marlow at
least, is to go back to the imperial idea before its decay, to be
Doughty, not Lawrence. One must have "a firm conviction
in the truth of ideas racially our own, in whose name are
established the order, the morality of an ethical progress.
. . . We want a belief in its necessity and its justice, to
make a worthy and conscious sacrifice of our lives. Without
it the sacrifice is only forgetfulness, the way of offering is
no better than the way to perdition. . . . we must fight in
the ranks or our lives don't count. . . . of all mankind Jim
had no dealings but with himself. . . ."[53] Neither Lawrence nor Jim can gain this conviction, can feel that they
fight in the ranks.

There are other revealing parallels between the two
heroes. Both Lord Jim and Lawrence emulate Christ in their
sacrifices, Jim in act, Lawrence in act and, more clearly, in
the parallels to Christ he establishes in his analysis of act.
Like Lawrence, Jim projects upon others his own complexity, even on Gentleman Brown. Both Jim and Lawrence
resemble the Byronic hero in their secret flaw, their egotism,
their complexity. Finally, action should fashion doubt into a
certainty and the end of man is an action, not a thought,[54]
but in both Lawrence and Jim there is action, then doubt and
reflection. Lawrence never examines his motives before
action except in the simplest imperial terms.

The reader's relationship to Lawrence's confession is like
Marlow's to Lord Jim's. In the modern confession the reader
has a greater role than in a novel. Lawrence cannot step back
from his egotism or his love of domination even slightly.
Thus the absurdity of the political redeemer is more obvious
in the confessional genre. Marlow properly distances
himself from Lord Jim's psychological imperialism as the
reader must do from Lawrence's.

Regardless of the effect of Lawrence's actions on others,
their effect on the self is pernicious. In rejecting the
possibility of a redeemer's role in society, Lawrence declines

any further active participation. Again he vacillates from highest to lowest. No matter what Lawrence as redeemer does, others can only copy and the world "is more plagued by the disciples than benefited by its prophets."[55] Unless a man uses his own will, his act can earn no merits: "It was a theft of souls to make others die in sincerity for my graven image. Because they accepted our message as truth, they were ready to be killed for it; a condition which made their acts more proper than glorious, a logical bastard fortitude, suitable to a profit and loss balance of conduct. To invent a message, and then with open eye to perish for its self-made image— that was greater" (550). Every imitative act damns rather than redeems. The characteristic paralysis of the Romantic redeemer is expounded by Morse Peckham in terms remarkably similar to Lawrence's:

> the imposition of the will upon reality, when given political and social instrumentality, meant the denial to others of their own moral responsibility. To redeem society could only mean to do for others what the nineteenth-century vision had made possible for the alienated individual to do for himself: the creation of genuine moral responsibility in everyone. The difficulty of this aim was not only that these "others" did not want it; it was also that to create the social conditions necessary for the assumption by all men of moral responsibility meant a temporary and perhaps permanent—who knew?—denial of the very responsibility the imposition of the will was designed to create. . . . his actions, through the exercise of power, reinforced the egocentricity which his beliefs were designed to break down.[56]

The introspective hero of *Seven Pillars* believes that use of will in the outside world has no absolute value. Lawrence proposes a new extreme solution, a new absolute: complete subjugation of the will. Despite his professed hatred, flesh is wholly embraced in a spirit of masochism: "man hangs in his body, crucified" (*M* 231). If Lawrence as redeemer has hung upon the cross of will and action, in the future he will "wallow in the physical which could be only a glorification of man's cross" (566). According to Frederick Garber, "the sickness unto death for the romantics comes when the [outward] direction of energy is reversed and the world impinges upon the self. The self . . . can disintegrate under pressure into a madness. . . . But those situations are comparatively rare, and when no recovery is possible, or the impingement becomes intolerable, one can usually choose retirement or annihilation."[57] Lawrence feared madness and contemplated suicide (*L* 416, 477), but he settled for an ostentatious withdrawal into the ranks of the R.A.F., which he documents in *The Mint*.

NOTES TO CHAPTER VI

1. Garber, "Self, Society, Value, and the Romantic Hero," p. 213.

2. Peckham, *Beyond the Tragic Vision*, pp. 93-99.

3. *The Statesman's Manual*, in *The Complete Works of Samuel Taylor Coleridge*, ed. W. G. T. Shedd (New York: Harper and Brothers, 1878), I, 458.

4. Garber, pp. 214-26.

5. *Ibid.*, p. 221, and Peckham, p. 236.

6. Thorslev, pp. 88-89.

7. *T. E. Lawrence to His Biographers*, I, 16, 55.

8. *Letters to T. E. Lawrence*, pp. 60-61.

9. Boston: Beacon Books, 1967, pp. 95, 205-06.

10. Lawrence's praise of the beauty of the dead may also have been inspired by

11. "The Everlasting Effort: A Citation of T. E. Lawrence," in *The Lion and the Honeycomb* (New York: Harcourt, Brace, 1955), p. 101.

12. Letter to Charlotte Shaw, 21 April 1927.

13. Letter to Charlotte Shaw, 3 August 1927.

14. *The Picture of Dorian Gray* (New York: New American Library, 1962), Ch. 10. Lawrence's praise of the beauty of the dead may also have been inspired by Coleridge's *The Rime of the Ancient Mariner*, II, 236-39. Lawrence greatly admired the poem and at times identified with its hero.

15. Stekel, I, 285. See also Leiris, *Manhood*, pp. 138-39.

16. Letter to Charlotte Shaw, 20 March 1928.

17. Posthumously published review of *The Works of Walter Savage Landor*, in *The Essential T. E. Lawrence*, ed. David Garnett (New York: E. P. Dutton, 1951), p. 283.

18. Letter to Charlotte Shaw, 20 March 1928.

19. Introduction of Doughty, *Arabia Deserta*, I, 22.

20. *Ibid.*, I, 20.

21. Note on a letter by Lawrence, 30 November 1922, Jesus College Library MS. J.160/20.

22. *Letters to T. E. Lawrence*, p. 169; see also *L* 262.

23. *T. E. Lawrence to His Biographers*, I, 116.

24. *The Lion and the Honeycomb*, p. 98.

25. *Private Shaw and Public Shaw* (New York: Braziller, 1963), p. 88.

26. *Abinger Harvest*, p. 135.

27. *Private Shaw*, p. 129.

28. "The Suppressed Introductory Chapter for *Seven Pillars of Wisdom*," in

Oriental Assembly, pp. 144-45. Subsequent references to this chapter in the next paragraphs are to pp. 139-46.

29.   "France, Britain, and the Arabs," [London] *Observer*, 8 August 1920; rpt. in Weintraub, ed., *Evolution of a Revolt*, p. 93.

30.   As noted in Chapter II above, many introspective passages removed from the manuscript version of the first two-thirds of *Seven Pillars* were reinserted here.

31.   *The World as Will and Idea*, I, 524.

32.   *Sartor Resartus*, Book Second, Ch. IX.

33.   *The Other Victorians*, pp. 23-24.

34.   *The Will to Power*, ed. Walter Kaufmann, trans. Walter Kaufmann and R. J. Hollingdale (New York: Vintage Books, 1968), p. 52. Nietzsche opposes his view to "Schopenhauer's basic misunderstanding of the will (as if craving, instinct, drive were the essence of will). . . ."

35.   *The World as Will and Idea*, I, 140-41.

36.   *Ibid.*, I, 490-91.

37.   *The Divided Self*, pp. 65, 69, 88.

38.   *Ibid.*, pp. 37, 113, 127, 109, 174, 71.

39.   *Ibid.*, pp. 93, 129, 112.

40.   Letter to Charlotte Shaw, 21 May 1928.

41.   *Home Letters*, p. 355.

42.   *The Anatomy of Human Destructiveness*, p. 201.

43.   *T. E. Lawrence to His Biographers*, I, 55, 17. For Lawrence's contradictory comments on S. A., see also II, 64, 68, 143, 156, 169, and Lawrence's record of the writing of *Seven Pillars* in the *Texas Quarterly*, V (Autumn, 1962), 48. For further speculation about S. A., see Knightley and Simpson, *Secret Lives*, pp. 176-81, and Meyers, *The Wounded Spirit*, pp. 67-71.

44.   *Heart of Darkness*, in *The Portable Conrad*, p. 495.

45.   Letter to Charlotte Shaw, 31 December 1928. D. H. Lawrence is less ambivalent in these matters. In 1914 he declares that "the Egoist as a divine figure on the Cross, held up to tears and love and veneration, is to me a bit nauseating now. . . ." Such egoism ends in "the passion for the extinction of yourself and the knowledge of the triumph of *your own will* in your body's extinction." See *The Collected Letters of D. H. Lawrence*, ed. Harry T. Moore (New York: Viking, 1962), I, 300-04.

46.   *T. E. Lawrence by His Friends*, p. 482.

47.   *Lord Jim*, Chs. XXIII, XXVII.

48.   *Ibid.*, Chs. XXIV, XXXV.

49.   For a discussion of Lawrence's resemblance to Philoctetes, see James A. Notopoulos, "The Tragic and the Epic in T. E. Lawrence," *Yale Review*, LIV (Spring 1965), 331-45.

50.   *Lord Jim*, Chs. IX, VII.

51.   *Ibid.*, Ch. XXII.

52.   *The Eighteen Nineties* (New York: Capricorn Books, 1966), p. 64.

53.   *Lord Jim*, Ch. XXXVI.

54.   Thomas Carlyle, "Characteristics," in *The Works of Thomas Carlyle*, ed. H. D. Traill (London: Chapman and Hall, 1896-1901), XXVIII, 25-26.

55.   Letter to Charlotte Shaw, 1 July 1926.

56.   *Beyond the Tragic Vision*, p. 236.

57.   "Self, Society, Value and the Romantic Hero," p. 214.

VII

Nebuchadnezzar Among the Animals:
"An Answer to the Ideals of the Desert"

To record the acts of Hut 12 would produce a moral-medical case-book, not a work of art but a document. (L 414)

BOTH *Seven Pillars* AND *The Mint* DISPLAY A PRECIOUS style, reveal Lawrence's inability to characterize, emphasize the effects of discipline on the common soldiers, and dramatize the hero's alienation from his comrades. These similarities might be expected, for Parts One and Two were composed at the same time as extensive revisions of *Seven Pillars* were going forward. *The Mint*, like *Seven Pillars*, focuses intensely on the self, and the reader's interest is in the impact of this brutal life on a man of sensitivity.[1] Never was there a documentary with less detachment or objectivity. The form also has parallels to that of *Seven Pillars*. Though the whole of *The Mint* portrays the private self, direct introspection increases as the strain of Lawrence's enlistment is relieved. The final third of the book is decidedly less concrete and less concerned with any specific event than the first third. Like the last books of *Seven Pillars*, by Part Three "the note season is over" (*L 620*). But formal differences from *Seven Pillars* are also significant, for the complex dramatic design and balance of the earlier work is absent. What Forster said of *Seven Pillars* is more appropriate for *The Mint*; Lawrence presents "life as a succession of items which are organically connected but yet have some sort of intervals between them, i.e., you give a series of pictures."[2]

Lawrence's will is not destroyed after Deraa nor is its strength lessened. Rather the object of the will has changed from domination of the outside world to domination of the inner. He asserts that the lesson of Arabia is that the body does affect the will, that there is flesh, perhaps only flesh. The

165

boundaries of the self contract. Now the "circle centres bit by bit on myself: and therefore turns faster and is dangerous. People who lived in Nitrea, in the old days, to fight down the world, did grow their eyes inward: only inside me is too vacant a place to take much exploring" (*L* 591-92). Contraction of self is at once punishment for his expansive role as redeemer and a means to restrain his will. Morse Peckham finds that when the expansive drive of the Romantic hero breaks down, the "individual is sustained more and more feebly, by behavior at the automatic level, but the relentless knife of self-probing strikes deeper and deeper; and more and more of civilization and acquired culture is cut out. Or the individual can sustain himself by forcing upon himself a purely external discipline accepted and self-imposed solely as a means to keep going the processes of life at their basic biological levels."[3]

The effect of military discipline on will is the subject of much introspection in the confessions. Lawrence discusses discipline in the first books of *Seven Pillars*, but delays direct application of his observations to his own case until the last ones. His descriptions of the psychological effects of discipline are clear. The Arab army "had no discipline in the sense in which it was restrictive, submergent of individuality, the Lowest Common Denominator of men. In peace-armies discipline meant the hunt, not of an average but of an absolute . . ." (339). Many Bedouins were "not soldiers, but pilgrims, intent always to go the little farther" (510). In fact the Arab War was "simple and individual" (339). But the English army is radically different:

> For discipline seemed a training to obliterate the humanity of the individual. . . . It was a process of the mass, an element of the impersonal crowd, inapplicable to one man, since it involved obedience, a quality of will: and will itself seemed to become manifest only when a command has been obeyed, to exist only in the plural, to be a mysterious double faculty, comprising a part which gave command and a part which executed it. In the army an effort, more or less conscious, was made to persuade the recruit to surrender one half of his will. . . . It demanded a surrender, for the term of service, of reason and initiative: the making of each soldier, or rather of each subordinate, an empty harp through which the will of the commander in chief could blow. (MS 324; cf. text 510-11)

Lawrence uses ironically the "empty harp," the Eolian Harp of the Romantics, for the wind is not Nature, but the Romantic will, and the harp is not the symbol of a mind that half-creates and half-perceives: it is wholly passive. The solution to the difficulties of the expansive stage is clear: to surrender reason and initiative, to institutionalize Lawrence's becoming half-himself, destroying formally his will, the half of his "double faculty" which he had prematurely pronounced dead at Deraa.

Perhaps in determinism "there lies the perfect peace I have so longed for. Free-will I've tried, and rejected: authority I've rejected (not obedience, for that is my present effort, to find equality only in subordination. It is dominion whose taste I have been cloyed with): action I've rejected: and the intellectual life: and the receptive senses: and the battle of wits. . . . obedience, nescience, will also fail. . . ." He does not seek restraint of will but intends to extinguish it totally, to burn it out (*L* 419). *The Mint* is "an answer to the ideals of the desert."[4] Relentlessly he emphasizes that his personality is to be destroyed. In the ranks he learns to be sterile; after a time "troops' intellects and wills go back to God, who made them. It's queer to see our minds bend when we lean on them. As walking sticks to stay instinct or character over a rough place they are now as useless as a stem of ivy. . . . The person has died that to the company might be born a soul" (*M* 191).

The process of self-extinction is admittedly pleasurable; means becomes end: "I liked the things underneath me and took my pleasures and adventures downward. There seemed a certainty in degradation, a final safety. Man could rise to any height, but there was an animal level beneath which he could not fall. It was a satisfaction on which to rest" (564; cf. *M* 135). Implicit is Lawrence's desperate cultivation of an oceanic sense of self, a feeling that he cannot fall out of the world,[5] though he may dangerously ascend from it. The masochistic desire existed well before the war. No act generated it; at best Deraa could confirm it.

The conviction that the will is absolute yields to a belief that the body is absolute and to a projected "mind-suicide,

some slow task to choke at length this furnace in my brain"
(564-65; cf. *L* 411). The absolute of the Bedouin becomes that
of women and animals. The senses and the body are to be a
base from which he will attempt to build a new relationship
to the world—one in which he is absorbed, passive, an
object, rather than absorbing, active, a subject. Theoretically, withdrawal results in extinction of the personality and
absorption of the self by other men and the universe. In the
R.A.F. Lawrence is to give up his "rights to personality."[6]
He intends to carry to fruition the solution proposed in
Books VIII and IX of *Seven Pillars,* passages on military
discipline which provide an "explanation of the renunciation which followed."[7] In analyzing the failure of the
expansive stage Lawrence contemplates the end of the new
process:

> To our strained eyes, the ideal, held in common, seemed to transcend
> the personal, which before had been our normal measure of the world.
> Did this instinct point to our happily accepting final absorption in
> some pattern wherein the discordant selves might find reasonable,
> inevitable purpose? Yet this very transcending of individual frailty
> made the ideal transient. Its principle became Activity, the primal
> quality, external to our atomic structure, which we could simulate only
> by unrest of mind and soul and body, beyond holding point. So always
> the ideality of the ideal vanished, leaving its worshippers exhausted:
> holding for false what they had once pursued. (467)

Lawrence's intentional emphasis on "Activity" as the
reason for his failing to achieve harmony suggests passivity
as the only possible path to "final absorption." Later he
gives an example of those already on the path: "We
westerners of this complex century who, monks in our
bodies' cells, searched and searched for something unknown
which should fill our being full to speechlessness and
senselessness were by the mere effort of our search shut out
from it for ever. It came to children like these Ageyl, sitting
still with their spirits' doors open: stronger than the actors of
life" (MS 322; cf. text 509).[8]

The Mint serves as a public penance for the metaphysical
crime of abusing others by use of one's will: "It's an odd

penance to have set oneself, to live amongst animals for seven years. Nebuchadnezzar did it, I suppose . . ." (*L* 410). By being broken off from the confessions of *Seven Pillars, The Mint* is intended to separate sin from expiation, crime from punishment. Thus Lawrence as a Romantic hero exhibits inordinate pride in Arabia, remorse and expiation after the war, harmony in his imputed final absorption. Of course expiation is gradually transformed, becoming positive rather than compensatory or penitential as it becomes more complete and extreme. But the first two-thirds of *The Mint* is only potentially in the stage of absorption and is intended as a means to the end of harmony with other men and the universe. Only in the final third of the work is harmony said to be achieved.

The Mint is a confession, and has a single, unifying pattern: the process of stamping out personality, of annihilating the self by giving it over to the R.A.F. machine, for he had "struck a false image" of himself on the coin current.[9] But it is more clearly a private confession than *Seven Pillars* and depends heavily on the reader's close familiarity with the earlier book and Lawrence's biography. For instance, he assumes his reader will know that the marks on his back queried by an officer in the book's opening chapter are from the beating at Deraa; otherwise his dry remark that the beating was not intended as punishment, but was "more like persuasion" would be meaningless. His audience is to be Forster, David and Edward Garnett, the Shaws—literary figures.[10] Besides, he writes Forster, "it isn't a book. It's a note for your private eye: a swollen letter" (*L* 596).

The Mint begins with Lawrence's defecating as a nervous response to his enlistment in the ranks of the Royal Air Force; the "melting of the bowels before a crisis" supposedly illustrates the moral that he is not a man of action (19). Then he is stripped naked and his body scrutinized, as if it were an object. The body and its functions are to be the subject of *The Mint,* its image of the absolute; everything in it is "designed to emphasize the flesh of men, leading a life which is only of the body, and therefore growing . . . very natural souls."[11] R. P. Blackmur finds in *The Mint* "the continuous cultivation of the intolerable."[12] Lawrence says this more precisely: he displays the "attraction of unlikeness" (*M* 35). Lawrence, for instance, describes "a little streak of what seemed gross" in an airman who would come in from the latrine "all uncleaned, with his dropped breeches flouncing round his knees. He'd throw down the blankets of the first empty bed and squat there with a leer on his mouth, rocking and rubbing his nakedness on the sheets. When this had cooled him enough, he'd slide his heavy body by his hands over the bed-end, to stand crowing and pointing with a happy finger. 'Oh, shitty,' he'd say, 'he's shit the bed' " (*M* 193-94). The airman then urinates in the shoes of each member of the squad. Lawrence's revulsion and concomitant awareness of his fascination illustrate his principle that "any conscious quality presupposed the presence of its opposite" (MS 357).

To define the self, Lawrence sets out to eliminate the subject of definition. He has "passed a lot of self-denying ordinances" (*L* 575), yet he is ambivalent about their effects. It is "not good for anyone to be so self-denying. They may lose their self in the end."[13] The final purpose of these ordinances is clear. He writes of uniformity in the ranks, "Chaos breeds life: whereas by habit and regularity comes death, quickly" (*L* 529). As Gertrude Himmelfarb says of the Victorian atheist, "The ultimate abnegation, beyond food, dress, pleasure, even sex, was the abnegation of self; and this was the basic moral principle, the basic affirmation of the unbeliever."[14] It is this ultimate abnegation Lawrence seeks.

In the final pages of *The Mint*, Lawrence writes: "As we gain attachment [to the R.A.F.], so we strip ourselves of personality" (248). He portrays himself as

too utterly content to speak, drugged with an absorption fathoms deeper than physical contentment. Just we lay there spread-eagled in a mesh of bodies, pillowed on one another and sighing in happy excess of relaxation. The sunlight poured from the sky and melted into our tissues. From the turf below our moist backs there came up a sister-heat which joined us to it. Our bones dissolved to become a part of this

> underlying, indulgent earth, whose mysterious pulse throbbed in every
> tremor of our bodies. . . . Such moments of absorption resolve the
> mail and plate of our personality back into the carbo-hydrate elements
> of being. . . . In winter we struggle undefended along the roadway,
> and the rain and wind chivy us, till soon we are wind and rain. . . .
> Everywhere a relationship: no loneliness any more. (*M* 250)

He tells Charlotte Shaw, "I feel absorbed," and declaims
"the unity of mind and matter, of intellect, soul, body, spirit,
of imagination and experience, of colour, taste, smell, touch,
of god and man."[15] It is a stage Lawrence finds in a Romantic poet: "In time I'll join, concerning them, in Blake's
astonishing cry 'Everything that is, is holy!' " (*L* 411). But
there is an implicit love of death, of dissolution. He finds that
"the equilibrium between conditions and expectations of
life is so fine that I shun all disturbances."[16]

The assertion of absorption with which *The Mint* ends
seems to be belied by the form and style of the work, as well as
by Lawrence's own admission in his correspondence that
this absorption has not in fact occurred. The conviction of
separation from other soldiers, openly stated in Parts One
and Two, is implicit in Three. E. M. Forster finds the
affirmation less successful than the expiation; he prefers "the
3rd part, as a whole, less than its predecessors." The
transition to Part Three, Forster believes, "is into another
medium, into a sort of comforting bath water, where I sat
contented and surprised, but not convinced that I was being
cleansed. You hadn't . . . communicated your happiness
to me."[17] The form of *The Mint* militates against the self's
achieving absorption, for at the beginning of Part Three the
narrator steps forward, out of character, to declare that this
section is not based on his Depot notes, like the previous two,
but only on a few "extracts, mainly from letters to my
friends. . . . There is no continuity in these last pages.
. . . How can any man describe his happiness?" (*M* 200).
The inability to complete the intended form of the work, the
destruction of the continuity of the process, demonstrates
that Lawrence has not joined the men, that his conviction of
being absorbed is questionable at best. The relation of the

third part to the first two is that of "benediction after a com-
mination service" (*L* 612).

The title of the minor work is as ironic as that of the major
one. In his letters, Lawrence repeatedly asserts that he feels
separate from the men. He has lived five years in the barracks
and "can honestly confess that I've never been really one
with my fellows. I have sometimes, for a moment, imagined
myself into a unity with them: and before I could seize it and
settle down into it, like a rabbit into a burrow, I'd be whisked
off to another existence, incontinent" (*L* 554). Frequently in
The Mint he shows himself at the center of events busily
recording them (e.g., 98, 124). He has "learned solidarity
with them here. Not that we are very like, or will be. I joined
in high hope of sharing their tastes and manners and life: but
my nature persists in seeing all things in the mirror of itself,
and not with a direct eye" (*M* 195). Lawrence finds himself
odder in the ranks than before (*M* 183); only the pattern of
physical movement "could momently absorb my mind" (*M*
119).

The use of "we" in *The Mint* seems contrived and, as in
Seven Pillars, jars the reader throughout the work. The style
of *The Mint* constantly pulls away from the content. Yet
Lawrence believes that its "style well fitted its subject: our
dull clothed selves; our humdrum, slightly oppressed, lives;
our tight uniforms: the constriction, the limits, the artificial
conduct, of our bodies and minds and spirits, in the great
machine which the R.A.F. is becoming. I had to hold myself
down, on each page, with both hands." There are two styles
in the work: "A painted or sentimental style, such as I used in
The Seven Pillars, would have been out of place in *The
Mint*, except in the landscape passages, where I have used it.
But I doubt whether any un-versed reader would be able to
connect the two books by any tricks of authorship" (*L* 596-
97). In fact, mannered throughout, *The Mint* generally has
only a painted style. Of course this quality is heightened in
landscapes (e.g., *M* 24-25), but there is no real division in
style because no significant public action is narrated. The
book is primarily introspective, or at least reflective, in
purpose, and direct emotional expression is not checked, as

it is in the war narrative of *Seven Pillars*. *The Mint* heals the split in *Seven Pillars* by eliminating its active side, for this narrator is always his literary, introspective self, always filtering out those passages which do not confirm this self.

When he describes breakfast in *The Mint* it becomes a rather elegant affair: "Give to a table twelve spindly brine-sodden rashers, and a tin of stale eggs noisomely splattered in the grease which a half-hour ago had been frying fat—and twelve men will roll out of Mess Deck, ripe-feeling and full, with praise of the messing officer. 'Bon' are bacon and eggs" (72). "Bon" conveys vividly the disparity exhibited throughout *The Mint* between Lawrence's style and his subject. The style is tense, broken, but it expresses only Lawrence's perception of the ranks and his own character, not the attitude of the soldiers themselves. His vocabulary reveals his distance from the games of the men: "The ball at intervals plonked musically against men's boots or on the resistant ground: and each game was edged by its vocal border of khaki and blue" (24). He wanders among the barracks: "the appellant moon easily conjures me outside. . . . I slouch meditatively, my head ever forward, eyes on the ground, to give my negligent feet unconscious warning of obstacles. Wits inwardly turned cannot watch a man's path" (137). As in *Seven Pillars*, Lawrence exhibits little feeling for nature. The sentimentality, the pathetic fallacy, the gloomy Romantic figure contrast strongly and consciously with the crude barracks and the animals inside.

The distance between Lawrence's elaborate prose and the soldiers' speech, fucking this and fucking that, is immense, even comic. Yet Lawrence's ear for speech rhythms in *The Mint* is remarkable; he seldom uses this faculty in *Seven Pillars*. The authenticity of the cadences of the obscenities is indisputable. Nonetheless Lawrence records only exclamations and isolated sentences, not conversations. Perhaps he is not interested in dialogue, for it would distract from the focus on himself.

Virtually no significant public events are narrated in *The Mint*. As heroic events become anti-heroic in *Seven Pillars*, here anti-heroic becomes heroic—or, more accurately, mock-heroic—by virtue of the style. There is no clear, direct, vigorous style, no war narrator certain of his identity who dominates a scene. The narrator expresses his feelings openly and directly about each event; he is angry, frightened, meditative by turns, and he analyzes each emotion: "I do try and feel every article or emotion which comes into the book . . ." (*L* 624). He tells of a cruel commander whom he observes insulting a soldier: "I found myself trembling with clenched fists, repeating to myself, 'I must hit him, I must,' and the next moment trying not to cry for shame . . ." (*M* 87). In *Seven Pillars* he distrusts instinct, for "Reason seemed to give men something deliberately more precious . . ." (511), but in *The Mint* he yields to emotion, condemning the "vanity in which we thinking people sub-infeudate ourselves, . . . judging myself now carried away by instinct, now ruling a course by reason, now deciding intuitively: always restlessly cataloguing each aspect of my unity" (*M* 178).

Lawrence must constantly call attention to himself, peek out from his hiding place among the common airmen and declare himself. He shows his lack of integration with the men by repeated references to his past glory. Sometimes he makes himself ridiculous; on the walls of the canteen he sees among the paintings of war heroes "a small picture of me, a thing later conveyed slyly to the ever-open incinerator" (60). Later a postwar proclamation of the King declaring him Minister Plenipotentiary falls open on the floor of the barracks, nearly destroying his incognito (77). On garbage detail, "shit-cart," he receives notice of an offer to edit a "projected highbrow monthly 'Belles-lettres' " (82; cf. *L* 365-66). Such scenes virtually parody his early insights into his character. Of course there is a sense in which he intends all this to be an elaborate joke and finds humor in the disparity between his potential and his circumstance.[18] Lawrence sometimes makes "a joke of this depot life, and of myself, the slowest and silliest thing in it" (182), but he never successfully integrates this perspective with the whole of *The Mint*.

Even in the benediction of Part Three, when he attends a

funeral service in honor of Queen Alexandra, he emphasizes his separation from the men by recounting memorably his meeting the Queen in a private audience (221). At times he steps completely out of character to declare, without any intimation of irony, that he can help the soldiers of the ranks survive against their non-commissioned officers "by using my powers (so sharpened by experience and success in war and diplomacy)" (195). He illustrates his dictum that "voluntary slavery was the deep pride of a morbid spirit . . ." (565). In seeking to become like the airmen, Lawrence emphasizes his essential difference and consistently defines himself against them. Theoretically the self would be representative if this were truly a minting process. Lawrence seeks the convergence of private and public self, but part of him remains willful, undegraded, unbroken, as style and form demonstrate. Indeed, if the form of the work is fragmentary (*L* 596), as Lawrence declares, using this form to express harmony of body and spirit is incongruous.

Absorption is never achieved by *The Mint*'s hero, and the search for the absolute again ends in failure. In a single letter Lawrence says ambiguously that Part Three is "vamped up," but "sincere." He "shrank from digging too deep into the happiness, for fear of puncturing it" (*L* 620). In fact in his confessions Lawrence never moves beyond the stage of withdrawal and contraction of the self. The confessions of Augustine, Bunyan, and Rousseau portray the inner life absorbing and eventually transforming the outer. In Lawrence the outer life simply withers away. Unlike the cenobite monks whose method he professes to imitate (*L* 853), for Lawrence the means of discipline becomes the end. What he writes of the days of medieval chivalry is true of his own monasticism: he engaged in "revivals and legends or reminiscences or ridicule of them, but never the real thing" (*M* 227).

The pattern Lawrence imitates is derived from nineteenth-century narratives of spiritual growth. To be regenerate for Schopenhauer, Carlyle, Mill, and Lawrence is to be reborn without the Byronic or Romantic egoistic will. Lawrence says of Carlyle's *Sartor Resartus*, "To start requires courage, to finish folly" (*L* 402). This is precisely Lawrence's attitude toward the process of regeneration described in Carlyle. In theory Lawrence follows Carlyle's hero out of the Everlasting No, out of exile and division, but only to the Center of Indifference, the "first preliminary moral Act, Annihilation of Self."[19] Lawrence does argue that man can pass through thought into comprehension, a oneness with other men and the universe, but, while he pretends to comprehension in Part Three, he actually ends *The Mint* emphasizing annihilation of self. Lawrence portrays no development from the Center of Indifference to the Everlasting Yea, from Part Two to Three in *The Mint*. Lawrence cannot document or dramatize a process he has not lived through.

The clearest evidence that Lawrence does not and cannot go beyond the Center of Indifference is his praise of the machine. Lawrence ends where Carlyle begins, consciously accepting as safe a universe "all void of Life, or Purpose, of Volition, even of Hostility: it was one huge, dead, immeasurable Steam-engine, rolling on, in its dead indifference, to grind me limb from limb."[20] Lawrence is not, in Carlyle's words, among those "to whom a higher instinct has been given; who struggle to be persons, not machines."[21] Rather he now happily serves a mechanical purpose (*L* 853), for, in the parlance of the airmen, even male genitals are reduced to a "bicycle pump and tool-bag" (*M* 114).

Attraction to the machine is, according to Erich Fromm in *The Anatomy of Human Destructiveness*, an extreme to which the sadomasochistic character may go. Necrophilia, which develops out of the sadistic character, is "the passionate attraction to all that is dead, decayed, putrid, sickly; it is the passion to transform that which is alive into something unalive; to destroy for the sake of destruction; the exclusive interest in all that is purely mechanical."[22] It is the malignant form of the anal character. From Marinetti's *Futurist Manifesto* Fromm derives "the essential elements of necrophilia: worship of speed and the machine; poetry as a means of attack; glorification of war; destruction of culture;

hate against women; locomotives and airplanes as living forces." Fromm's list of characteristics differs in some respects from Lawrence's presentation of self in his confessions, but there are significant parallels. Certainly Lawrence does worship speed and the machine, expresses contempt for women, and glorifies war. The necrophiliac "turns his interest away from life, persons, nature, ideas—in short from everything that is alive; he transforms all life into things, including himself and the manifestations of his human faculties of reason, seeing, hearing, tasting, loving."[23] Lawrence himself asserts that he loves "objects before life or ideas" (549). The man who turns away from life in the manner of the necrophiliac is an extreme instance of a general psychological trend: "Thus far we have considered the connection: mechanical—lifeless—anal. But another connection can hardly fail to come to mind as we consider the character of the totally alienated, cybernetic man: his *schizoid* or *schizophrenic* qualities. Perhaps the most striking trait in him is the split between thought-affect-will. . . . The cybernetic man is almost exclusively cerebrally oriented: he is a *monocerebral man*. His approach to the whole world around him—and to himself—is intellectual; he wants to know what things are, how they function and how they can be constructed or manipulated."[24] In the same letter in which he discusses most explicitly his desire to become a machine, Lawrence states that in his creative work he sought "to be perhaps an artist . . . or to be at least cerebral. . . . What I was trying to do, I suppose, was to carry a superstructure of ideas upon or above anything I made" (*L* 853).

Fromm's observations clarify Lawrence's assertions that there are "no women in the machines, in any machine. No woman, I believe, can understand a mechanic's happiness in serving his bits and pieces" (*L* 853). Lawrence implies that the machine is essentially male. The human male then, if fully male, has the qualities associated with the machine: he is cold, dead, aggressive, dominating, exploitive, implacable, relentless, inorganic, multiple, a thing of bits and pieces. Henry Adams, who seeks to distance himself from his own diagnosis and does not apply it to himself as Lawrence does, sees this in historical terms; the unity of the Virgin has given way to the horrifying multiplicity of power, the Dynamo. In Lawrence's exaggerated sense of being male, the woman has emotions and softness; the man must not yield to such feelings, must guard against hysteria, the prime instinct of his nature.

The Mint, like the introspective passages in *Seven Pillars*, is written in a cypher that disguises true emotion. There is no woman in the machine, but Lawrence fears sudden and complete yielding to the emotional part of himself or to the woman within. One need not believe that these veiled emotions are so base that they must be disguised or suppressed, nor that what Lawrence has done in Arabia contaminates and destroys his power to act. It is not the power he has used, not what he has done, that causes remorse; rather it is what he feels about his acts. Not the power but the fantasy about the power generates remorse, and that fantasy or myth is what Lawrence presents to the reader in the confessions. Emotion must at every point be segregated from act for fear that what he does will be tainted by the emotion he fantasizes is present. Thus Lawrence makes his acts effete and harmless by withdrawing emotion from them. But so treated they become meaningless, mechanical, dead. That which is alive is elsewhere, and Lawrence tries "never to dwell on what was interesting" (563). Act is impoverished by Lawrence's inability to give it affect without guilt and emotion is made sterile without any meaningful relationship to act.

Lawrence writes that "one of the benefits of being part of the machine is that one learns that one doesn't matter" (*L* 853). The annihilation of self described by Carlyle and Schopenhauer parallels Fromm's and Karen Horney's descriptions of masochism. All masochistic strivings, writes Horney, "are ultimately directed toward satisfaction, namely, toward the goal of oblivion, of getting rid of self with all its conflicts and all its limitations." Masochism is "a striving toward the relinquishment of self."[25] By annihilation of self all these writers seem to mean the extinction of desire or will. Extinguishing desire for nineteenth-century writers means a temporary and unwilled loss of intellect which allows natural feeling to flow in and regenerate the self. The feeling must come unbidden from the unconscious. The regenerate self can then overcome the isolation which bedevils it and can assume its place in the human community. But for Lawrence this loss of control is illusory, for he plans it, wills it. He controls even the process of letting go. The style of *The Mint* reveals his intense fear of yielding to emotion. Like the cactus he admires, Lawrence's "general attitude is stubborn, and his parts are fleshy and weak. Also he holds up those maimed, gangrenous fingers of his stiffly and protestingly against the wind. Ordinarily plants wanton so, when the wind comes. There is hostility and independence in the cactus. . . ."[26]

If Lawrence's becoming a machine is a negative way to view the course of his life and the pattern he makes of it in his confessions, there is a more positive way. His intention to transform the self into a machine is not different from his artistic purpose. Both machine and art slay the beast of the will. Schopenhauer, from whom Lawrence's concept of will is derived, defines this function of art; the artist

> is chained to the contemplation of the play, the objectification of will; he remains beside it, does not get tired of contemplating it and representing it in copies; and meanwhile he bears himself the cost of the production of that play, i.e., he himself is the will which objectifies itself, and remains in constant suffering. That pure, true, and deep knowledge of the inner nature of the world becomes now for him an end in itself: he stops there. Therefore it does not become to him a quieter of the will, as . . . it does in the case of the saint who has attained to resignation; it does not deliver him for ever from life, but only at moments, and is therefore not for him a path out of life, but only an occasional consolation in it, till his power, increased by this contemplation and at last tired of the play, lays hold on the real.[27]

The greatest art, according to Schopenhauer, can "become a *quieter* of all will, from which proceeded the complete resignation, which is the innermost spirit of Christianity, as of the Indian philosophy; the surrender of all volition, conversion, the suppression of will, and with it of the whole inner being of the world, that is to say, salvation."[28]

It is this triumph of art over will that Lawrence seeks in his confessions, where, by shaping his own life into art, he can escape the stream of willing. Lawrence entered the R.A.F. "to write a real book" (*M* 199). In Arabia Lawrence's strongest desire was for "the power of self-expression in some imaginative form" (549). Art exists, according to Morse Peckham, "in order to realize the existence of the artist, his will, his organizing powers, and his grasp of experience."[29] Though once Lawrence does assert that the Revolt itself "was something exterior which we had created, a work of art, in honouring which we glorified ourselves" (MS 400), he strikes the passage from the text. His general conviction is that action and art are incompatible and action must be sacrificed for the sake of art (MS 415).

As Lawrence understands it, action occurs because of the nature of the private self. The acts of war do not generate the private self. For the Romantic artist, according to Peckham, "Art and not religion . . . is the source of value; and the artist—not the priest, not the metaphysician—introduces value into the world."[30] The measure of the extraordinary importance Lawrence gives art is in his declaration that only to writing has he given his full strength (*L* 758) and that the failure of *Seven Pillars*, not the war, broke his nerve (*L* 456). In a complex sense this is true, for art replaces the nerve of action. Thus it is the process of seeking order in his life which produces remorse. Lawrence, in his own view, writes instead of acts; he abandons the authority and power he has won in the East in order "to create some lively thing of black marks on white paper" (MS 415). He feels that he gains control of his will in the creative process, which consists in the contemplation of his willing. In a very direct sense the subject of these confessions, the pattern they are intended to make, is simply the drama of damnation and salvation, the assertion and denial of the will.

Lawrence is the offspring of the literary and philosophical ideas of the nineteenth century, and by exaggerating them to destructive extremes he acts out the unconscious impulses of his age in a radical and direct way. Lawrence makes the creation and presentation of self his life's work after the war. His spiritual crisis—an inheritance from the nineteenth century—is never resolved. Indeed, his problem is the paralysis of will associated with the sadomasochistic character and cannot be resolved. Lawrence analyzes himself as a case-study of the abnormal. Yet as Emerson says of a writer's confessional impulse, "the deeper he dives into his privatest, secretest presentiment, to his wonder he finds this is the most acceptable, most public, and universally true."[31] It is Lawrence's unsystematic translation of the optimistic Romantic myth of self into the pessimistic psychological myth of our century that gives his confessions power, universality, and complexity.

NOTES TO CHAPTER VII

1. John Buchan in *Letters to T. E. Lawrence*, p. 22. For a biography emphasizing the period of Lawrence's life presented in *The Mint* see H. Montgomery Hyde, *Solitary in the Ranks: Lawrence of Arabia as Airman and Private Soldier* (London: Constable, 1977).

2. In *Letters to T. E. Lawrence*, p. 58.

3. *Beyond the Tragic Vision*, p. 92.

4. Letter to Charlotte Shaw, 19 June 1928.

5. Freud, *Civilization and Its Discontents*, p. 2, discusses this notion.

6. Letter to Charlotte Shaw, 20 March 1928.

7. Letter to Charlotte Shaw, 31 August 1924.

8. This passage illustrates Lawrence's deleterious revision of the manuscript. The text eliminates the word "actors," which reinforces the connection between the generalization and Lawrence, who frequently refers to himself as an actor. Further, the specific "century" becomes the vague "age" and the connotation of "spirits' door open" is lost.

9. Letter to Charlotte Shaw, 3 August 1927.

10. Letter to Charlotte Shaw, 20 March 1928. He does add Hugh Trenchard, Marshal of the Royal Air Force, to the list of permitted readers, but for an entirely different motive: *The Mint* appeals for reforms in the services. Trenchard, his friend, was frightened by the possibility of the book's publication, though Lawrence never considered this. See *Letters to T. E. Lawrence*, pp. 202-05.

11. Letter to Charlotte Shaw, 2 May 1928.

12. *The Lion and the Honeycomb*, p. 115.

13. Letter to Charlotte Shaw, 20 March 1928. This comment is made of Florence Hardy, wife of the novelist.

14. *Victorian Minds*, p. 309.

15. Letters to Charlotte Shaw, 7 July 1925, 16 March 1927.

16. Letter to Charlotte Shaw, 17 June 1926. In *The Mint* Lawrence writes that "happiness, while primarily dependent on our internal balance of desire and opportunity, lies also at the mercy of our external acquaintance" (238).

17. *Letters to T. E. Lawrence*, pp. 69, 67.

18. G. B. Shaw exploits this disparity in *Too True To Be Good*, whose Private

Meek is modeled after Lawrence. See *Complete Plays with Prefaces*, IV (New York: Dodd, Mead, 1963), pp. 633-720. For a detailed commentary on the play, see Weintraub, *Private Shaw*, pp. 196-230. Curiously, Weintraub can better demonstrate Lawrence's specific influence on *Too True To Be Good* than Shaw's on *Seven Pillars* (e.g., p. 217).

19.   *Sartor Resartus*, Book Second, Ch. IX.

20.   *Ibid.*, Book Second, Ch. VII.

21.   "Characteristics," *The Works of Thomas Carlyle*, p. 31.

22.   *The Anatomy of Human Destructiveness*, p. 332. The original passage is italicized.

23.   *Ibid.*, pp. 345, 350.

24.   *Ibid.*, pp. 351-52.

25.   *New Ways in Psychoanalysis*, p. 248.

26.   Letter to Charlotte Shaw, 16 March 1927.

27.   *The World as Will and Idea*, I, 345-46.

28.   *Ibid.*, I, 301.

29.   *Beyond the Tragic Vision*, p. 203.

30.   *Ibid.*, p. 98.

31.   "The American Scholar," in *Selections from Ralph Waldo Emerson*, ed. Stephen E. Whicher (Boston: Houghton Mifflin, 1957), p. 74.

BIBLIOGRAPHY

Works by T. E. Lawrence

Lawrence, Thomas Edward. "The Arab Revolt: A Personal Record." T. E. Lawrence Collection, Humanities Research Center, University of Texas at Austin.

_____. "Confession of Faith." British Museum Additional MS. 46355.

_____. *Crusader Castles.* 2 vols. London: Golden Cockerel Press, 1936.

_____. "Crusader Castles." Jesus College Library MS. 160/7.

_____. *Eight Letters from T. E. Lawrence.* Ed. Harley Granville-Barker. London: privately printed, 1939.

_____. *The Essential T. E. Lawrence.* Ed. David Garnett. New York: E. P. Dutton, 1951.

_____. *Evolution of a Revolt: Early Postwar Writings of T. E. Lawrence.* Eds. Stanley and Rodelle Weintraub. University Park: Pennsylvania State University Press, 1968.

_____. Field Service Diaries. British Museum Additional MSS. 45914-15.

_____, trans. [Pseud. John Hume Ross]. *The Forest Giant,* by Adrien le Corbeau. London: Jonathan Cape, 1924.

_____. Foreword. *Arabia Felix: Across the Empty Quarter of Arabia,* by Bertram Thomas. New York: Jonathan Cape, 1932.

_____. *The Home Letters of T. E. Lawrence and His Brothers.* Ed. Montagu R. Lawrence. New York: Macmillan, 1954.

_____. Introduction. *Travels in Arabia Deserta,* by Charles M. Doughty. Definitive edition in one volume. New York: Random House, 1936.

_____. Introduction. *The Twilight of the Gods and Other Tales,* by Richard Garnett. New York: Dodd, Mead, 1927.

_____. "Leaves in the Wind." British Museum Additional Manuscript 46355.

_____. Letters. Jesus College Library TSS. and MSS. J.160/19 and J.160/20.

_____. Letters. T. E. Lawrence Collection, Humanities Research Center, University of Texas at Austin.

_____. *The Letters of T. E. Lawrence.* Ed. David Garnett. London: Spring Books, 1964.

_____. *Letters from T. E. Shaw to Bruce Rogers.* New York: privately printed, 1933.

_____. Letters to Charlotte Shaw. British Museum Additional MSS. 45903-04.

_____. *Men in Print: Essays in Literary Criticism.* London: Golden Cockerel Press, 1940.

_____. *Minorities: Good Poems by Small Poets and Small Poems by Good Poets.* Ed. J. M. Wilson. Garden City, N.Y.: Doubleday, 1972.

———. *The Mint*. New York: Norton, 1963.

———. "The Mint," TSS. British Museum MSS. 45916-17.

———, trans. [Pseud. T. E. Shaw]. *The Odyssey of Homer*. New York: Oxford University Press, 1956.

———. *Oriental Assembly*. Ed. Arnold W. Lawrence. New York: E. P. Dutton, 1940.

———. Pocket diaries. British Museum Additional MS. 45983.

———. Record of the writing, printing, and distribution of *Seven Pillars*. *Texas Quarterly*, V (Autumn 1962), 48.

———. *Revolt in the Desert*. London: Jonathan Cape, 1927.

———. *Secret Despatches from Arabia*. London: Golden Cockerel Press, 1939.

———. "The Seven Pillars of Wisdom." Bodleian MS. Reserve d.33 (MS. English History d.112).

———. *Seven Pillars of Wisdom*. Oxford: privately printed, 1922.

———. *Seven Pillars of Wisdom*. London: privately printed, 1926.

———. *Seven Pillars of Wisdom: a triumph*. London: Jonathan Cape, 1935.

———. *Shaw-Ede. T. E. Lawrence's Letters to H. S. Ede, 1927-1935*. Ed. H. S. Ede. London: Golden Cockerel Press, 1942.

———. *T. E. Lawrence to His Biographers, Robert Graves and Liddell Hart: Information about Himself in the Form of Letters, Notes, Answers to Questions, and Conversations*. London: Cassell, 1963.

———. Two letters to R. M. Gouldby. Bodleian MS. English Letters e.91, fols. 71-76.

——— and C. Leonard Wooley. *The Wilderness of Zin (Archeological Report)*. London: Palestine Exploration Fund, 1915.

OTHER WORKS CITED

Abélard, Peter. *The Story of My Misfortunes*. Trans. Henry Adams Bellows. New York: Macmillan, 1972.

Adamov, Arthur. "The Endless Humiliation." Trans. Richard Howard. *Evergreen Review*, 2 (Spring, 1959), 64-95.

Adams, Henry. *The Education of Henry Adams: An Autobiography*. Boston: Houghton Mifflin, 1961.

Aldington, Richard. *Lawrence of Arabia: A Biographical Enquiry*. London: Collins, 1955.

Arendt, Hannah. *Origins of Totalitarianism*. New York: Harcourt, Brace, 1951.

Auden, Wystan H. "T. E. Lawrence." *Then and Now: A Selection of Articles, Stories, and Poems, Taken from the First Fifty Numbers of "Now and Then", 1921-35*. London: Jonathan Cape, 1935, pp. 21-23.

Augustine. *Confessions*. Trans. R. S. Pine-Coffin. Baltimore: Penguin Books, 1961.

Bergonzi, Bernard. *Heroes' Twilight: A Study of the Literature of the Great War*. New York: Coward-McCann, 1966.

Blackmur, R. P. *The Lion and the Honeycomb: Essays in Solicitude and Critique.* New York: Harcourt, Brace, 1955.

Bloom, Harold. Afterword. *Frankenstein: Or, the Modern Prometheus,* by Mary Shelley. New York: New American Library, 1965.

Bunyan, John. *The Pilgrim's Progress and Grace Abounding.* Ed. James Thorpe. Boston: Houghton Mifflin, 1969.

Carlyle, Thomas. *The Works of Thomas Carlyle.* Ed. H. D. Traill. 30 vols. London: Chapman and Hall, 1896-1901.

_____. *Sartor Resartus and Selected Prose.* Ed. Herbert L. Sussman. New York: Holt, Rinehart and Winston, 1970.

Carr, E. H. *What Is History?* New York: Knopf, 1961.

Coleridge, Samuel Taylor. *The Complete Works of Samuel Taylor Coleridge.* Ed. W. G. T. Shedd. 7 vols. New York: Harper and Brothers, 1878.

Conrad, Joseph. *Lord Jim.* Boston: Houghton Mifflin, 1958.

_____. *The Portable Conrad.* Ed. Morton Dauwen Zabel. New York: Viking Press, 1947.

Doughty, Charles M. *Travels in Arabia Deserta.* Definitive edition in one volume. New York: Random House, 1936.

Emerson, Ralph Waldo. *Selections from Ralph Waldo Emerson: An Organic Anthology.* Ed. Stephen E. Whicher. Boston: Houghton Mifflin, 1957.

Fanon, Frantz. *The Wretched of the Earth.* Trans. Constance Farrington. New York: Grove Press, 1963.

Fitzgerald, F. Scott. *The Crack-Up.* Ed. Edmund Wilson. New York: New Directions, 1956.

Forster, E. M. *Abinger Harvest.* New York: Meridian Books, 1955.

Freud, Sigmund. *Civilization and Its Discontents.* Trans. Joan Riviere. Garden City, N.Y.: Doubleday Anchor, n.d.

_____. *Collected Papers.* Trans. Joan Riviere. 5 vols. London: Hogarth Press, 1933.

_____. *A General Selection from the Works of Sigmund Freud.* Ed. John Rickman. Garden City, N.Y.: Doubleday, 1957.

_____. *A General Introduction to Psychoanalysis.* Trans. Joan Riviere. New York: Washington Square Press, 1960.

_____. *New Introductory Lectures on Psychoanalysis.* Trans. and ed. James Strachey. New York: Norton, 1965.

_____. *Three Essays on the Theory of Sexuality.* Trans. and ed. James Strachey. New York: Avon, 1965.

_____ and Albert Einstein. *Why War?* Dijon, France: League of Nations, 1933.

Fromm, Erich. *The Anatomy of Human Destructiveness.* New York: Holt, Rinehart and Winston, 1973.

_____. *Escape from Freedom.* New York: Avon Books, 1965.

Frye, Northrop. *Anatomy of Criticism: Four Essays.* New York: Atheneum, 1968.

Garber, Frederick. "Self, Society, Value, and the Romantic Hero." *The*

Hero in Literature. Ed. Victor Brombert. Greenwich, Conn.: Fawcett, 1969.

Gebhard, Paul H. "Fetishism and Sadomasochism." *Science and Psychoanalysis*, XV (1969), 71-80.

Genet, Jean. *The Thief's Journal*. Trans. Bernard Frechtman. New York: Grove Press, 1973.

Goffman, Erving. *The Presentation of Self in Everyday Life*. Garden City, N.Y.: Doubleday, 1959.

Graves, Robert. *Lawrence and the Arabian Adventure*. New York: Doubleday, 1928.

Hart, B. H. Liddell, *'T. E. Lawrence': In Arabia and After*. London: Jonathan Cape, 1964.

Hart, Francis R. "Notes for an Anatomy of Modern Autobiography." *New Literary History*, I, No. 3 (1970), 485-511.

Hegel, G. W. F. *The Phenomenology of Mind*. Trans. J. B. Baillie. London: Allen and Unwin, 1949.

Himmelfarb, Gertrude. *Victorian Minds*. New York: Knopf, 1968.

Holland, Norman. "Prose and Minds: A Psychoanalytic Approach to Non-Fiction." *The Art of Victorian Prose*. Eds. George Levine and William Madden. New York: Oxford University Press, 1968, pp. 314-37.

Horney, Karen. *Self-Analysis*. New York: Norton, 1942.

––––––. *The Neurotic Personality of Our Time*. New York: Norton, 1937.

––––––. *New Ways in Psychoanalysis*. New York: Norton, 1939.

Howe, Irving. "T. E. Lawrence: The Problem of Heroism." *Decline of the New*. New York: Harcourt, Brace, 1970, pp. 294-326.

Hulme, T. E. *Speculations*. Ed. Herbert Read. London: Kegan Paul, Trench, Trubner, 1936.

Huysmans, Joris Karl. *Against Nature*. Trans. Robert Baldick. Baltimore: Penguin, 1959.

Hyde, H. Montgomery. *Solitary in the Ranks: Lawrence of Arabia as Airman and Private Soldier*. London: Constable, 1977.

Jackson, Holbrook. *The Eighteen Nineties: A Review of Art and Ideas at the Close of the Nineteenth Century*. New York: Capricorn Books, 1966.

Keppler, C. F. *The Literature of the Second Self*. Tucson: University of Arizona Press, 1972.

Knight, G. Wilson. *Neglected Powers: Essays on Nineteenth and Twentieth Century Literature*. London: Routledge and Kegan Paul, 1974.

Knightley, Phillip, and Colin Simpson. *The Secret Lives of Lawrence of Arabia*. New York: Bantam Books, 1971.

Laing, R. D. *The Divided Self: An Existential Study in Sanity and Madness*. Baltimore: Penguin Books, 1965.

––––––. *The Politics of Experience*. New York: Ballantine Books, 1967.

Lanham, John. "The Genre of *A Portrait of the Artist as a Young Man* and 'the rhythm of its structure'." *Genre*, X, No. 1 (1977), 77-102.

Lawrence, Arnold W., ed. *Letters to T. E. Lawrence*. London: Jonathan Cape, 1962.

————. *T. E. Lawrence by His Friends.* London: Jonathan Cape, 1937.

Lawrence, David Herbert. *The Collected Letters of D. H. Lawrence.* Ed. Harry T. Moore. 2 vols. New York: Viking Press, 1962.

————. *Phoenix: The Posthumous Papers of D. H. Lawrence.* Ed. Edward D. McDonald. New York: Viking Press, 1972.

————. *Women in Love.* New York: Viking Press, 1960.

Legman, Gershon. *Rationale of the Dirty Joke: An Analysis of Sexual Humor.* New York: Grove Press, 1968.

Leiris, Michel. *Manhood: A Journey from Childhood into the Fierce Order of Virility.* Trans. Richard Howard. New York: Grossman, 1963.

Lévi-Strauss, Claude. *The Savage Mind.* Trans. George Weidenfeld. Chicago: University of Chicago Press, 1966.

————. *Tristes Tropiques.* Trans. John Russell. New York: Atheneum, 1969.

Mack, John E. *A Prince of Our Disorder: The Life of T. E. Lawrence.* Boston: Little, Brown, 1976.

————. "T. E. Lawrence: A Study of Heroism and Conflict." *American Journal of Psychiatry*, CXXV (1969), 1083-92.

Mailer, Norman. *The Armies of the Night: History as a Novel, The Novel as History.* New York: Signet, 1968.

Malraux, André. "Lawrence and the Demon of the Absolute." *Hudson Review*, VIII (Winter, 1956), 519-32.

Mannoni, Dominique O. *Prospero and Caliban: The Psychology of Colonization.* Trans. Pamela Powesland. London: Methuen, 1956.

Marcus, Steven. *The Other Victorians: A Study of Sexuality and Pornography in Mid-Nineteenth Century England.* New York: Bantam Books, 1966.

Marinetti, F. T. *Marinetti: Selected Writings.* Ed. R. W. Flint. Trans. R. W. Flint and Arthur A. Coppotelli. New York: Farrar, Straus, and Giroux, 1971.

Marx, Leo. *The Machine in the Garden: Technology and the Pastoral Ideal in America.* New York: Oxford University Press, 1964.

Meinertzhagen, Richard. *Middle East Diary: 1917-1956.* New York: Cresset Press, 1960.

Meyers, Jeffrey, "E. M. Forster and T. E. Lawrence: A Friendship." *The South Atlantic Quarterly*, LXIX (Spring, 1970), 205-16.

————. *The Wounded Spirit: A Study of Seven Pillars of Wisdom.* London: Martin Brian and O'Keeffe, 1973.

Mill, John Stuart. *Autobiography and Other Writings.* Ed. Jack Stillinger. Boston: Houghton Mifflin, 1969.

Mills, Gordon. "T. E. Lawrence as a Writer." *Texas Quarterly*, V (Autumn, 1962), 35-45.

Miyoshi, Masao. *The Divided Self: A Perspective on the Literature of the Victorians.* New York: New York University Press, 1969.

Montaigne, Michel de. *The Essays of Montaigne.* Trans. E. J. Trechmann. New York: Oxford University Press, 1927.

Morris, John N. *Versions of the Self.* New York: Basic Books, 1966.

Nietzsche, Friedrich. *The Will to Power.* Ed. Walter Kaufmann. Trans. Walter Kaufmann and R. J. Hollingdale. New York: Vintage, 1968.

Notopoulos, James A. "The Tragic and the Epic in T. E. Lawrence." *Yale Review,* LIV (Spring, 1965), 331-45.

Olney, James. *Metaphors of Self: The Meaning of Autobiography.* Princeton: Princeton University Press, 1972.

Pascal, Blaise. *Pascal's Pensées.* Trans W. F. Trotter. London: J. M. Dent, 1932.

Pascal, Roy. *Design and Truth in Autobiography.* Cambridge, Mass.: Harvard University Press, 1960.

Peckham, Morse. *Beyond the Tragic Vision: The Quest for Identity in the Nineteenth Century.* New York: George Braziller, 1962.

Peyre, Henri. *Literature and Sincerity.* New Haven: Yale University Press, 1963.

Read, Herbert. *English Prose Style.* Boston: Beacon Books, 1967.

————. Review of *Seven Pillars of Wisdom. The Bibliophile's Almanack,* 1928, pp. 35-41.

Renza, Louis A. "The Veto of the Imagination: A Theory of Autobiography." *New Literary History,* IX, 1 (1977), 1-26.

Richards, Vyvyan. *Portrait of T. E. Lawrence.* London: Jonathan Cape, 1936.

Rousseau, Jean-Jacques. *The Confessions of Jean-Jacques Rousseau.* Trans. J. M. Cohen. Baltimore: Penguin Books, 1954.

Sayre, Robert F. *The Examined Self: Benjamin Franklin, Henry Adams, Henry James.* Princeton: Princeton University Press, 1964.

Schopenhauer, Arthur. *The World as Will and Idea.* Trans. R. B. Haldane and J. Kemp. 3 vols. London: Routledge and Kegan Paul, 1883.

Shaw, George Bernard. *Complete Plays with Prefaces.* 6 vols. New York: Dodd, Mead, 1963.

Shaw, W. David. "*In Memoriam* and the Rhetoric of Confession." *English Literary History,* 38 (1971), 80-103.

Shumaker, Wayne. *English Autobiography: Its Emergence, Materials, and Form.* Berkeley: University of California Press, 1954.

Sontag, Susan. *Against Interpretation and Other Essays.* New York: Dell, 1969.

Spender, Stephen. *The Making of a Poem.* New York: Norton, 1963.

Sprigg, Christopher St. John. [Pseud. Christopher Caudwell]. *Studies in a Dying Culture.* London: The Bodley Head, 1938.

Stekel, Wilhelm. *Sadism and Masochism: The Psychology of Hatred and Cruelty.* New York: Washington Square Press, 1968.

Stewart, Desmond. *T. E. Lawrence.* London: Hamish Hamilton, 1977.

Stoller, Robert J. *Perversion: The Erotic Form of Hatred.* New York: Delta, 1976.

Sussman, Herbert L. *Victorians and the Machine: The Literary Response to Technology.* Cambridge, Mass.: Harvard University Press, 1968.

Tabachnick, Stephen E. "The T. E. Lawrence Revival in English Studies." *Research Studies*, 44, No. 3 (September, 1976), 190-98.

Thorslev, Peter L. *The Byronic Hero: Types and Prototypes.* Minneapolis: University of Minnesota Press, 1962.

Trilling, Lionel. *Sincerity and Authenticity.* Cambridge, Mass.: Harvard University Press, 1972.

Vernon, John. *The Garden and the Map: Schizophrenia in Twentieth-Century Literature and Culture.* Urbana, Ill.: University of Illinois Press, 1973.

Villars, J. B. *T. E. Lawrence, or The Search for the Absolute.* Trans. Peter Dawnay. London: Sidgwick and Jackson, 1958.

Watt, Ian. *The Rise of the Novel: Studies in Defoe, Richardson, and Fielding.* Berkeley: University of California Press, 1957.

Weintraub, Stanley. *Private Shaw and Public Shaw: A Dual Portrait of Lawrence of Arabia and G. B. S.* New York: George Braziller, 1963.

———, and Rodelle Weintraub. *Lawrence of Arabia: The Literary Impulse.* Baton Rouge: Louisiana State University Press, 1975.

Wilde, Oscar. *De Profundis.* New York: Vintage Books, 1964.

———. *The Picture of Dorian Gray and Selected Stories.* New York: New American Library, 1962.

Wordsworth, William. *Poetical Works.* Eds. Thomas Hutchinson and Ernest de Selincourt. London: Oxford University Press, 1969.

Young, Hubert. *The Independent Arab.* London: John Murray, 1933.

INDEX